Dearest Children

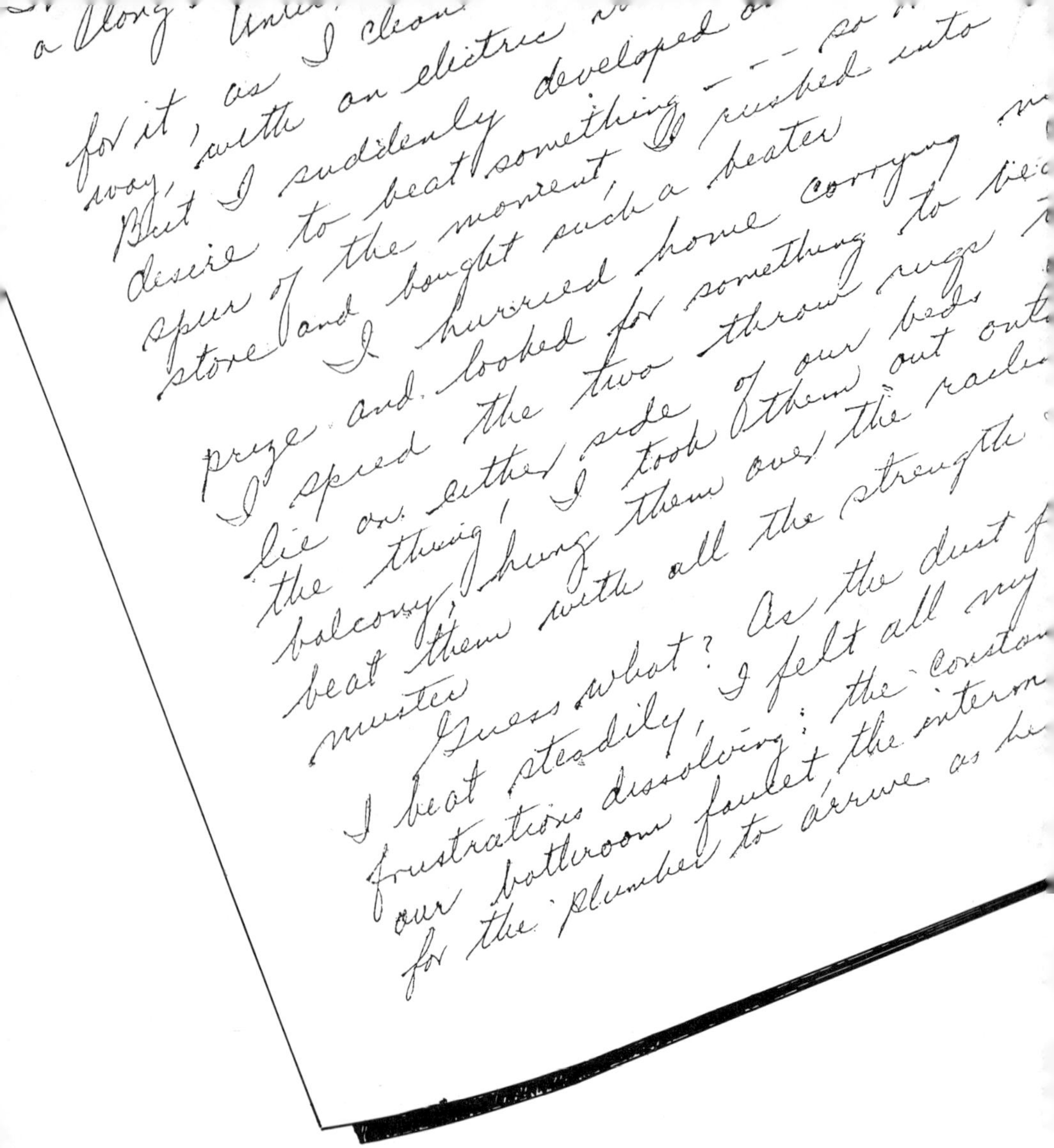

FELDHEIM PUBLISHERS
Jerusalem / New York

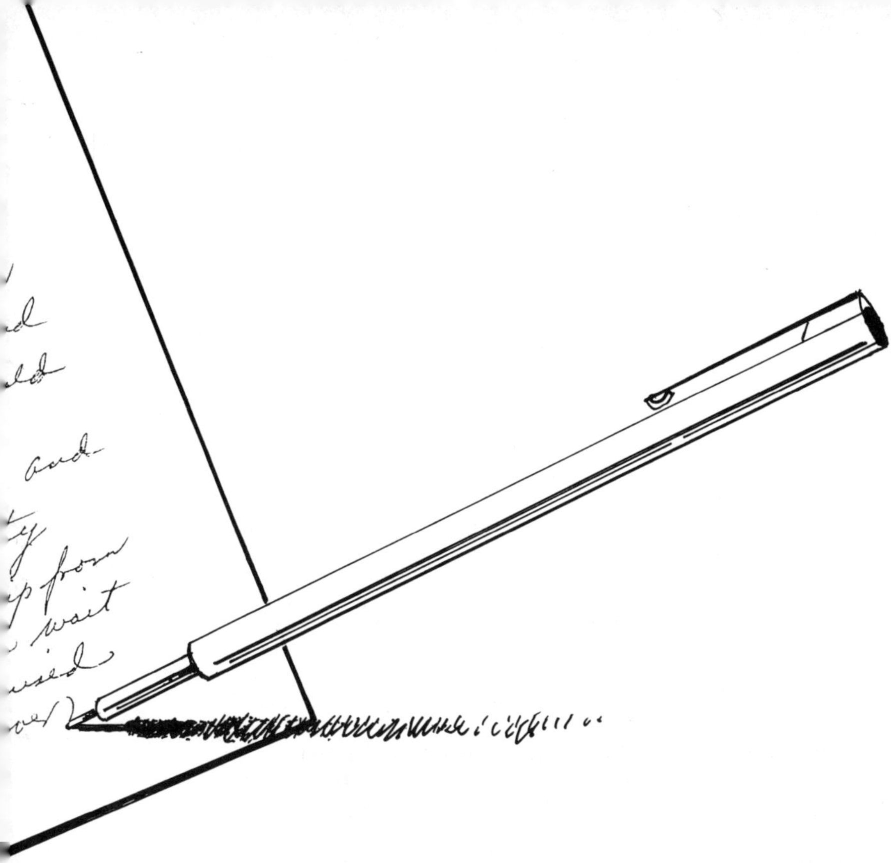

Dearest Children, ...

RUCHOMA SHAIN

Library of Congress Cataloging-in-Publication Data

Shain, Ruchoma.
Dearest children / by Ruchoma Shain.
p. cm.
ISBN 0-87306-610-3 (hc). — ISBN 0-87306-611-1 (pb)
1. Shain, Ruchoma—Correspondence. 2. Jews—Jerusalem—Biography. 3. Jews—Jerusalem—Social life and customs. 4. Jerusalem—Biography. I. Title.
DS109.86.S54A3 1992
956.94'42—dc20 91-13103

First published 1992

FELDHEIM PUBLISHERS
POB 35002 / Jerusalem, Israel

200 Airport Executive Park
Spring Valley, NY 10977

Printed in Israel

This book is dedicated to my dearest children:

Yisroel Meyer and Chaya
Elimelech and Mashi (Willner)
Raphael Yitzchok Isaac and Yehudis

Though we have been physically apart
for over twenty years,
our loving letters to each other have been like a life line,
connecting us across the ocean.

Acknowledgments

Dear Readers,

Some of you may be tempted to skip the Acknowledgments and jump right into the book itself. But please consider: this book would not be in your hands were it not for the following people who made it possible. Please take the time to read their names and give them your nod of approval as well.

Reb Yaakov Feldheim, my publisher and good friend. I consider it a privilege to be one of the authors whose books he publishes.

Marsi Tabak, editor par excellence. Her wise and prudent advice enhanced my book by far, and I should add "by near" also.

Joyce Bennett, assistant editor. Her constructive and clever suggestions were a "joy" to follow, because she knew me so well and knew exactly what I wanted to convey.

Harvey Klineman, graphic artist. I can always depend on him for attractive, creative designs of my books and their jackets.

And all the Feldheim staff members involved in producing my book: Sarah and Dubba-Raisel, who prepared my manuscript; Dina, whose cheery hello always greets me when I call; Hannah, who did the typesetting; Bracha, the production editor; Menachem, Feldheim's fantastic production manager who routinely makes the impossible happen; Yitzchak, who is in charge of the warehouse, and Moshe, his assistant; Chaim, in the accounting department; and Dov, in the graphics department. Although I know that they always treat authors with kindness and respect, I feel that I get extra-special treatment from each and every one of them.

Chana Levitt, my adopted granddaughter. Knowing that

Chana was at my side throughout the entire writing of this book, which she read page by page, gave me the encouragement to keep going.

Tzur and Hemla Levitt, devoted and loving friends. Their moral support lifted my spirits when I went into a low, and Hemla's physical support lifted my nutrition level to a high.

Reb Chaim Dov and Frume Altusky, my nephew and my niece. They opened their hearts and home to me every Shabbos. With Reb Chaim Dov's food for thought and Frume's delicious meals, I replenished my strength to continue my writing during the week.

Mindy Altusky, my great-niece, who generously provided many of the photographs in this book.

Batsheva, whose continued encouragement and interest in my writings spurred me on.

Rabbi Zelig Pliskin, well-known author. His new book, *Consulting the Wise*, has been published recently, and I consult him for sound advice.

Contents

Introduction

When my mother passed away in 1945, I realized how very lonesome Papa* would be, all by himself in Yerushalayim with all of us children living in the United States. I wrote him immediately that I would, God willing, write him a letter every single week. When Mama was alive, I had been a little lax in writing letters. Since I was so busy with three lively youngsters and household chores, I just did not get around to writing that often. Now my conscience bothered me terribly, and I hoped that by writing weekly letters to Papa, it would make up for the time I neglected to write, and that Mama, *a"h*, would forgive me.

Thus each week without fail my letter was mailed to Papa, and I allowed nothing to deter me. I recall one *erev Pesach*, when Reb Moshe was ill and I had to finish the cleaning up and all the final preparations myself. I even had to do the *bedikas chametz*, searching for any signs of *chametz* by myself. When I finally collapsed into a chair at 3:00 A.M., I was too tired to move. However, I knew that the next day was the day my weekly letter to Papa had to be mailed. In the morning I would be rushing, cooking, and making all the preparations for the Seder — and with Reb Moshe ill, and the children underfoot, I realized I would surely not find the time to write during the day — so out came my pad and pen, and I wrote my weekly letter to Papa then and there.

Twice, during the twenty-two years that I wrote my weekly

*I use the word "Papa" in this book to refer to my beloved father, in the narrative section, as well as to my husband, in the letters to my children. I hope this is not confusing, but it should be clear from the context each time.

letters, Papa revealed to me how very much they meant to him. The first time I visited him in Yerushalayim, in 1954, I noticed some of my letters lying on the cupboard. As I looked through the pile, Papa walked into the room.

"Ruchoma," he asked, "what are you going to do with all the *berachos* you merit in *olam ha-zeh* and in *olam ha-ba,* for writing to me every week?" Papa saw my writing to him as such a wonderful thing, that he was sure God's blessings were due me not only in this world but also in the world-to-come!

On another occasion, I received a letter from Papa, and I quote: "I have not received your letter this past week. I need the letter of my dear *tuchter* to her Pops (I had reverted to using his nickname), because if I don't receive it, my spirit is not 100 percent. Please find a few minutes to send me your letter and tell me how everything is going with our families." On the sealed envelope, Papa had added a little notation: "Received your weekly letter before dropping this letter into the mailbox. Thank Hashem..."

I kept up my weekly letters until Papa passed away in 1967.

For many years, I had yearned to live in Yerushalayim, but Reb Moshe was hesitant, and there were always valid reasons for delaying it. After Mama passed away, we received a moving letter from Papa asking us to come and settle in Yerushalayim: "I need my children nearby now that Mama is not here with me." His letter touched us deeply, and Reb Moshe and I sat for hours discussing the pros and cons of leaving the United States.

Finally, we wrote Papa that as much as we wanted to be with him, we simply could not make the move at that time. Our children were very young, we had no savings, and Palestine (the State of Israel had not yet come into being) was in a difficult plight both politically and economically.

When I visited Papa in Yerushalayim for the first time, he broached the subject again. Since our financial situation had not changed significantly, our children were in the midst of their schooling, and Israel was a fledgling State beset with many problems, I was in a quandary.

I decided to ask advice from Reb Chatzkel Levenstein. Reb Moshe and I had become very close to him and to his family in Mir, Poland, when we lived there, and now he was the *Mashgiach* of the Mir Yeshivah in Yerushalayim. (Afterwards he moved to Bnei Brak where he was *Mashgiach* of the Ponevez Yeshivah for the rest of his life.)

In reply to my query, he said, "If you have the *bitachon* of your father, then there is no problem, and you can come right away." We did not have that degree of faith and trust, and once again we decided that the time was not ripe for us to immigrate to Israel.

Two weeks before Papa passed away, Reb Moshe and I, and my oldest sister, Esther, were told that Papa was very ill and weak. Although it was difficult to get immediate accommodations since this was right after the Six-Day War, we booked the earliest flight to Israel that we could. My brother, Reb Nochum Dovid, and his wife Chaye Dube, and my sister Bessie and her husband, Reb Chaim Scheinberg, had settled in Yerushalayim a few years earlier, so that all the children were near him until the very end.

After Papa passed away, and we had been in Yerushalayim for several weeks, Reb Moshe and I came to the conclusion that we were finally ready to make the move. Being there made us realize what a natural thing it would be, and an overwhelming love for Yerushalayim simply captivated our hearts. We decided that by Papa's first yahrtzeit, we would — God willing — be living in Yerushalayim.

It had been a very difficult decision, for it meant leaving our beloved children and grandchildren, our relatives and friends. It also meant leaving our students and teaching positions: Reb Moshe had been teaching for many years in the Rabbi Jacob Joseph Yeshivah during the day, and was assistant principal in the Beth Jacob Seminary in the evening; and I was teaching secular subjects in a religious high school. We were both in our fifties, and had lived all our lives in America, except for our almost six years in Mir. It would mean a complete metamorphosis for us.

However, though we took all this into consideration and understood that it would not be easy for us, we both had set our hearts on it — to live our remaining years in Yerushalayim. Eretz Yisrael had charmed us, beckoned to us, spoken to our souls, and we could not resist the pull.

Our children accepted our decision, knowing how much it meant to us. Though it was a bitter pill for them to swallow, none of them tried to dissuade us.

Before we left, I made three photocopies of the letter that my father had written to me about how much he needed my weekly letters, and I handed a copy to each of our couples.

"Children," I said, "we shall miss you terribly. And not seeing our grandchildren as they grow will be especially painful. You can make our loneliness easier to bear by writing letters regularly and sharing your lives with us." Then and there, the children undertook to write weekly letters to us, and they have continued to do so for more than twenty years.

I like to think that the blessing of "this world" that Papa gave me for writing to him each week, was realized with the letters my children have been sending to us — and now to me alone — all these years.

Though this book depicts my letters to our children, it was in fact their weekly letters, sharing each phase of their lives with us, that gave me the impetus to share our lives with them.

✍ ✍

In March 1989, I visited the United States for a family *simchah* — the wedding of my grandson, Avrohom Yitzchok

Willner. Of course, I made the rounds and stayed with each of my children for two weeks.

While I was with my youngest children, Raphael Yitzchok, Yehudis, and their family, it was only a few weeks before Pesach and Yehudis had begun the many preparations. "You certainly have a lot to do," I told her, "and believe me, I know it's not an easy job."

"You know, Mama," she smiled, "even though there's a lot of work, it always brings us a special compensation. Every year, when all the work is done, Raphael Yitzchok and I take out all your letters and reread them. You know, we laugh and cry as we go through each letter, because they are so special."

"Yehudis," I said in amazement, "do you mean to say that you have actually saved all the letters I've written you through all the many years that Papa and I have lived in Yerushalayim?"

"Of course, Mama. Do you think that we would discard a letter of yours?" She looked at me in surprise.

I was stunned. "Can I see them?"

Yehudis lugged a large carton up from the basement and opened it. There, before my eyes, were twenty years of letters, and as I opened one after another, I soon became deeply engrossed.

When my son returned from the Yeshivah where he teaches, we all sat down to dinner. "Raphael Yitzchok," I said, "Yehudis told me that you've saved my letters all these years, and I've spent the whole afternoon reading them. I have an idea, and I want your opinion. I feel that there's material here for a third book. Not only do these letters depict the personal experiences that Papa and I had, but they are also a record of twenty years of life in Yerushalayim.

"You know," I went on, "in the last few hours, I have relived the Yom Kippur War, the *shemittah* years, the *Yamim Tovim*, everything — above all, the specialness of Yerushalayim itself."

Raphael Yitzchok caught my excitement. "Great, Mama!"

"It's an excellent idea," Yehudis agreed.

And even the grandchildren chimed in: "Bubbie, go to it! It sounds terrific."

And so the idea of this book was born.

I subsequently discovered that my other children had also been saving my letters, and within a short time after my return home, copies of all my old letters found their way back to Yerushalayim through kind-hearted friends who were visiting Israel.

For weeks and weeks I pored over them, selecting the incidents and experiences that I felt would be of interest to my readers. It is my fervent hope, dear readers, that as you read each letter, you will experience the ups and downs, the joys and sorrows, not only of our personal lives in Yerushalayim, but of the unique quality of life in Eretz Yisrael as well, and will feel as if my letters were written to you also.

Ruchoma Shain
Rosh Chodesh Tammuz
Yerushalayim

PART ONE:

Homecoming

Homeward Bound

IT WAS 4:00 A.M. as the plane flew toward Israel and brought us closer to our new home in Yerushalayim. Reb Moshe was dozing, and so were most of the other passengers, including my sister Esther (who had chosen to settle in Yerushalayim at the same time). Sleep eluded me, as I have never been able to sleep on a plane, and I watched with envy as they napped all through the plane trip. But was I really envious? Surely I would not want to sleep through something as momentous as this.

My thoughts returned to the moment of parting with our beloved children. Reb Moshe and I sounded so brave as we bade them farewell: "No tears, children. You should be thankful that we have the *zechus,* the privilege, to settle in Yerushalayim. May our going be the forerunner for all of you, and in the near future, God willing. We are following our heritage — Zaidie and Bubbie Andron left all their children in 1921, and settled in Eretz Yisrael. Zaidie and Bubbie

Herman left all of us children in 1939, and now it is our turn."

I ended with the encouraging words that my father had said to his children when he and my mother left America twenty-nine years before. "*Chazak, chazak* — Be strong, be strong! We shall meet in Yerushalayim."

Though my father did not see his fervent wish come true during his lifetime, I hoped that he was gaining spiritual sustenance in Heaven knowing that now, finally, all his children would be living in Yerushalayim.

The first of my "Israeli letters" to our loving children was written as soon as we were airborne.

July 17, 1968

Dearest Children,

We salute you for walking off like courageous soldiers. We were proud that there were no tears — just a few hugs and kisses. Papa and I stood for a few minutes, watching you recede from our sight, and then you were gone. We sat down on the nearest sofa and cried and cried. Papa kept blowing his nose as if that would stop his tears, while I used tissue after tissue to dry my eyes. I said half-jokingly to Papa, "Moshe, we'd better stop crying! We're using up all our tissues, and I heard that they cost a lot of money in Israel." It cleared the air, and the tears stopped.

I realize that we shall have great periods of loneliness, but, as you know, our Sages taught that settling in Eretz Yisrael is one of the three experiences that comes with suffering. Many of our relatives and friends tried to talk us out of leaving, pointing out the many good reasons there were for us not to go. In fact, we were advised by many of our relatives to take a year's leave of absence from our schools and to sub-lease our apartment, so we could at least have the alternative of returning to America if life in Israel proves too difficult for us. I told Papa, though, that if we have one foot in Yerushalayim and the other in the States, we'll never be able to overcome the hardships — so we pulled up our stakes, knowing we cannot backtrack.

And so here we are, children. Your parents are being borne on the wings of eagles — or rather on the wings of El Al — to Eretz Yisrael.

Papa just awoke, and I read this letter to him. Since I will be signing my letters "Papa and Mama," he should know the contents.

All our love,
Papa and Mama

As the flight went on and the miles between us continued to grow, I kept on writing, and that gave me the emotional strength that drew us even closer.

Dearest Children,

Your Mama and Papa are now in England! We've just made a stopover at the airport, so I'm writing to you again. Do you know, Mr. and Mrs. Dubin are also on our flight. Our friendship goes back to the time when I was a young girl. It turns out that they've rented an apartment in Kiryat Mattersdorf, just across the street from us. How nice it will be to have good friends close by.

And speaking of old friends, I don't think I ever told you about the humorous experience I had when Osna came all the way from the Bronx to help me pack. She had been telling me I was positively "nuts" to leave my children and everything else behind — including her, as we have been dear friends from the time we were born. However, when I asked for her help, she came early in the morning and told me she would spend the whole day with me. I suspected that she still hoped to change my mind.

I put her to work and sent her into the master bedroom

with instructions to take all the boxes out of our closet. You remember that I had a conglomeration of everything under the sun in there. In fact, I hardly remembered what I had.

I was in the kitchen trying to make some semblance of order, choosing which of the pots and pans I wanted to pack, when I heard Osna call out, "Racoma, what's in the two large cardboard boxes tied with blue and pink ribbons, marked His and Hers?"

Osna's question refreshed my memory. Several years ago, I had bought *tachrichim* for Papa and me. I recalled the day Aunt Bessie had phoned to tell me that the woman who sewed these special burial shrouds was leaving for Israel, and still had a few sets to sell. "She uses the best quality linen," Bessie had told me, "and she is a *tzaddekes.* It's a *segulah* for long life, so I'm ordering two sets for Reb Chaim and me — may we live till 120." Aunt Bessie had convinced me, and so I also ordered two sets. When I told Papa, he got all jittery at the idea, so I hid the boxes on the top shelf of our closet, tied them up prettily with the pink and blue ribbons, and marked them accordingly.

Well, I went into the bedroom and told Osna matter-of-factly, "These are our *tachrichim.*" Children, her reaction was something I had not bargained for. "I knew it!" she screamed. "You're going to Israel to die, and don't expect me to be a party to it." With that, she quickly put on her coat and dashed out the door. That was the end of her help. For days she would not even talk to me, until I finally convinced her that buying these garments is a special good omen for long life. Many people are so frightened at the thought of death, though we all know it is inevitable.

Children, as we near Eretz Yisrael, our hearts and minds are filled with the glory of *living,* not dying, in Yerushalayim. May Hashem bless us with long and healthy years.

The loudspeaker has just announced that we should board our plane. We are on the last leg of our trip...

Love, Papa and Mama

This letter jogged my memory of another humorous, but embarrassing, incident that occurred a few weeks after I had ordered the sets of *tachrichim.* I went to the wedding of a young friend of mine, and when I entered the wedding hall, the ceremony was already taking place. The elderly woman from whom I had ordered the sets was among the guests.

Since she was very hard of hearing, she did not realize the impact it made in the hushed quietness of the hall when she spied me and called out loudly, "Rebbetzin Shain, your *tachrichim* are ready. You can pick them up!" For a moment there was stunned silence, and then a burst of laughter with an added "shhhh." I quickly sneaked out, my cheeks burning. I don't think the *chasan* or the *kallah* will ever forget this incident, and neither will I.

✍ ✍

Dearest Children,

It was night when we finally arrived at Lod Airport. Aunt Bessie and Aunt Esther's children — Moshe Aaron, Yossie, Shmuli, and Minna — were on hand to greet us. Since Shmuli has a car, Aunt Esther and her children rode together. The Dubins, Aunt Bessie, and Papa and I hired a *sherut.*

By the time the taxi had brought us to our apartment, Papa and I were so tired that we could hardly say "Hello" to the many relatives who were awaiting us there.

Our apartment is still empty, except for a double hi-riser and clothes rack in our bedroom, and a cot in the other bedroom for Aunt Esther, since her apartment is still occupied by the family who has been renting it.

We will be eating our meals at Aunt Bessie's this week, and for Shabbos we are going to Uncle Davie [Nochum Dovid] and Aunt Chaye Dube. Papa and I were very disappointed that we missed Zaidie Herman's first yahrtzeit — the seventeeth of Tammuz — by just five days. As much as we tried to apply pressure to the Jewish Agency to get us on a plane the week before, it just did not work out.

I guess the *Satan* had to win something in his battle to prevent us from settling in Yerushalayim! However, we did go to Zaidie's grave on Har Hamenuchos yesterday, the day after we arrived, which happened to be Uncle Lipman's yahrtzeit. His grave is right near Zaidie Herman's. And Reb Aaron Kotler, *zt"l*, and other very great *tzaddikim* are close by.

Papa and I are waiting anxiously for your first letters. We miss you and our grandchildren terribly.

Love, Papa and Mama

Dearest Children,

Though I wanted to share with you my first thoughts about our arrival, I was too overwhelmed emotionally and too tired physically to find adequate words. Therefore, my first letter to you just detailed the "bare facts" of our first days in Yerushalayim.

It is only now, several days later, that I am able to sort out my impressions and to express my feelings of elation as we drove from Lod Airport to Yerushalayim. I will share them with you.

As we sped along the Tel Aviv highway toward Yerushalayim, the age-old, lofty mountains on either side of the road stood at attention and shielded us from the shadows of the night.

The first breathtaking view of the Holy City, with her myriad lights sparkling and twinkling her message of welcome to us, brought tears of joy to my eyes.

My peaceful heart softly beat out our reply: "Thank you! Thank you! Thank you! We have at last reached HOME!"

Love, Papa and Mama

Klitah: An "Absorbing" Experience

COMING FROM BUSY, bustling New York City to Kiryat Mattersdorf brought a great change into our lives. Here was a sense of spaciousness, the stillness of strolling down a country lane, where the pure, clear air almost begs to be breathed and the clutter of life fades slowly into the distant horizon.

Kiryat Mattersdorf overlooks a large expanse of fifteen kilometers (about nine miles) of stony, sandy land that extends all the way to the city of Ramallah. Before the Six-Day War, this was known as "no-man's land," and it marked the boundary between Jordan and Israel.

On a clear day, one can see in the very far-off distance the tomb of Shemuel *Ha-Navi* high on a mountain, almost touching the horizon.

When we first arrived, Kiryat Mattersdorf was a very small community — if it was even big enough to be called that. It consisted of five apartment buildings, all told. On our side of the street, there were two buildings, A-1 and A-2, with twenty-four apartments in each, and these were considered luxurious at the time, because they were the only ones to have elevators. Our elevator can carry only four passengers at a time, and skinny ones at that. It stops only on the floors of the larger apartments, so that the residents who live in smaller apartments have to walk up half a floor or down half a floor after getting out. Although it seems rickety, it is still a boon for the residents, especially those who live on the higher floors. The three buildings, B-1, B-2 and B-3, on the other side of the street, each have thirty-two apartments. There was a grand total of one hundred forty-four religious families back then, a good part of them blessed with many children, and indeed it was "grand": these families comprised a very warm and vibrant neighborhood.

There was a fruit-and-vegetable store and a small grocery which stocked basic staples, bread and *lachmaniyot* (rolls), and dairy products. One could get filled in on all the news of the town during a visit to the grocery store, as the neighbors were very friendly. This remains true to today, although the community has expanded greatly.

The shul played a vital part of our Kiryah right from the beginning, and one could find a minyan for morning prayers continually, from daybreak on, with *Minchah* prayers in progress from early afternoon until sunset. *Ma'ariv* services would begin at nightfall but minyanim gathered until very late at night. One could always catch a minyan whenever he needed it. There was a separate room for women which was usually crowded on Shabbos.

The shul also had a special place for holding *simchahs*, making it very convenient for celebrating joyous occasions like a bris, a bar mitzvah, or a special Shabbos when a prospective bridegroom would be called up to the Torah. Each *simchah* on Shabbos was followed by a kiddush, with the traditional Yerushalmi kugel as the main dish. This traditional noodle kugel would be kept warm from *erev Shabbos* until it was delivered steaming hot to the shul for the kiddush. (Of course, there was an *eruv* so that carrying on Shabbos in the Kiryah did not present a problem.)

Dark brown, sweet, and quite peppery, Yerushalmi kugel leaves a burning sensation on the tongue. Israelis go for it in a big way, and eat large portions and even second helpings.

Dearest Children,

Last Shabbos when we attended a kiddush in our shul for a *chasan* who was called up to the Torah, Yerushalmi kugel was served and it brought back "spicy" memories of how we were first initiated to this dish. Do you remember the Shabbos *sheva berachos* at Chaya's parents' home? Since her mother was born in Yerushalayim, she had prepared a large Yerushalmi kugel for this special occasion.

I remember that we had no idea what to expect when Chaya's father, Rabbi Berman, announced enthusiastically, "Now comes the best part of the meal — the Yerushalmi kugel." Papa, Yisroel Meyer, and I were served large portions, and Mashi and Raphael Yitzchok got smaller ones.

Now, since I always baked sweet noodle-and-raisin kugel, I assumed that this, too, would be a sweet one. Well, it was surely sweet, but also the most peppery kugel we had ever tasted — how it burned our tongues! Papa and I bravely suffered and ate our portions, not wanting to dampen the enthusiasm of Chaya's parents and her family, who were eating it with gusto. But you, children, took one bite and looked at me helplessly as you tried to swallow it. I gave you the "high sign" to let you know that you did not have to eat it, and you politely put your forks down.

The next day Chaya called me and tactfully asked, "Mama, what kind of kugel does Yisroel Meyer like?"

By the way, speaking of shul, I want to tell you that Papa has a built-in minyan in our own building every morning for *Shacharis,* and for Shabbos as well. The Isbees, Reb Zvi Yakov and Mollie (with whom I have become very friendly), settled here several months before we did. Since he is ill and cannot get to the shul, there is a steady minyan right in their apartment.

Love, Papa and Mama

After Reb Zvi Yakov, passed away, the daily minyan and the Shabbos minyan were kept up for the first year. After that, it was decided to continue the minyan, which caters to many *bnei Torah,* for Shabbos and every *Yom Tov.* It was a great blessing for my husband who found it difficult to climb the stairs to the shul across the street.

✍ ✍

Dearest Children,

Papa and I are trying to get acclimated to life in Yerushalayim. It is actually not a fair trial, since our belongings have not arrived yet, and we are really not settled in.

I had such an embarrassing experience today. I was rushing home from the grocery store with fresh milk and rolls for Papa's breakfast. By mistake, I dashed into building A-2, which is identical to ours, and ran up the two-and-a-half flights of stairs, not even waiting for the elevator. "Our" door was locked, so I pounded very hard, yelling, "Moshe, where are you?" When the door opened, and a startled woman gaped at me, I realized immediately what I had done and explained my mistake to her. We have since become friends!

I am sure you are waiting to hear all about our apartment. You know, in the States, we always lived in a rented one, and now for the first time in our lives we actually own an apartment — Papa and I feel rich!

It is a three-room, sunshiny one with excellent exposures: the living room and the larger bedroom, ours, face south, getting sun all day, while the small bedroom — which is reserved for you when you visit, God willing — faces east, getting all the morning sun and no wind. In the meantime, I am planning to set it up as my typewriting room.

Our kitchen (which is not counted as a room when giving apartment sizes in Israel) is a small one but ample for our needs. A small porch, built out from the kitchen, is designated for our sukkah. This means that on Sukkos, we shall not have to leave our house as we always did, but we'll just walk out of our kitchen straight into the sukkah. We can hardly wait!

Porches and balconies are very important features of Israeli apartments, as everyone wants to extend their limited living space to include the outdoors. We're lucky to have not one, but three balconies: the small one off the kitchen, a long one facing the garden, and another off the bathroom. From the big one off the living room we can see the children from the school nearby as they play and frolic during their recess time. We can even hear their lively chatter, and this does my heart good, as I miss my teaching very much. The third porch is specially built to hold our washing machine; however, since it is completely exposed to the elements (which means that during the winter rainy season our machine can get soaking wet) we shall have to enclose it before winter comes.

The walls are bare, with no built-in closet space at all, and the kitchen has no cupboards. We shall have to invest in clothing wardrobes and build cabinets in the kitchen. As Americans, we were used to built-in closets almost the size of a typical Israeli room, and wall-to-wall cupboards in the kitchen. We were also used to being provided with a refrigerator and stove, which, of course, is not the case here. We're looking forward to getting our electrical appliances with our lift. But I never forget, children, that the above is a small price to pay for the great *zechus* of living in Yerushalayim.

Love, Papa and Mama

Some of the incidents described in the following letter appear in the Introduction to Part 2 of my book *Reaching the Stars.* I am repeating them here, since the source of these experiences was my letters to our children.

Dearest Children,

None of your letters have arrived yet. Papa and I keep checking the mailbox several times a day. Compared to New York, everything here seems to move in slow motion, so I guess the mail follows that pattern too.

Aunt Bessie told me a story that illustrates the snail's pace in which things get done (or not) here! When she settled in Yerushalayim several years ago, and her lift finally arrived, she hired a carpenter to do several jobs for her. She asked him, among other things, to hang her large mirror over the dresser. He replied that he was too busy to get to it that day but that he'd return in a day or two to attend to it. Aunt Bessie waited patiently for two whole weeks, but he did not show up. Of course, he had no phone, so there was no way to reach him. Since she was worried that the mirror might break, she finally hired another carpenter to do the job. About a month later, the first carpenter showed up and walked in briskly with his bag of tools, ready to hang up the mirror. He was quite surprised to learn that Aunt Bessie had not waited for him. "Didn't I tell you that I'd come back?" he complained. "What was your hurry?" I guess you get the idea!

Our painter is also a slippery guy, who disappears regularly for a week or so at a time and then returns to do his painting, at his convenience. However, we are stuck with him, because we naively paid him the entire amount for the painting job when he began. One certainly learns the art of *savlanut* here. Patience is good for one's heart and blood pressure, they say. (You might say that taking things in stride — patience — will keep Papa and me from becoming *patients* at Kupat Cholim!)

Love, Papa and Mama

Dearest Children,

Your first letters have arrived! Papa was at the Yeshivah when they came, so I was able to read them alone, fortunately — for my tears flowed. By the time Papa returned, my eyes were all bloodshot. When he asked me why, I gave him a flimsy excuse about some dust that had blown into my eyes. I then handed him your letters, and he took them out to the porch to read them. His eyes were wet with tears when he came back into the living room, and his excuse was that his allergies were bothering him! I guess we both get 100% for acting our parts...

Love, Papa and Mama

P.S. I should add that having devoted relatives who live in our building helps us greatly to cope with our loneliness. Aunt Esther lives right above us, and Uncle Chaim and Aunt Bessie live on the fifth floor. Their children, Reb Simcha and Rochel and their family, live right next door to them. And Reb Chaim Dov and Frume and their children live one floor down from them. In essence, we are part of a loving family here, and have much to be thankful for.

✍ ✍

Dearest Children,

Our lift finally arrived! It was a grand show for all the children from the neighboring streets, who quickly gathered. My neighbors also peeked from their windows to see the goings-on. Thank Hashem, everything arrived in pretty good shape. There were a few minor dents in the stove and in a metal cabinet, but nothing major.

I may have told you that before we left New York a well-meaning friend had advised me, "Racoma, I understand that the toilet paper in Israel is very rough, and expensive too. Why don't you buy a case of it and stuff every crevice of your lift with rolls of tissue?"

I thought it was excellent advice. Papa and I went to the

warehouse where our lift was being constructed around our belongings, arriving in a taxi filled with cartons and cartons of toilet paper!

As the workers built our crate, and stored our possessions, I tucked a roll of toilet paper into every available space. By the time we left the warehouse, I had a sense of great accomplishment.

Well, when our lift arrived and was opened out on the street, and the movers started to unload our furniture and cartons, the many rolls of toilet paper that I had so carefully tucked into every nook and cranny started to roll away in every direction. The children had a field day, as they scooped up my precious American toilet paper and ran off with it! Like bees, they swarmed around the lift, and the word was out: "Come and get it!"

I chased after them wildly, screaming at the top of my lungs, "*Ganavim*! *Ganavim*!" — the only word in Hebrew I could think of. The little "thieves" thumbed their noses at me, and kept grabbing the rolls of tissue as more and more filled the streets. Somehow, none of our furniture, nor even the beautiful gifts and sets of china we received as going-away presents, were of any value to me at that moment: all that mattered was retrieving my rapidly-rolling-away toilet paper. The movers looked on with amusement, as they watched a hysterical middle-aged woman making such a fuss over some toilet paper.

When it was all over, I had salvaged only a few rolls of the precious stuff. As I entered our apartment, Papa glanced at me with alarm. "Racoma, what on earth has happened to you?"

"Moshe," I gasped, "it's all gone — all our precious toilet paper! I guess I'll just have to buy whatever they sell here."

Now, looking back, I can laugh at the spectacle I made of myself, but then it seemed one of the many hardships of settling in Yerushalayim.

Love, Papa and Mama

The painters finally finished their job, but left a big mess. The floors needed a good scrubbing afterwards, and my neighbor recommended a cleaning lady to do *sponja* (Israeli-style floor washing). She arrived at 7:00 A.M., ready to begin. I found it difficult to understand her accent, as it was different from my Ashkenazi Hebrew. However, I understood enough to be able to hand her the items she needed to do the job: a large pail, a *sponja* stick (a squeegie with a long handle), two *sponja* rags, liquid floor detergent, and plenty of hot water, for which I had turned on my boiler the night before.

I asked her to start with the living room, while I went into the kitchen to make breakfast. A few minutes later, I heard tremendous splashings and sloshings. I hurried into the living room to find it flooded — the water had risen to the lower shelves of our floor-to-ceiling walnut bookcases, and the *seforim* were sopping wet. There was a flow of water cascading through the open door of our balcony and pouring down onto my neighbor's balcony below.

The *sponjerka* was just about to pour another pail of water onto the floor, when I cried out sharply, "*Atzor! Atzor!* — Stop! Stop!" I knew that word from the sign on the bus that lit up when I rang the bell to get off at my stop. She looked at me questioningly, as I pointed frantically at the bookcases and at the armchairs which were beginning to float by then. She did not seem to get the message, so I ran to my neighbor and asked her to please come over and explain in her more fluent Hebrew that I wanted my floors washed but not flooded!

The *sponjerka* was very put out by this, and told my neighbor in a rapid burst of Hebrew that she always does *sponja* this way and no other way. She left in a huff, after I paid her for an extra hour. It took me a few hours of sopping up and wringing out the *sponja* rags to get all the water out of the living room and the balcony.

I then went to my downstairs neighbor to ask her forgiveness for the water that had run onto her porch. She was very understanding when I told her what had happened. She enlightened me by explaining that Israeli furniture is usually moved out of the room before the *sponja* is done, and then when the pails of water are poured onto the floor, and "squeegied" dry, nothing is damaged. Nevertheless, I decided that from then on I would use American methods and my American mop, which fortunately came in my lift.

✍ ✍

Dearest Children,

Our house is slowly shaping up. Most of the cartons have been unpacked, and it feels homey to be surrounded once again by our own furniture and dishes. As I wrote in a previous letter, our apartment did not come with any closet space, so we bought two second-hand closets that hold Papa's suits, my dresses, and the rest of our clothes. They each have a bottom drawer for shoes. We also had cabinets built in the kitchen, and one built in the foyer for our linens.

Living in Mir after our marriage was really good preparation for life in Israel, which is a Garden of Eden compared to the primitive conditions we had there.

Love, Papa and Mama

Dearest Children,

Papa has been trying to find a teaching position, but apparently there is nothing available at this time. He was offered a job teaching very young children, but it was not suited for him. We had thought that finding a job would not be a problem at all, since he is a wonderful teacher with many years of experience in administration as well. But it's not so simple.

We had a long talk about the situation, and Papa expressed

a desire to attend Uncle Chaim's yeshivah, Torah Ore, and learn there for the morning session. So Papa has become a *yeshivah bochur* once more, and finds it very gratifying. When he leaves the house every morning, with a bag of nosh, it reminds me of the years when I saw you all off to yeshivah with your bags of goodies for recess time.

So, you may wonder, if Papa is not earning money, how are we managing financially? First of all, Papa and I know that on Rosh Hashanah, Hashem prepares *parnassah* for the entire year. Of course, we have to make an effort ourselves and not just sit back, so I decided to try to find a job as quickly as possible. And Hashem sent me the exact one geared to my needs.

I am now working in Bayit Lepletot Orphan Home as an English secretary. I wanted very much to be near children, and I was given my wish — the children flit in and out of my office, enjoying the attention I give them. There are two other secretaries as well, young ones, so I sort of adopted them too, and they look to me as their "mother hen," which is also good for my emotions, as I miss you all very much.

I write personal letters for our three directors, which is very interesting, as each one dictates in a different manner: the senior director emigrated from Hungary, one director came from Austria, and your cousin Shmuel Yitzchok Stern [my sister Esther's son] is American. My job also entails public relations work, which means that when English-speaking visitors come to the Home, I show them around and explain our goals.

The hours are very convenient: I leave after Papa does, and I am home soon after he gets home, so we have the afternoons to spend together, and time for our other activities. *Chasdei Hashem*!

Love, Papa and Mama

✍ ✍

In America, we took many material possessions for

granted, that were considered luxuries here. For instance, when I first shopped at our grocery store and asked for a plastic bag for my loaf of bread, I was looked upon as a "spoiled American." The women simply carried the unwrapped loaves of bread in their hands or put them into the shopping baskets they always brought with them.

Another luxury was having a telephone. In our building of twenty-four families, there were only two telephones at the beginning. My sister Bessie had one, and a neighbor on the ground floor had the other. Consequently my sister had a full-time job notifying the neighbors every time someone called them on her telephone, or graciously allowing the neighbors to use her phone. In fact, I went up to her one Friday just to relieve her from phone duty! There were quite a number of calls for our neighbors that morning, but then just before candlelighting time, someone phoned asking for a certain person I did not know. When I inquired where he lived, I was told he lived in B-3, on the top floor. Well, I knew I wouldn't be able to get to him in time, and the caller was quite disappointed when I told him to call back after Shabbos! In a way, Reb Moshe and I enjoyed the quiet of not having a phone, though sometimes it was a necessity.

Transportation from Kiryat Mattersdorf was also a problem. At the beginning, there was only one bus a day that came down to our Kiryah, and when we had to go into town, we had to trudge up a steep hill to get it. The neighborhood submitted a petition asking for the bus to come down into Mattersdorf. The bus company agreed and this was already a great improvement. In general, we do a lot of walking in Israel, which keeps us in good shape.

Dearest Children,

Hooray! After waiting impatiently for three months, we finally have a telephone. We can now call each other once in a while, and it will be wonderful to hear your voices. Of course, it was only the emergency of Papa's tachycardia attack that made it possible for us to get it so "quickly." Other people sometimes have to wait for six months to a year. However, since the head of the cardiology department gave me a letter to the telephone company stating that it was urgent for us to have a telephone because of Papa's heart condition, we were given priority.

Can you imagine that it cost over one hundred dollars to install!! And I had gotten so used to not having a phone that the first time a call came through, it rang a number of times before I realized that I was hearing our phone ringing! It was Aunt Bessie wishing us mazal tov on our new acquisition. Actually we don't expect too many calls, as telephones are still scarce in Yerushalayim.

May we share many happy tidings through our phone.

Love, Papa and Mama

✍ ✍

In my home in America, I had a special wall dispenser for rolls of aluminum foil, wax paper, and paper towels. Whenever I saw they were getting low, I would make a note to replenish them on my next trip to the supermarket. It never entered my mind to consider these items as luxuries.

When we settled in Yerushalayim, and I priced paper goods and aluminum foil, I realized that here they were very expensive and that the locally produced brands were of inferior quality as well. Suddenly, the little "necessities" of life became extravagances.

A friend of mine who was visiting from New York thoughtfully brought me a large roll of "silver foil," which I guarded as if it were *sterling* silver. In fact, it was so precious to me that after I used some of it, and it was still in good condition, I would wash it and hang it out to dry.

Dearest Children,

A young, newly married couple from the States recently moved into our building. I met the young woman and welcomed her warmly. The next morning she knocked at my door and asked if I had any aluminum foil, confiding in me that she was attempting to bake a chocolate cake for the first time, as a surprise for her husband.

"Yes, I do have a roll," I said hesitantly, but she didn't seem to sense my reluctance. I handed her the roll, and as I watched in despair, she kept unrolling and unrolling it. "I guess this should be enough to line my pan, and I'll take a little more, if you don't mind, to keep the cake fresh in the refrigerator after it's done," she said. Then with a breezy, "Thank you very much," she hurried out of the house.

Looking back now, I am amazed at my uncharacteristic response. Usually I feel great pleasure in lending things and helping people. But at the time, that roll of aluminum foil seemed to symbolize for me the security of doing things the way I knew, the way I had been used to. My insecurities as a new immigrant came to be centered on that precious roll of "silver" foil, and the thought of watching it get used up so quickly just overwhelmed me.

A few days later, in walked my neighbor with a piece of chocolate cake, and a penitent look on her face. "Mrs. Shain," she blurted out, "I had no idea that aluminum foil is so precious here! I happened to mention to a friend of mine about my chocolate cake, and how very kind you were to supply me with enough aluminum foil. My friend was astounded, and explained to me that in Israel you don't borrow foil and that these things are not taken for granted. Please forgive me, and I'll gladly buy some aluminum foil and return it to you," she ended apologetically.

"Oh, just forget about it," I told her. "It's my welcoming gift to you, and thanks for the chocolate cake, which really looks delicious. Will you give me the recipe?"

Love, Papa and Mama

P.S. Children, if you get the opportunity, please send me a box of aluminum foil...

✍ ✍

When we arrived in Yerushalayim in 1968, very few families owned air conditioners. Since we were living in the mountains, 830 meters (over 2,700 feet) above sea level, we did not suffer from the often unbearably hot, humid weather that characterizes summertime on the coast. However, in the spring and the fall, the *chamsin*, with its scorching dry desert winds from the east, parched Yerushalayim and us along with it. We were advised — rather, warned — to drink at least three or four liters (quarts) of liquid each day during this period.

After Reb Moshe had his tachycardia attack, the cardiologist advised him to be careful during a *chamsin*, for it was a strain on the heart. He was to stay indoors and we were to keep the windows closed, so that the dry air would not penetrate. The doctor also suggested that we install an air conditioner.

Dearest Children,

Amid dust and dirt, breaking and building, questions and queries, our air conditioner at last is safely embedded in the living-room wall.

I ordered the unit from a catalog at a local electrical appliance store, whose owner knew as much about air conditioners as an Eskimo does. He told me he would find me workmen to prepare the wall before the delivery of the air conditioner, which would be in about a week or so.

Several days later, two workmen arrived laden with tools and a piece of paper on which were written the exact measurements of our air conditioner. I got Papa safely out of the house so he would not be exposed to the dirt and dust.

The men then began the arduous job of breaking through the twelve-inch-thick stone wall in our living room. (In our apartment, the unit could not be placed in a window, as is done routinely in the States.) The deafening noise reverberated throughout our entire building, so that all twenty-four neighbors knew that the Shains were having an air conditioner installed. The stones piled up, and the fine white dust settled on everything.

Several hours later, a shape started to emerge, but what a shape! When the workers left to take a lunch break, I measured the space, which was over two feet long and about a foot wide. I could not imagine that any air conditioner could possibly fit into that space.

When I questioned the workers afterwards, they looked at me with scorn. "*Geveret,*" one said confidently, "we know what we are doing, and we are following the measurements exactly. Why don't you just relax and wait until the job is all finished." Against my better judgment I waited. They left in the early afternoon, and said they would return the next morning to finish their work.

Well, the next morning the workmen arrived early as they'd promised, and started their hammering right away. They had just about completed breaking out the last part of the wall when the air conditioner arrived. I asked them to stop their work and lift the air conditioner out of its carton, so I could see it. Well, children, as soon as they took it out, I saw immediately that it would not fit into the hole they had prepared for it. The workers looked at each other queerly and rechecked their measurements. They did not wait for me to confront them — one of them hurried to the phone and telephoned the store owner.

After an agitated conversation in rapid Hebrew, and a comparison of the unit's measurements with those of the hole, the worker banged down the phone and said grumpily, "The owner made a *slight* mistake and gave us the width for the length and vice versa. It will take us several more hours of work now — we'll have to break more of the wall in the width and rebuild the wall in the length."

You might imagine that they would feel somewhat contrite and express remorse, since I had warned them that it did not look right — but no! Instead, *they* acted like the injured parties! The final blow came when they insisted that I pay them for the extra hours they had to work repairing the damage they had caused in the first place. They argued that it was not their fault at all, but the store owner's, since he had made the mistake, and that I should have it out with him.

Since I was too weary to fight them, I paid them the entire amount. When I turned to the owner with my complaint, he put me on the defensive, saying, "I only sold you the air conditioner and I was kind enough to get you workmen." As for his mistake with the measurements, he dismissed it casually: "The directions were not in Hebrew, so I got them mixed up."

I've discovered, since living in Yerushalayim, the wisdom of the old adage, "If you can't lick 'em, join 'em."

I like Papa's reaction: "Racoma, we are in Yerushalayim, where the *churban Beis Ha-Mikdash* took place. We have to be reminded of this over and over again, and know there cannot be complete satisfaction without *tza'ar,* especially in material things." How right Papa is! The workmen left an ugly patch on the living-room wall, adding another *zecher l'churban* in our home.

Today it was very hot, and I turned on the air conditioner for the first time. Thank Hashem, it really works!

Love, Papa and Mama

✍ ✍

I have written about experiences which, although they taxed my patience, I have learned to take in stride. Now, in fact, when a workman shows up on time, I am so appreciative that I never haggle over the price. An incident which I like to call "finishing touches" — and you will see why — proved once again that material possessions acquired here seem to come with some sort of suffering.

Dearest Children,

Last year I bought a second-hand clothes closet, with an attractive walnut finish, which seemed to be in very good condition. A short while after the closet was delivered, the finish started to wear off, and white streaks showed through here and there.

Since the store where I bought it had no telephone, I went back and told the owner in person what had happened. He was very agreeable and sympathetic. "Don't worry," he assured me, "I am responsible and I'll take care of it."

I waited for two weeks, and then visited his store again. He assured me again that he would come to refinish my closet as soon as possible. After my fourth trip to his store, I realized that his "possible" was becoming impossible, and I accepted the inevitable and learned to live with the white streaks, which became more numerous and prominent as the months went by.

Recently my neighbor mentioned that she had bought some furniture from the same place, and the man would be delivering it soon. I asked her if she could please remind him that I had been waiting for an *entire year* for him to refinish my closet. She conveyed my message, and he told her that when he delivered her furniture, he would come over and take care of the closet.

Lo and behold! He appeared a week later with a large bottle of wood alcohol and a bottle of walnut finish. He set about his work, and I watched him happily, hoping that at long last our closet would have a nice finish. He smeared the wood alchohol on the doors to remove the old finish.

As he was working, he lit a cigarette and accidentally tripped, knocking over the bottle of alcohol, which shattered into pieces, scattering glass and alcohol all over the bedroom floor. The alcohol burst into flame, but fortunately, he doused the flames before the house went up in smoke!

We both worked for almost an hour to clean up the mess, as a result of which he cut his finger, the house reeked from the alcohol fumes, and the closet doors are now a dull gray. He left with the assurance that he would return. Of course, I really don't expect him to come in the foreseeable future. Maybe I'll try to apply the walnut finish myself, for he left the bottle behind!

I would recommend to all would-be settlers, that it is important to have some knowledge of carpentry, plumbing, electricity, doctoring, and other essential services in order to keep their homes and themselves in shape.

Love, Papa and Mama

Instead of feeling frustrated by incidents like this, I learned to accept that living in Yerushalayim has a price, and, as I have already mentioned, it is little enough to pay for the ultimate peace of mind at being here.

The fact is that we were never bored, and each challenge was stimulating. Though Reb Moshe and I were in our middle years when we settled in Yerushalayim, for us it was not the "finish," but rather the start, of an exciting, stirring, bright and wonderful life.

Uncommon Utilities

WE ARE SURROUNDED by various sounds in our lives: the soothing rustle of leaves, the happy gurgle of a baby, the twitter of birds, the comforting sound of approaching footsteps, the honking horns of traffic. There is the sudden cry of pain, the whimper of a child, the raucous laughter of youth, and the soft sigh of old age. The list is endless, and I have always accepted the sounds of life with equanimity.

However, the deafening rat-a-tat-tat of drilling in the street, which awakened me very early in the morning, grated on my eardrums.

Workmen were busy breaking up the road, trying to get to the pipes underground. After completing whatever it was they were doing, they cleaned up the mess and repaved the street. A few days later, we were once more subjected to the racket of the jackhammer and to the dirt and mess of the same area being torn up. This time, there were different laborers, who had to reach other installations underneath the street. Somehow, there had been no coordination with the previous workers. Perhaps they belonged to different municipal departments or different utility companies.

In fact, it seems that the streets of Yerushalayim are in constant repair. Either new sidewalks are being put in or old ones are being ripped up, new cables and pipes are being laid or old ones fixed. It would be a good idea if our streets had built-in zippers to make them easier to open and close whenever necessary.

When utility companies attack the streets, and a whole neighborhood becomes a "battle zone," the residents commiserate with one another. However, when a utility singles out a newcomer like me for its attack, it can be a very lonely war. Like any front-line soldier, I took solace in letter-writing.

Dearest Children,

I've always taken it for granted that only human beings have distinct personalities, but since settling here, I've discovered an unusual phenomenon: animals — cats, especially — and even inanimate objects — like our plumbing — appear to have their own personalities.

Yerushalayim has an abundance of stray cats who strut through the streets as if they own them. In the States, whenever I shooed a cat away, he quickly fled. Here, when I enter the garbage cubicle, there is always a congregation of cats barring my way. When I try to disperse them, they stare me straight in the eye and refuse to budge, their haughty expressions suggesting that *I'm* disturbing *them.* I guess they must be unique if they have the *zechus* to be in Eretz Yisrael.

And now on to plumbing: in Yerushalayim, a small drip in a faucet becomes a major event. Not only are we warned to conserve water for obvious reasons but we also pay for our water, which we did not have to do where we lived in the States.

The other day, I heard a steady drip coming from our

bathroom faucet, and as much as I tightened it, the dripping would not stop. I could see Israel's precious water resources declining, and our water bill growing, with every *plop*. I realized that this required drastic steps, so I ran to the plumber (called an *installator* in Hebrew!) who lives in our neighborhood and impressed upon his wife that her husband must come as soon as possible, since it was an emergency.

In the meantime, I placed a large bucket under the leaky faucet to save the water. When it reached overflowing, I decided to do *sponja* (wash the floors), even though they were clean. I also washed our bedspreads and bathmats with the next few buckets of water. By that time, Papa forbade me to go near the faucet, and I was so "washed out" that I did not argue with him.

Late the next afternoon, the plumber finally put in an appearance, equipped with a large box of tools, expecting to see a waterfall. He strode over to the leaky faucet, turned it on and off several times, and the drip stopped! We waited in mute silence for a few seconds. "You have to learn to turn off your faucet properly," he chided me, making me feel like a foolish child who had made a fuss over nothing. He kindly refused any payment. I told Papa that we should not use this faucet for a while as it deserved a rest. Fortunately, we have another little sink right outside our bathroom.

Love, Papa and Mama

✍ ✍

A large-capacity water tank is situated on our roof. If for any reason the city water supply is cut off, this tank contains enough reserves to sustain us for a few days. After the War of Independence, when Yerushalayim was under siege and water had to be rationed, tanks like these were installed on the roofs of most of the buildings. This feature has become more or less standard in all new construction as well.

Our roof is only accessible by climbing a rickety ladder

and crawling through a trap door. It is therefore impossible for me to check our water tank. A neighbor who climbed up to check his found that ours was leaking badly. He kindly shut it off and informed us; otherwise, our water tank would have continued to leak, running up an enormous bill, and eventually leaving us "high and dry."

We called the *installator*, who wriggled his way onto the roof and brought back the report that we needed a new tank. It was hoisted up to the roof from the street below with heavy rope.

In Yerushalayim, it is necessary to be prepared for every eventuality: not only water shortage, but also a sudden shut-off of gas or electricity. One *erev Shabbos*, a short time before candlelighting, the gas suddenly ran out in our entire Kiryah. There was a hue and cry, as most of us use a *blech* over the gas to keep the cholent hot over Shabbos. It seems that this had happened several times in the past on *erev Shabbos*, but for us it was the first time. After an emergency call to the gas company, the gas came back on partially, but many residents — including us — remained without any.

When we came to Israel, I had bought a two-burner electric hotplate to use until our gas stove arrived. Several weeks before our gas shut-off occurred, I had lent it to a friend, telling her she could keep it as long as she needed it. That very Friday she returned it, as her stove had finally been repaired. Thus it was available just when this emergency arose, and thank Hashem, we had good hot meals on Shabbos.

The electricity also plays tricks, stopping without prior notice. These power failures play havoc with our electrical appliances, and our nerves, the electricity going off in the midst of washing cycle, or when I'm mixing a cake. "Time and time again," the electric clock and the Shabbos clock have to be adjusted.

In addition to water, gas, and electricity, heating our

house during the cold, rainy months posed another problem. Though we had steam radiators, the building's furnace was on for only a few hours in the early morning and in the evening. We understood that to heat the entire building all day long would be prohibitively expensive, but the apartment would get freezing cold in the afternoons — too cold for comfort.

We were advised to buy a kerosene stove and a supply of kerosene, which was considered to be a relatively inexpensive and effective means of providing supplemental heat. Although kerosene fumes are not healthful, we were accustomed to a heated apartment, and couldn't take the cold, so this seemed the lesser of two evils. We did have a small electric heater, which we had shipped with our belongings, but we used that just for spot heating, as electricity is costly.

They say that Yerushalayim is one of the rare cities where a person has to go outside on a sunny winter's day to warm up, because the houses, built of thick stone, retain their cold.

Dearest Children,

There was excitement in the "Israeli branch" of the family about our great nephew (Avremal's son) getting married. This was our first family wedding since settling here, so we really looked forward to a Yerushalmi affair. Of course, Papa wore his Shabbos suit, and to please me he even put on a tie, which he has stopped wearing since living here. I dressed up in a special outfit, and had my wig combed out for the occasion. Though it was a very cold night, I wore my Shabbos shoes instead of my lined boots.

The *chupah* was held in the courtyard of the Yeshivah, but the reception was in the basement, or rather, the bomb shelter. (All the buildings here have basement bomb shelters which, thank Hashem, are used mostly for storage; the ones that are spacious enough are used for regular minyanim and for *simchahs*.) Little did we know that there would be no heat, and the place was icy cold. Not only did I not take off my winter coat throughout the whole evening, but I wore my woolen scarf wrapped around my neck and my gloves the entire time. I tried wiggling my toes every so often so they would not get frostbitten. By the time the meal was served, I had to pry open my frozen lips to get the warm food down.

When we finally got home, and warmed up a bit, Papa told me that at one time he had such a case of shivers that he wanted to leave, but did not want to spoil my "fun." I had the same idea, but had thought that Papa probably wasn't that cold, since he was wearing a heavy woolen suit and a vest. At the next winter wedding, I could wear a warm flannel nightgown and bathrobe under my coat, and no one would be the wiser.

I was surprised to see that very young children and even infants were brought to the wedding. In fact, the children could not find empty seats when the meal was being served, so they seated themselves at the bride's table. When the *kallah* returned from the *yichud* room, it took a lot of coaxing to get the little ones to relinquish their seats.

I just reread what I've written, children, and it sounds very negative. So I should point out that the wedding itself was a very happy and *freilich* one, and Papa and I enjoyed the opportunity of meeting many of our relatives and friends. Surprisingly, the *kallah* and many of the guests (I presume sabras) did not seem to suffer from the cold at all — they actually took off their coats! However, they did a lot of dancing, which kept them warm, something Papa and I could not do.

May we share many "warm" *simchahs* with each other.

Love, Papa and Mama

Growing Up with Mattersdorf

EXCITEMENT REIGNED IN Kiryat Mattersdorf when our street was finally given a name: Panim Me'irot — "radiant face." After inquiries about the significance of this name, I discovered the following about both our street and our Kiryah:

Rabbi Shmuel Ehrenfeld, who founded Kiryat Mattersdorf, was the Grand Rabbi of the *kehillah* of Mattersdorf, and also the *Nasi* of the seven *kehillos* in the area of Burgenland, Austria, with Mattersdorf the largest and most prominent of them. When he immigrated to the United States, he established the Yeshivah Chasan Sofer and was also the rabbi of the Etz Chaim shul. He was a descendant of the great sage, the Chasan Sofer.

Panim Me'irot is the title of an eighteenth-century volume of responsa on the *Shulchan Aruch*, written by Rabbi Meir Eisenstadt of the seven *Kehillos*. It was rewarding to have our street named after a holy book.

In fact, the streets of Yerushalayim bear many inspiring names. A walk through the neighborhood of Geulah, for example, can be very spiritually uplifting as one passes Zechariah, Yechezkel, Amos, Malachi, Yonah, Tzefaniah, and other streets named after the great and holy Prophets. A casual glance at the street sign when one is waiting to cross the road reveals the depths of the tradition and holiness that surrounds our every moment in Yerushalayim. We are thus constantly reminded of the message they convey: "We are a holy people."

Dearest Children,

It is exciting to watch Kiryat Mattersdorf grow. As you know, Papa and I were the very first to buy an apartment here, when there were only bare hills and dales, sand and stone. In fact, when we bought our apartment from a sketch, many of our friends and relatives scoffed when we told them, "We have an apartment in Yerushalayim!" Frankly, even I looked a little skeptically at the architect's drawing of several high-rise buildings with cars parked nearby.

Now that we are living here and watching it develop, we are optimistic that in time it will grow by leaps and bounds into a large community, spreading far and wide.

Buildings A-3 and A-4 on our side of the street are almost completed. The plans call for the building of A-5 and A-6 to start very soon. On the other side of the street, C-1, C-2, and C-3 are in the midst of construction. I heard that there will also be three D-buildings, which will be more luxurious, with larger apartments, and, hopefully, larger elevators too. There are also plans to build private, one-family cottages which will command a majestic view of the entire mountainside, and be the most luxurious of all.

A playground for young children is also in the offing. It will be a welcome benefit for both the children and their mothers who will be able to sit and relax while their little ones romp and play together.

We are very much looking forward to having Rebbetzin Hollander, and Eleanor and Dave Mandel as new neighbors. They will be settling here shortly. You know, it was with our encouragement that they bought an apartment in A-4, and they are hoping to come as soon as they receive word that it's ready. Having these devoted friends of many years living close by will be a great pleasure for Papa and me. Rebbetzin Hollander's fondest dream was to spend her later years in Yerushalayim, and now her wish is about to come true, God willing, when she settles here with her daughter and son-in-law.

Love, Papa and Mama

Dearest Children,

Our wonderful new neighborhood is continuing to develop, and each addition is thrilling for Papa and me. What a *zechus* it is to be seeing with our own eyes the rebuilding of Yerushalayim! Bus number 7 now comes down to our Kiryah to pick up passengers, so we don't have to climb the hill to get it. We also have a *second* grocery store, and the competition keeps prices stable and eases the pressure of everyone buying in the same place and having to wait a long time for their turn to check out. A chicken and fish store, and a variety store that sells miscellaneous items have now become part of our neighborhood.

The way our shopping center is developing reminds me of the nursery rhyme about "the butcher, the baker, and the candlestick-maker." We also have other "makers" here — like the wig-maker, the shoemaker, and the marriage-maker! And we have another convenience in our Kiryah — a doctor! Dr. Shusheim, a very fine surgeon and general practitioner, has opened an office just across the street from us.

Last but not least, I just saw a notice that a bank will be opening in our shopping district. This is exciting progress...

The apartments in Kiryat Mattersdorf are very much in demand and are being snapped up as soon as they are built. I recall that Rabbi Akiva Ehrenfeld (the son of the Mattersdorf Rav), who sold our apartment to us, advised Papa and me to encourage you all to buy apartments when we did. I wish we had heeded his advice, as they cost much more now. However, none of you had available funds anyway, and, at that time, it seemed only a dream on a sketch, so we did not pursue it.

Love, Papa and Mama

✍ ✍

From 1968 to the present, Kiryat Mattersdorf has developed from a few buildings perched on the edge of a bare mountainside into a large, active community.

What Reb Moshe and I thought was a dream in the distant future has in twenty years become a reality far surpassing our greatest expectations. Kiryat Mattersdorf is a bustling, vibrant, flourishing community of hundreds of religious families living together in harmony.

There are myriad activities for everyone: *shiurim* for men and for women, charity drives, *oneg Shabbos* parties for the children, and more and more and more...

A few years ago this was brought home to me, as I was sitting at our bus stop in the early morning waiting for bus number 3 to take me to Meah Shearim to do some shopping.

Boys and girls were streaming from their homes on the way to the Kiryat Mattersdorf *cheder* and to Bais Yaakov. Fathers and mothers were pushing strollers to the many day nurseries in the neighborhood. School buses were picking up children for schools in other neighborhoods.

Traffic was heavy, with several buses stopping at our bus stop. Bus number 16, coming from Bayit Vegan on its way to Ramot, picked up many passengers. Bus number 2, from Har

Nof to the *Kosel* had standing-room only. I noticed bus number 7, on the other side of the street, heading toward the center of town, crowded with students and many young people going to work. Finally, my bus came and I boarded it.

We passed the very busy commercial center, which always gives me a sense of satisfaction when I see the throngs of people frequenting the stores. Reb Noson Greenberg has a thriving real estate agency in the midst of our shopping center.

The bus rode by Panim Meirot 17, the last building on our street, and turned the corner into Sorotzkin Street, named after Rabbi Zalman Sorotzkin, a great Torah Sage from Lutsk, Poland.

We passed Nevei Simcha, a Senior Citizens' Home, which also has hospital facilities for the chronically ill, and its own clinical laboratory. Rabbi Simcha Bunim Klein, the nephew of the Mattersdorf Rav, is the director of Nevei Simcha, and he has overseen all the construction of Kiryat Mattersdorf from its beginning.

As the bus wound its way around the mountain, there came into view Torah Ore Seminary, whose *Rosh Yeshivah*, as I've mentioned, is Rabbi Chaim Scheinberg, my sister's husband. It occupies a large building and has hundreds of *talmidim* both in the Yeshivah and in the *Kollel.* It is adding a new wing to accommodate many more *talmidim* who are anxious to enroll in the Yeshivah. The building is at the boundary of Kiryat Mattersdorf.

We were now in Kiryat Itri, which consists of five large apartment buildings on one side of the street, and a large supermarket on the other side.

The community of Unsdorf begins right after Kiryat Itri, with the impressive Machon Sarah Schneirer dormitory jutting out on the hill. It houses foreign students and out-of-town Israelis who attend the Bais Yaakov Seminary. Children's Town came into view next, a yeshivah with dormitory facilities, founded by Rabbi Menachem Porush of the Agudas Yisrael, and member of the Knesset.

As the bus continued its route, we passed other yeshivos that have sprung up over the last few years, and a pharmacy and another supermarket were evident. Girls' Town Jerusalem, founded by Bayit Lepletot, came into view. It has a full program of academic studies and vocational training, and is home for many Russian girls and other new immigrants, who have recently come home to our shores.

We rode into Kiryat Sanz, which was built about the same time as our Kiryah. Near it is Ezrat Torah, and overlooking these communities is Kiryat Belz, which was built only recently. On Shabbos it is paradise to see and to feel that there is no *chillul Shabbos* from Kiryat Mattersdorf all the way to Ezrat Torah, several kilometers away.

The golden stone of all these buildings glowed against the clear blue sky, as the bus slowly climbed and descended the hills of Yerushalayim.

Yes, Reb Moshe and I witnessed the growth and development of Kiryat Mattersdorf almost from its inception, and many of the other neighborhoods as they grew and transformed the once-barren mountains into thriving communities. I thought of the prayer we recite on Rosh Hashanah and Yom Kippur, asking Hashem to "grant...joy to Your Land and gladness to Your city..."

As we neared my bus stop in Meah Shearim, it took a few moments for my thoughts to return to the everyday world. May Yerushalayim continue to spread far and wide!

PART TWO:

Festival Firsts

"Heading" for Rosh Hashanah

THE CHANTING OF *SELICHOS* at dawn,* and the blowing of the shofar right after morning prayers usher in the month of Elul. It brings with it an intangible, trembling feeling that it is time for us to prepare for the coming of the Day of Judgment. It is also customary to recite Psalm 27 after *Shacharis* and after *Ma'ariv*, from the second day of *Rosh Chodesh Elul* through *Hoshannah Rabbah.* This Psalm was chosen because of its connotation, according to a comment from the Midrash:

"A Psalm of David — Hashem is my light [on Rosh Hashanah] and [on Yom Kippur] He is my salvation."

The month of Elul has its physical qualities also. A few stray clouds sail bravely through the clear blue sky, making

*It is the custom of the Sephardim to start reciting *Selichos* from the first day of Elul, while the Ashkenazim start only during the last week of the month.

us aware that summer is waning. The parched, cracked earth looks up expectantly toward the heavens for the first signs of the early rains to quench her thirst after the hot, dry summer. The stately olive trees (one of the seven species with which Eretz Yisrael is blessed [*Devarim* 8:8]) wave their silvery branches laden with the green fruit that will be ready to pick after the first rain.

The days grow shorter, and the nights' cool breezes bring relief from the heat of the summer.

The month of Elul prepares us spiritually and physically for the approaching "Days of Awe" — Rosh Hashanah and Yom Kippur.

Dearest Children,

A happy, healthy New Year to you and to all of our beloved grandchildren. We are now in the midst of *Asseres Yemei Teshuvah* [the Ten Days of Repentance between Rosh Hashanah and Yom Kippur]. Every morning at 6:00 A.M. Papa and I go down to the Isbee minyan to recite *Selichos* and then daven *Shacharis.* Though it is very early in the morning, "the women's section" — which consists of the Isbee kitchen and sukkah porch — is crowded with women and children.

And now, children, I want to tell you something about Rosh Hashanah in Yerushalayim. As a child and later as a teenager, every Rosh Hashanah at shul I heard Zaidie Herman's melodious and spiritual intonation of the *Shacharis* service, which had a lasting effect. In Mir, Poland, I davened on Rosh Hashanah with the greatest *Gedolim* of our time and over five hundred *bnei Torah,* an experience which I shall never forget. But, somehow, on a sunny morning in the Isbee kitchen in Yerushalayim, it was even more inspiring for me. I felt that I had a "hotline" straight to "the Boss."

After *Ma'ariv* on the first night of Rosh Hashanah, before leaving the shul, we all greeted one another with the traditional New Year blessing: "May you be inscribed and sealed immediately for a good life."

We continued to observe the customs we always had observed on the first night of Rosh Hashanah. We dipped the challah into honey, and then we made the blessing on an apple, which we also dipped into honey, saying, "May we have a good and sweet year." We ate fish to symbolize our wish that the Jewish nation should multiply like fish in the sea, and we also ate the head of the fish, so that we would merit to be "at the head and not at the tail."

But here in Israel, I learned that there are many other special foods eaten for the symbolic significance of their Hebrew or Aramaic names. Rochel (Edie) Landsberg, who has become a very close friend of mine since working in Bayit Lepletot with me, graciously sent me all the different kinds of foods — along with a chart of the different blessings that are said over each one. She has become a pro, as she was married here and knows all the many customs. (Sometimes different foods are used for the same words.)

I am sure you will be interested in learning about them, as Papa and I found them very enlightening:

Kara (pumpkin): May it be the will of our Father in Heaven that You tear up — *she-tiKRA* — the evil judgment and recall — *ve'yiKARu* — before You our meritorious deeds.

Ruvyah (black-eyed peas): ...that our merits be numerous — *yiRBU.*

Karti (leek): ...that our enemies be torn asunder — *she-yiKARTu.*

Silki (spinach): that our enemies and adversaries be no more — *she-yiStaLKu.*

Temarim (dates): that our enemies be nullified— *yiTAMu.*

Rimonim (pomegranates): that our merits be as numerous as the seeds of the pomegranate.

Well, children, after Papa and I and Aunt Esther, who ate with us, partook of all the above *simanim,* we were left with very little room for all the festive holiday food I had prepared.

Love, Papa and Mama

Dearest Children,

You know, Rosh Hashanah is a different color here in Israel! In the States, the holiday clothes are in dark-toned autumn colors or classic black. But here every shul and street shines with white; from grandmothers to infants, all of *am Yisrael* is dressed in the color of purity for Rosh Hashanah.

Just before the blowing of the shofar, the Isbee shul became so crowded with mothers and children, that they were standing lined up in the hall. Mollie Isbee had thoughtfully prepared loads of lollipops and cookies to keep the little ones quiet during the blowing of the shofar. It worked, as their mouths were stuffed and busy with the goodies. Most of the mothers and children cleared out right after the first shofar blowings.

As you know, one is not allowed to talk from the start of the blowing of the shofar until the end of prayers, when the last blasts are sounded. This always gives me a chance to really concentrate, but here in Yerushalayim as I reflected upon the lyrical words of the *Musaf* prayers, I understood them even more profoundly. As our Sages say: "The air of Eretz Yisrael makes one wise."

After *Minchah* we set out for *Tashlich,* and let me tell you, it certainly was very different from going to *Tashlich* in New York. There, you know how thousands crowd the East River Drive to throw their sins into the murky depths of the East River, which certainly had enough water to accept them all. Here, since Yerushalayim is not near any bodies of water, we had to make do with a distant little pond that was so far away we could hardly see it. I certainly hope it had room for our sins...I can't imagine how it did, but maybe that's part of the wonder of Eretz Yisrael.

We wish you all a *Gemar Tov,* an easy fast, and a very joyful Sukkos.

Love, Papa and Mama

P.S. Chana telephoned to wish us a "Happy New Year," and

told me about a lively experience she had on *erev Rosh Hashanah.* I must share it with you.

She had spent Shabbos in Safed with some close friends, and since Rosh Hashanah was on Sunday night, she was anxious to get back to Yerushalayim in plenty of time for the *Yom Tov.* She got to the bus station in Safed early Sunday morning, and as she waited in line for the bus to Yerushalayim, she noticed a young religious man in heated conversation with the bus driver. The bus driver kept shaking his head in adamant refusal. Then the young man went over to a few of the men who were about to board the bus, and again Chana witnessed the same reaction. Whatever it was he was asking for, no one was willing to comply.

Finally he approached Chana, and pleaded, "Please, Miss, could you do me a favor and take this package with you to Yerushalayim? It is for my father, who must have it for tonight, for Rosh Hashanah."

"What's in the package?" asked Chana.

"I've just slaughtered a sheep," the young man replied casually, "and this is the head, which my father is waiting for."

Although Chana felt queasy just thinking about the contents of the package, she understood that this was the custom of some Jews and agreed to take it, handling it gingerly.

"My father will be at the central bus station in Yerushalayim to accept it," the young man explained happily, and blessed her many times. Chana boarded the bus, and deposited the unpopular package near her seat, as the bus driver and passengers looked warily in her direction.

No sooner had the bus started on its way, than the package started to ooze, slowly but surely staining the floor of the bus a deep pink. To make a long story short, hours later, by the time the bus was approaching Yerushalayim, the wet wrapping paper had all but disintegrated and the fresh sheep's head ogled Chana ungratefully. The sheep then stuck her rosy tongue out and wagged it reprovingly at the bus driver and the passengers, who stared back in utter disgust.

When the bus finally arrived at its destination and pulled in to the central bus station in Yerushalayim, Chana leapt up with the dripping sheep's head, and flew off the bus. An elderly, bearded man hurried over to her, grabbed the sheep's head, blessed her profusely, and went on his way.

I told Chana that in the merit of doing this act of *chesed*, she will be blessed to be at the head...

Children, this unique experience could only happen in Eretz Yisrael.

Love, Papa and Mama

"This is Our Atonement"

Erev Yom Kippur
October 5, 1973

Dearest Children,

Just a few words before Papa and I sit down to eat the *seudah ha-mafsekes* —

When we lived in the States, on *erev Yom Kippur* our home reflected the holiness of the approaching day, but just outside our door the cars whizzed by without a stop, and it was "business as usual."

In Yerushalayim, however, *erev Yom Kippur* is an entirely different experience. In the very early morning, the streets were full of men and women coming from *Selichos* and morning prayers, frantically doing last-minute shopping, and hurrying to the mikveh.

At 2:00 P.M. life suddenly ground to a halt. The radio went off the air. Buses stopped running. The streets were emptied, and a heavy silence pervaded every nook and cranny.

I went out onto our balcony. The trees seemed to be

standing at attention, still and tall, ready for the Day of Atonement. Not a leaf stirred on their branches. The birds had stopped their chirping. Our roses silently nodded to the tiny blades of grass: "We are ready."

I asked myself, "Am I ready?"

May Hashem answer the many prayers that we all will beseech Him with on Yom Kippur. We only ask from Him what He wants from us: that we be able to learn Torah, to obey His commandments, and to serve Him with joy. In order for us to accomplish this, He has to bless us with clear minds, healthy hearts and bodies, livelihood, and *Yiddishe naches* from our children and grandchildren. Why should He not answer us? He surely will!

Love, Papa and Mama

None of us had the faintest inkling of the tumultuous events that would take place on that Yom Kippur. Who would have imagined that the deep and utter silence would be shattered by the wail of air-raid sirens? That the clear blue sky would be filled with the roar of warplanes? And that the men who stood in shul praying would rush to the front before the fast was over, some never to return?

When we heard that Egypt had attacked us at the Suez Canal and that the army was being mobilized and all the reserve troops called up, we were shocked and terrified. The army sent jeeps to all the shuls in the entire country to round up the reservists — that is, every able-bodied man in Israel. *Roshei Yeshivos* and *Rabbanim* urged the men who were called up to leave immediately to join their army units, even though it was Shabbos and Yom Kippur — this was a matter of *pikuach nefesh*, of life and death!

Dearest Children,

The start of the Yom Kippur War caught everyone

ill-prepared. Papa and I were jolted into a realization of the gravity of the situation when the air-raid siren went off with its shrill, piercing, rising-and-falling wail which clearly announces danger. There was near panic in our shul as everybody cleared out and ran down to the air-raid shelter in the basement.

Papa and I faced a problem: I knew that if he went down to the shelter two floors below, it would be a strain for him to climb up again, because of his fasting and his heart condition. So I suggested that we remain in the Isbee apartment, and sit it out in the foyer, which seemed a protected place since it had no windows facing the street. Papa agreed.

While we were waiting there, without thinking of the possible consequences I jumped up and went out to the front balcony and searched the deep blue sky to see if any enemy planes were approaching. A Civil Guard, patrolling the streets, spied me and yelled out in Hebrew, "*Geveret,* go down to your shelter immediately!" I hurried back to Papa and said, "It looks quiet outside." He was relieved.

Of course, at that time we had no idea of Israel's precarious position and the extent of our losses, but this was the first time in our lives that we were faced with war close at hand. About an hour later, the "all clear" siren sounded, and everyone trooped up the stairs from the shelter, huffing and puffing.

We started *Minchah* with heart-rending prayers, but soon the siren went off again, and the shul emptied out. Once again, Papa and I remained in our foyer saying *Tehillim.* This time, though, the "all clear" came after a short while.

It was a frightened, anxious congregation that finally started *Ne'ilah* prayers. By that time, the Isbee's kitchen and sukkah porch were packed with women and children who had come from neighboring shuls and Torah Ore Yeshivah to be closer to their homes in case another siren went off and they had to run. Our cries split the heavens; our tears flowed unchecked. How could this have happened on Yom Kippur, the day of forgiveness? This was the day of the year when Hashem was closest to us and answered our prayers. Was this His judgment for us this year? My questions were suspended in air, looking down accusingly and mocking me.

Love, Papa and Mama

Chol Ha-Mo'ed Sukkos

Dearest Children,

Papa allowed me to write to you even though it is *Chol Ha-Mo'ed,* as long as I write with a *shinui* — the difference is that I am writing in pencil. Because of the war, I don't know when my letters will reach you, but I hope you will receive them eventually. We ourselves haven't received any mail since the war started. I guess even the mailmen must be at the front.

Right after breaking the fast, we turned on the radio and we've been glued to it ever since. Now we have begun to hear the tragic news that many of our soldiers have fallen, and many others are wounded or missing in action.

You will have read all about the Egyptian and Syrian attacks. We were prepared for Jordan to follow suit, as she did in the Six-Day War, but so far she has not become involved.

The day after Yom Kippur, I received a call from the Orphan Home, informing me that I would be picked up by car to come to the office. (It may be wartime, but there was a lot of correspondence to take care of.) The city buses were hardly running, I learned, as most of the bus drivers had been mobilized. At a time like this, you realize to what extent ours is a citizens' army — and we are such a little country! In the streets, only older men, women and children walk about.

The Orphan Home was a somber place indeed that day, with the childrens' fear evident, and the directors tense. All the excitement in the Home that would normally precede Sukkos was sorely lacking. And we secretaries were very troubled and could hardly concentrate on our work.

When I returned from work in the early afternoon, I went

to the local grocery store to shop for some items I needed for Sukkos. The scene that awaited me was unbelievable. The store looked as if it had been ransacked, with all the shelves emptied of staples. No flour, sugar, oil, canned vegetables, noodles, etc., etc. The owner of the store was sitting dejectedly with his head resting on the cash register.

"Are you moving your store?" I asked innocently.

For a moment he gazed at me in astonishment, and then exclaimed, "Don't you know there's a war going on?" When he saw my bewilderment, he explained. "Ah, you're an American, and don't know what war means." He then gave me a detailed description of what had gone on that day.

Most of the residents of Kiryat Mattersdorf were already grouped outside the grocery store when he arrived early in the morning to open up. They had been there from the crack of dawn. He had barely unlocked the door, when they charged inside, emptying the shelves within minutes and grabbing whatever they could get their hands on. There was a frenzy of pushing and shoving.

There was no way for him to get payment then and there, but that did not trouble him. "They are all honest, and will pay me for everything they took," he went on, "but just to watch the panic was terrible. You see, Mrs. Shain, most of my customers have lived through a few wars already, so how can I blame them? They have large families and *Yom Tov* is coming, and they need food." He sighed and shook his head sadly. "It is a pity that we shall have such an unhappy Sukkos."

I went home without any groceries.

I realized that although there have been wars that America fought, the United States had never been under attack — except for far-off Pearl Harbor. The lives of civilians were not threatened. But for each of us living in Israel, this is a personal war. We mourn each Jewish soldier killed, we cry for each one wounded, and we worry for each one missing. May Hashem have pity on His Jewish Nation and bring us peace.

Love, Papa and Mama

✍ ✍

On *erev Sukkos*, when I went to buy challahs, the area near the grocery store was crowded with people impatiently awaiting the delivery. When the bakery truck finally pulled up, the crowd quickly clambored aboard, and it was "first come, first served." Since I could not possibly attempt such gymnastics, I called out to one of my neighbors to get me some challahs. She threw down one small challah, which I fortunately caught. I guess my basketball-playing in high school paid off! That was it. I had a few whole matzahs in the house, so we had enough for *lechem mishneh.* But somehow, even though it was *Yom Tov*, food did not seem that important to us.

Preparations for Sukkos were made with heavy hearts. The Civil Guard had ordered that after nightfall, no lights should be seen from any house. Heavy blackout curtains were hung on all the windows and in all the sukkos, and most of our shutters were closed.

Despite all this, it was wonderful to see how the women of Israel managed. Although their hearts were heavy with fear and anxiety for husbands and sons and fathers at the front, nevertheless they put up their sukkos and decorated them together with the children in great joy. But the joyous sounds of *zemiros* that usually filled the sukkos were muted.

Dearest Children,

Since settling in Yerushalayim, I have gone to the *Kosel* every year during *Chol Ha-Mo'ed Sukkos.* I did not allow the war to keep me from going this year.

It took three buses and a very long time to get there. I cried when I saw that there were only a handful of older men and a few women there. For usually, the crowds are so large that it is difficult to get near the *Kosel* on *Chol Ha-Mo'ed*, with people from all over the country as well as many tourists who come for *Yom Tov.*

I davened *Minchah*, and prayed to Hashem to protect us from our enemies, and watch over our soldiers. The *Kosel* looked forlorn, and seemed to share my despair. For almost two thousand years, she has stood silently listening to our pleas and cries. I could hear her whispering to me, "Be comforted, redemption is on the way."

Going home proved an even greater problem than getting there. I had to walk part of the way because there was no bus to Kiryat Mattersdorf. Papa greeted me at the door looking very worried, because I had been gone for many hours. He wisely did not comment when he saw my strained and tired look. May our prayers be answered.

Love, Papa and Mama

P.S. As you know, we always spend one evening during Sukkos with Reb Chaim and Chani Kass. This year we kept up the tradition. Reb Chaim came for us with a very small flashlight — for the blackouts are very much in effect. The streets were pitch black, and Papa and I groped our way slowly to their home, which is quite near ours.

Although Chani had prepared a delicious *Yom Tov* meal, the music was muffled, the children — who usually make a rumpus — were subdued, a single candle flickered in the darkened sukkah, and our moods reflected the war that has become part of our lives.

✍ ✍

As the war raged on, certain food items became rationed, and eggs were limited to five a week per family. For Reb Moshe and me, this was not a problem, as we watched our cholesterol intake and ate few eggs anyway, but for large families, it was a real hardship.

There was a feeling of isolation and vulnerability as night fell and the blackouts continued. It was only the morning sunshine hopping and skipping all over our home, and the lovely sukkah that lifted our spirits.

Throughout Jewish history, in times of trouble, the yearning for *Mashiach* and the final Redemption is intensified, and people look for signs that his arrival is imminent. That Sukkos, during the Yom Kippur War, many felt that the time was ripe.

Motza'ei Sukkos

Dearest Children,

I want to tell you about a rumor with a Yerushalmi touch! I haven't the slightest idea how this started, but somehow word got around that on Hoshannah Rabbah at 2:00 P.M. every man, woman and child should be sitting in his sukkah, because something miraculous would happen then. (There have been other rumors floating round that *Mashiach* was about to come. We certainly need him!)

Well, promptly at 2:00 P.M. I left my cooking in the kitchen and went into our sukkah. Papa sits there anyway most of the time, and even has a study session with his *chavrusa* there every day. I started saying my *Tehillim* and sat expectantly awaiting some sort of a sign from Heaven. After an hour, when there was none forthcoming, I asked Papa what to do, as I had a lot to finish before *Yom Tov.* Papa told me to go back to the kitchen. "Don't worry," he reassured me, "I'll call you." Well, children, nothing happened, and I was very disappointed. But I don't think Papa took it that seriously.

Later Aunt Bessie told us about her experience. She, too, had gone into her sukkah at two o'clock, telling Uncle Chaim that she still had a lot of cooking to do. He advised her to go back to the kitchen and her cooking. Aunt Bessie retorted, "You'll be saved, and what will happen to me??" And she had remained sitting in the sukkah...

Love, Papa and Mama

As more details about the attack on Yom Kippur began to be heard, we realized that our tiny country could have been overrun by the enemy in a matter of hours. Somehow, the bits and pieces of the puzzle had not yet fallen into place, but we knew they would at the proper time. However, the miracles and *chesed* of Hashem were evident throughout this traumatic period.

One of the miracles I heard about had to do with the *Shema*. The *Shema Yisrael* prayer brings Hashem and His People together in a holy bond. Every day we recite the *Shema* in our prayers during the morning *Shacharis* and the evening *Ma'ariv*. Before we close our eyes for the night, we repeat it again.

For those of us who were born into a religious home, the words of the *Shema* became rooted in our early childhood, when we had no concept of the depths of its meaning. It is stamped on our hearts and in our minds in times of joy and times of sorrow.

Through every generation, the *Shema* has kept the Jewish Nation strong in their faith and brought them closer to Hashem. As they were led to the gallows or to the ovens, by the Romans, the Spanish, the Germans, Jews went to their deaths with the *Shema* on their lips. And in other instances, reciting the *Shema* proved to be the catalyst that led to miraculous life-saving events.

We read in the Torah about Ya'akov *Avinu*'s emotional meeting with his beloved son, Yosef, after enduring twenty-two years of not knowing if Yosef were dead or alive.

Our Sages teach that at the moment that Yaakov *Avinu* set eyes on Yosef, who had become the Viceroy of Egypt, instead of immediately clasping his loving son to his heart, he recited the *Shema*, to show that his first love and devotion was to Hashem.

One of the wonderful things about living in Israel is starting my day when the radio goes on the air at 6:00 A.M.

and the first portion of *Shema Yisrael* is recited in meticulous Hebrew before the opening news broadcast. I listen carefully to every word, and it brings home to me how blessed I am to be living here. There are many problems which beset our little country, but where else but in Eretz Yisrael can one awaken to hear *Shema Yisrael* coming over the air waves.

Dearest Children,

I want to tell you about a dramatic experience which I am sure will move you as much as it did us.

Five soldiers were traveling on a lonely road somewhere in Israel. Suddenly, they heard cries of "Help, help!" They stopped their car and tried to discover where the cries were coming from. Looking everywhere, they finally spied two soldiers far off on a lone outpost on a hilltop.

As the five climbed up to reach them and came closer, they were horrified to see one of the soldiers trembling and pointing to his terror-stricken companion, who had a large, poisonous snake coiled tightly around his leg.

The soldiers realized that trying to shoot the viper could endanger the soldier's life. They were in a quandary and there was very little time to decide what action to take. If the snake dug his poisonous fangs into the soldier, he could die in a short while.

One of the five soldiers was a religious man. He called out to the terrified soldier, "Say the *Shema*!" The soldier gasped, "Say it with me." And there, before their eyes, as the soldier repeated word after word of the *Shema*, the snake uncoiled itself from his leg and slithered away. The soldiers fired several shots in the snake's direction, but it disappeared into a hole in the ground.

The miracle of the *Shema* was so evident that on the spot the soldier whose life was saved undertook to become a *ba'al teshuvah.*

We Jews recite the *Shema* daily, confirming that our hearts and souls are fully with Hashem. He is Supreme both in the

Heavens above and the earth below. This is the essence of our faith, and it has sustained our Jewish Nation.

Love, Papa and Mama

✍ ✍

Dearest Children,

Shemini Atzeres, which is also Simchas Torah in Eretz Yisrael, was an experience I won't forget.

The men gathered at the Isbee minyan for prayers and *hakafos.* All the children from our building, and many others from the neighborhood, came with their mothers. Many of their fathers were in the army, and the older men "took over" and danced with the little boys. As they raised their voices in song, and danced with the *sifrei Torah,* we, the women, cried softly.

Although it is a mitzvah to rejoice on this Festival, how can one be fully joyous when there is war and sorrow all around us? I think of the men who were singing and dancing joyously, without any outward show of sadness, as being soldiers too, doing their duty bravely and faithfully. I recall that Zaidie Herman used to say, "I'm a soldier of the Boss." How lovingly Hashem's children follow His commandments!

I heard a wise explanation about the mitzvah of rejoicing on Simchas Torah: There is a song that is repeated during *Simchas Beis Ha-Sho'evah* and during Simchas Torah, which starts with "*Ach, ach, mesame'ach* — make merry," and then a phrase in Yiddish is added: "*A gans yahr freilich* — A whole year happy." What does the happiness of the entire year have to do with the mitzvah of rejoicing on Simchas Torah? The answer is that if we observe Hashem's commandments to be really joyous on Sukkos — even though sometimes we are very saddened by certain events, which makes it difficult — then Hashem will bless us with joy and happiness throughout the entire year. Amen!

Love, Papa and Mama

P. S. The yeshivos are continuing their full learning schedules even though it is *bein ha-zemanim.* May the Torah learning be a *zechus* for *Klal Yisrael* and bring peace to our land.

✍ ✍

Israel's 25th Independence Day was celebrated in May, a few months before the Yom Kippur War broke out. There were elaborate ceremonies and festivities. Soldiers paraded; bands played patriotic songs; airplanes flew overhead in dazzling formation; the Navy opened its ships to hundreds of visitors. There was a "State of Euphoria."

It seemed that we were declaring to the entire world: "We won the Six-Day War with *our army, our air force, our navy, our might, our strategy.*"

I feared that many had forgotten that Hashem was the true Chief of Staff! I prayed that His troops would continue to merit His mercy and guidance.

✍ ✍

Dearest Children,

Now that the cease-fire has gone into effect, it can be told: The morning after the war broke out, Yosi, a young friend of ours came over to discuss a problem with me. "As you know, Mrs. Shain, my wife is in her ninth month. She's in a panic about the possibility that she will give birth during the night when the blackout is in force, and might not get to the hospital in time. Since this is her first pregnancy, she wants us to leave immediately for the States.

"I, too, share her fears," he continued breathlessly, "but I also know that if we leave, the chances of our returning are slim. I'm gaining so much in my Torah studies here in the Yeshivah, that I'm really in conflict. I've made inquiries, and it is possible to get a flight out today, but after that it's likely that the airport will close down. What should we do?" He looked at me questioningly.

Now, children, I don't know what came over me, but I said glibly, "Oh, you have nothing to worry about, Yosi. Just tell Etta that I know all about childbirth. Why, I was present when my sister, Rebbetzin Scheinberg, gave birth in Mir."

Yosi perked up considerably. "Oh, thank you, Mrs. Shain! I'll send Etta to you, and you tell her yourself," he beamed. "She'll be so relieved!"

When he left, Papa gazed at me in amazement. "Racoma, what on earth are you getting into? You are not a midwife and you have no experience whatsoever."

I was having second thoughts when Etta rang our doorbell loudly. She plopped down on the couch, all out of breath. "Mrs. Shain, can I really rely on you to be with me if I can't reach the hospital in time? I hate to make Yosi leave the Yeshivah, but I'm scared stiff." She looked at me anxiously.

I was about to confess that indeed I knew very little about birth, but I held back and said instead, "Etta, Hashem will help, and you will have an easy birth. You can call me if you need me."

"Oh, thank you very much, Mrs. Shain." Etta smiled in obvious relief.

After she walked out, Papa shook his head, without saying anything. The next few weeks played havoc with my nerves. I scoured a book that describes the birth process, but I was still not sure about cutting the cord and other "minor details" too numerous to mention.

Every phone call after dark got me trembling. Besides the tragedy of war all around us, I was facing my own war of nerves. Though I prayed with all my heart that Hashem should end the war quickly because of our soldiers, I added a prayer that Etta's baby should stay in until a cease-fire is declared.

Thank Hashem, both my prayers were answered! A cease-fire was declared, and Etta gave birth a few days later.

MAZAL TOV...IT'S A BOY! Yosi and Etta have been telling their friends that they were very calm about the impending birth, because they knew that I was on hand in case of an emergency. What they didn't know is that although they were calm, I was a wreck!

Children, I realize that it was foolhardy behavior on my part and could have even had serious consequences. I don't recommend this action to anyone, and I certainly would never offer my services as a midwife again.

Love, Papa and Mama

Chanukah De-Lights

AS A CHILD, CHANUKAH was one of my happiest holidays. It meant watching my father light the tiny oil lamps near our dining-room window, and hearing his sweet, melodious voice recite the *berachos* on each of the eight nights. It meant feeling wealthy upon receiving my precious few pennies for *Chanukah gelt*, which I was free to spend in any way I wanted. It meant eating lots of hot potato latkes, which my mother prepared in amazing quantities for us, for all the regular *orchim*, and for the many visitors who came to wish us "Happy Chanukah."

Of course, as I grew older, my joy at Chanukah took on different aspects. Over and over again, I would ask my father to tell me about the great miracles that had taken place at that time. I swelled with pride that Hashem had championed our cause, so that our few and weak overcame the strong and mighty.

Living in Eretz Yisrael where the "action" actually took

place makes Chanukah very exciting. Weeks before the Festival actually arrives, we know it is in the air: hot, golden *sufganiot* — deep-fried jelly doughnuts that are the local substitute for latkes — appear at every corner kiosk, in bakeries and supermarkets.

On this Festival, the whole country is aglow. The Chanukah story is a victory and a miracle for the Jewish nation, and the whole nation proclaims its joy with thousands of Chanukah lights shining from windows, entranceways, porches, synagogues, and public buildings.

The glory of Chanukah leaves its special imprint on all those who are privileged to live in Eretz Yisrael.

Dearest Children,

Happy Chanukah!

The first Chanukah light that Papa lit about an hour ago is still burning with a soft glow near our window. Outside there is a cold wind blowing but the house is comfortably warm. Papa is sitting and learning, while I am typing this letter in triplicate.

Today, *erev Chanukah,* the 24th of Kislev, was my beloved mother's yahrtzeit. We arranged to meet at Uncle Nochum Dovid and Aunt Chaye Dube's house at 2:00 P.M. and go to the cemetery. Papa came straight from the Yeshivah, and I from the office. Aunt Esther and Aunt Bessie, and some of our nephews and great-nephews, were already there when we arrived, so we had a large minyan.

We hired a van, and together with Shmuel Yitzchok Stern's car, there was enough space for everyone. It was a cloudy day and quite cold, but the weather was dry. Though I have gone to Har Hazeisim a number of times, it has not diminished the sense of awe I feel when I stand near Bubbie Aidel's *kever,* which faces the *Makom Ha-Mikdash.*

I can see in my mind's eye the glorious, holy *Beis Ha-Mikdash* rebuilt in all its splendor, beckoning to us. We said the appropriate *Tehillim,* Psalm 119, spelling out Bubbie Aidel's name, which is the custom on a yahrtzeit. Then Uncle Nochum Dovid recited Kaddish, and his voice rang out in the mountains of Yehudah. Surely, Bubbie Aidel's spirit was there listening to our many entreaties.

Being near her grave always brings back vivid memories of my childhood. Her loving, understanding manner of dealing with us, and her extreme patience, are still something that I marvel at. Our house was a real "merry-go-'round," and sometimes not so merry, with the *orchim* coming and going at all times of the day and night.

When I came home from school every day and ran up the steps calling, "Mama, I'm home!" I always knew she would be there to greet me. I could not wait to share my day's experiences, and she listened with that attentive air of hers, that complete interest, that gave me a great sense of security.

Children, as you were growing up, I tried very much to follow in Bubbie Aidel's footsteps, and to make sure I was there when you got home from yeshivah and Bais Yaakov. May she be a *melitz yosher* for our entire family.

Now I want to share with you the exhilarating events of our first night of Chanukah in Yerushalayim. From Bubbie Aidel's *kever* on Har Hazeisim, we decided to go to the *Kosel* to watch the first light of Chanukah being kindled by the Minister of Religion, Rabbi Warhaftig.

The giant menorah was encased in glass, so that the flaming lights would not be blown out by the wind. We davened *Minchah,* and then with the crowds of people who had gathered at the *Kosel,* we awaited the moment of lighting.

We stood breathlessly as the wick burst into a flame and the blessings were recited, and then the assembled mass of people all answered with a resounding "Amen."

We davened *Ma'ariv,* and just as we were about to leave, a large group of Sephardim, singing and dancing around a *chasan* and *kallah,* arrived. A *chupah* was raised, and then and there the wedding ceremony took place. With the joyous cries of "Mazal tov!" ringing in our ears, we left the *Kosel.*

Our Chanukah was further enhanced when we got home and received your loving letters wishing us "Happy Chanukah."

Love, Papa and Mama

P.S. Only in Yerushalayim could one be at Har Hazeisim, witness the first light of Chanukah kindled at the *Kosel*, and take part in a wedding, all in one day!

✍ ✍

One Chanukah, since it was my birthday, I decided to go to the *Kosel* to daven and recite *Hallel*. I prepared breakfast for Reb Moshe, and with his birthday blessings ringing in my ears, I started off. Though it was December, the weather was still warm and Indian-summer-like. Instead of waiting for the number 7 bus near our house, which connected with the number 1 bus to the *Kosel* at the central bus station, I decided to walk to the central bus station, which took about fifteen minutes.

Dearest Children,

Today is my fifty-eighth birthday, and when I awoke early this morning I decided to count my blessings. *Baruch Hashem*, Papa and I are living in Yerushalayim, in our own home — a dream come true. Papa is occupied with his Torah learning and goes daily to the Yeshivah, which he finds most rewarding. I enjoy my work as secretary in the Orphan Home, and keep active going to *shiurim*, and attending classes in the *ulpan*, where I am making strides in improving my Hebrew.

We have been blessed with wonderful children, *baruch Hashem*, all *bnei Torah* who are following our path and bringing up their children as they were brought up. Although we are physically apart, we are very close emotionally and spiritually. I have seen families in which, although they live in close proximity, the parents and children are emotionally a great distance from each other.

I decided to go to the *Kosel* and give thanks to Hashem.

The morning sun had just risen above the hills, and the mist was still evident. As I made my way down the hilly path, the wet roofs of the houses reflected the golden sun, which enveloped me in its glory and brightness. The streets were quiet, and as I walked I basked in the loveliness of this special day.

One of the greatest blessings is finding emotional and spiritual satisfaction in life. This is a most precious birthday present, and I give thanks to Hashem!

My dear children, you were with me in spirit today, surrounding me with your special brand of love and birthday wishes, and filling my heart with inner gladness.

May Papa and I live to see the *geulah shelemah* with all of you together with us in Yerushalayim. Amen!

Love, Papa and Mama

When I returned from the Kosel, I felt like expressing my thoughts in a poem:

I walk the streets of Jerusalem,
With a song that sings in my heart;
And the birds chirp their good morning,
As the dawn of a new day does start.

The stately trees, a glowing green,
Wave their graceful, leafy arms;
And beckon to me to listen,
As they chant their Heavenly psalms.

The sun is a circle of fire,
In a sky of piercing blue;
That surrounds me with its radiance,
With colors of a rainbow hue.

You are my comfort, Jerusalem,

I no longer have to roam;
I walk your streets with a song in my heart,
For at last you have brought me home.

✍ ✍

My sixtieth birthday fell on *erev Shabbos Chanukah.* On Saturday night I sat down to write to my children, eager to share the exciting experiences of the day.

Dearest Children,

Gut voch! Papa just finished making *Havdalah.* Thank you for your loving letters and birthday cards, with their many special blessings for my sixtieth birthday. They arrived in record time — even before my birthday.

Now let me share with you the events of my birthday. As soon as I awoke, Papa started off my day with his cheery "Happy Birthday." When I told him that sixty sounds so old, he quoted *Pirkei Avos* 5:25: "At sixty years a person reaches *ziknah* — old age." Papa explained, however, that this word does not connote physical age only but, more so, "the qualities of wisdom and understanding that one gains through life's experiences." I hope I qualify!

To move from the wisdom of our Sages to more mundane matters, I had heard that women over 60 and men over 65 are eligible for special reduced-rate bus tickets. So on my birthday, I decided to take immediate advantage of the reduced bus fare by traveling to the Machaneh Yehudah open-air market to buy groceries. Great bargains are to be found there in fruits and vegetables on Fridays.

After breakfast, I set out with a large shopping bag. I boarded the number 7 bus, and in my best Hebrew announced proudly to the bus driver: "I am sixty years old today and would like to purchase a ticket for senior citizens." The driver graciously wished me "Mazal tov" on my birthday, and handed me the ticket. The bus was quite crowded, with standing room only, but some of the passengers in the front seats, who had heard my announcement, also joined in wishing me "Mazal tov!" A young man offered me his seat — I guess in deference to my advanced years. The friendliness of the driver and the passengers made me feel once again how blessed Papa and I are to be living in Yerushalayim.

Shopping in the *shuk* is always thrilling. Piles of beautiful and delicious fruits and vegetables surround one on all sides, while the vendors call out in Ladino, Yiddish, English, Hebrew, [and now Russian], trying to attract customers.

I came home laden with shining golden oranges, pink grapefruits, deep red apples from the Golan Heights, and several kinds of fresh green vegetables, all at bargain prices.

A few hours later, a friend of mine telephoned to wish me "Happy Birthday." She always remembered my birthday because we were both born in the same month, although she is two years younger than I am. I told her excitedly that I was now considered officially a senior citizen and was eligible for reduced bus fare, which I had already taken advantage of.

"Racoma," she said in surprise, "do you mean to say you *advertised your age*?! But you look so much younger."

I explained that I didn't think my age was anything to hide, and that in fact, a sixtieth birthday is very special. I hope it brings me more wisdom and understanding, I told her, quoting what Papa had explained to me in the morning. "And saving money on the bus fare," I added, "was a special present."

It seemed she did not share my enthusiasm. She was quiet for a minute, and then said, "Well, I myself will be content to go on buying a regular ticket until the driver himself notices my age — and I hope it won't be for several years."

I wished her success in keeping her age hidden.

I hope that Hashem blesses us both with many more healthful, joyous birthdays.

And may we all be blessed with many Happy Chanukahs.

Love, Papa and Mama

Purim Highs and Lows

THE JOY OF PURIM in Yerushalayim is catching. It invades the heart and soul and doesn't let go. The whole Jewish nation, not only the religious segment of Israel, takes part in the celebration and excitement of Purim.

Hamantashen appear in the bakeries, and shiny, colorful costumes and accessories are seen hanging in storefronts. The open market is dazzling, with its proliferaton of little satin outfits, and gleaming crowns and scepters. And then, after the mothers have spent money, time, and effort in providing their children with original and beautiful costumes, the children make their way to school. What a pleasure it is to watch this wonderful parade: miniature sailors, soldiers, doctors, nurses; gypsies, cowboys, witches, and an occasional angel; and, of course, the traditional little Hamans, Mordechais, and Queen Esthers.

Because Yerushalayim is a walled city, we celebrate the

holiday on Shushan Purim* — one day after it is celebrated almost everywhere else — and many people from different parts of Israel come especially to Yerushalayim to join the festivities. The day before is spent in hectic preparations, cooking and baking, and the halls and entranceways of every building are filled with tantalizing aromas.

Dearest Children,

The "onslaught" of *mishlo'ach manos* amazes me, and I need all my stamina to keep up with it, as four and five arrive at one time. The best I can do is to give *Purim gelt* to the children who happily deliver these lovely gift packages of cake and fruit and wine. By mid-afternoon we thought they had finished coming, but when we came home from Uncle Nochum Dovid's house after the *seudah,* we found our doorway blocked with many more baskets of *mishlo'ach manos.*

How I wish Pesach were half a year away instead of a month — for we surely have enough nosh to last us until then. I'll send a carton of goodies to the Yeshivah, where it will go fast.

Here are some interesting Purim sidelights that I want to share with you: When Papa and I pushed ourselves onto the crowded bus on our way to Uncle Nochum Dovid and Aunt Chaye Dube in the early afternoon, the bus driver was also in costume, wearing a wig, miniskirt, and high heels! And his face was heavily made up with cosmetics. When we stopped at one of the bus stops, a bearded man with long *payos* climbed aboard. As soon as he saw the bare legs of the driver, whom he mistook for a woman, he flew off the bus pell-mell!

Then there was a young couple we know, both barely

*Cities in Israel which were surrounded by walls "from the days of Yehoshua bin Nun" celebrate Purim on the 15th of Adar, just as was done in the ancient capital of Persia, Shushan, where Purim was celebrated one day later than everywhere else.

eighteen, who were married just before Purim. Since it was the week of their *sheva berachos,* they dressed in their most festive apparel: the *chasan* wore his *shtreimel* and a long, striped yellow robe, the customary dress of Reb Arale's chassidim, and the *kallah* wore a green velvet dress with elaborate embroidery. As they walked down Jaffa Road many people turned to gaze at them and remark, "Look at those beautiful and expensive costumes."

I hope your Purim was *freilich.*

Love, Papa and Mama

After Purim, Reb Moshe wrote the following letter to our children. I enclosed a note which read, "This is a letter from Papa: It is rare! Cherish it! Treasure it! Frame It!" Although Reb Moshe wrote very well, he always relegated the letter-writing to me. But he was so inspired by Shushan Purim, with all its interesting aspects, that when I suggested, "Moshe, why don't you write the children all about it?" — lo and behold! He agreed.

Dearest Children,

Today is the day after *Purim meshulash,* the three days of Purim celebrations that we had this year. This occurs rarely — once in about fifteen or twenty years, and only in cities surrounded by walls. You see, Purim — the 14th of Adar — can never fall on Shabbos, but Shushan Purim, the 15th, can. When this happens, the various *minhagim* and observances are spread out over three days. Friday, Megillah; Shabbos, *Al Ha-Nissim*; and Sunday, *mishlo'ach manos* and the *seudah.* To fulfill other halachic opinions, we sent *mishlo'ach manos* on both Friday and Sunday, but *matanos l'evyonim* we gave on Friday, the day of the reading of the Megillah. So much for the *halachos.*

Now, as to how we spent Shushan Purim: on Sunday the *mishlo'ach manos* started earlier than usual because there was no reading of the Megillah. I leave that to Mama, who tries to rise to the challenge, and she does a good job.

We had an interesting experience on the way to Uncle Nochum Dovid's house, where we have the *seudah*, which is always delicious, and the Purim talk inspiring. While waiting for the bus, a group of rowdy young boys came toward us, shouting and carrying on, obviously tipsy. They sat down on the stone wall near the bus stop and continued to make merry. Finally the bus arrived and we all got on. It was so crowded that there was hardly any standing room, but I was offered a seat right away. As the bus chugged along, the boys really acted up. One of them kept saying in Hebrew, "I'm not completely drunk." And then suddenly, he started to quote the Gemara in *Bava Kama*, in the portion *Basor Maikra*, explaining it in detail, with the Tosefos and the Rosh. It was a *Kiddush Hashem* to see such a Jewish drunkard, and watch his actions.

May we be *zocheh* to *Mashiach* and see *yeshuos* from our enemies. A happy and kosher Pesach to all of you.

Papa

Becoming drunk is part of the Purim festivities, and a custom that *Klal Yisrael* does with "spirit!" Our Sages prescribed the drinking of wine on Purim until intoxication, saying, "A person is obligated to drink on Purim until he no longer knows the difference between 'cursed is Haman,' and 'blessed is Mordechai.'"

✍ ✍

On Shushan Purim 1986, the funeral of the *gaon*, Reb Moshe Feinstein, *zt"l*, was attended by about 250,000 people from all over Eretz Yisrael, and from every sector of the population.

It was a *chamsin*, with unbearably hot, dry weather, which was quite unusual for Purim time, when rain and often snow are expected. I have heard that the traditional inclement weather on Purim is due to a prayer from the great Sage, the Rabbi of Yerushalayim, Reb Yosef Chaim Sonnenfeld. Since the destruction of the Holy Temple took place in Yerushalayim, he felt that the Purim festivities should accordingly be toned down a bit, and rainy or stormy weather certainly can "dampen" the spirits. The searing *chamsin* must also have been an answer to his prayer. However, nothing — not rain, nor sleet, nor even snow, would have deterred the thousands of people from coming to this great *tzaddik*'s funeral.

Dearest Children,

I am sure you all attended the memorial service for Reb Moshe Feinstein in New York, but you will be anxiously awaiting to hear the details of his funeral in Yerushalayim.

Reb Chaim Kass offered to drive Papa and me to the funeral, and we gratefully accepted. However, by the time we got to the Etz Chaim Yeshivah on Jaffa Road, where the funeral procession was scheduled to begin, the street was overflowing and jammed with thousands of people. He finally found a parking place about seven blocks away. Fortunately, we found a low stone wall on which to sit, with a tree nearby to provide us with some protection from the blazing sun. We watched as thousands of men and women (including mothers pushing baby carriages) streamed by us, intent on getting as close as possible to the Yeshivah.

Papa and I were too far from the speakers — *Roshei Yeshivos* and other *Rabbanim* — to be able to see or hear anything, and all we could do was wait for Reb Moshe Feinstein's coffin to pass by.

As I sat there, many thoughts of this great and holy man came to mind. Zaidie Herman had been very close to him and his family when they first arrived in New York. In fact, Reb Moshe Feinstein often relied upon Zaidie in certain matters of kashrus.

When Zaidie settled in Eretz Yisrael, he would send us *esrogim* to sell each year for Sukkos. One year, when Papa took one look at the *esrogim*, he was disappointed and asked, "How are we going to sell these? There is not one *mehudar* among them." I think that it was a *shemittah* year, and the produce was limited. We received a call from Rabbi Feinstein asking if Zaidie had sent us any *esrogim*. When Papa told him we had some, he came to our house right away. After looking over each one carefully, he selected one, saying, "I would rather buy a *vadai bilti murkav* from Reb Yonkev Yosef, than a *mehudar* that might be questionable." An *esrog* from Zaidie was definitely kosher, and that was preferable to a more beautiful one with questionable reliability. As soon as word got out that he had bought an *esrog* from us, we had no trouble selling the entire batch.

My thoughts also went back to the daily minyan we had in our house for *Shacharis* for the several years before we settled in Yerushalayim. It had started one Monday morning when there was a huge snowstorm, and many of our neighbors on the East River Drive could not get to a shul. Since we had the *sefer Torah* that Zaidie had sent us from Eretz Yisrael when we moved to the Drive, we organized a minyan in our house, and we kept up the minyan until we left for Eretz Yisrael.

The Mattersdorf Rav, who lived two floors below us then, became a steady congregant. And Rabbi Feinstein, who lived across the street from us, came to our minyan several times when stormy or snowy weather prevented him from getting to Yeshivas Tiferes Yerushalayim on time.

When we packed our lift for Eretz Yisrael, we decided to take along the two armchairs — though they were worn out — in which the Mattersdorf Rav and Reb Moshe Feinstein sat whenever they came to our house to pray.

Though Rabbi Feinstein was a *Gadol B'Yisrael*, he never failed to greet me when I passed him on the street. The greater the person, the more modest he is. People flocked to his home day and night for his *pesak* on every halachic problem, for personal advice, and for *berachos*. He accepted everyone with graciousness, and with extreme patience. Even when he became older and weaker, he did not allow his wife or family to turn anyone away.

My thoughts were interrupted by a cry: "The *aron* is on its way!" Papa and I stood and craned our necks to catch a glimpse of the coffin, but there was so much pushing and shoving, as thousands surrounded it, that we almost missed seeing it. As it passed by, Papa and I gave vent to our pent-up emotions. We both cried, and Papa sighed deeply. I felt a keen sense of loss, not only for the *Gadol Ha-dor,* but also for the loss of a close friend of our family.

He was short in physical stature, but a giant in Torah and *middos tovos. Klal Yisrael* has become bereaved and orphaned with the loss of this great *tzaddik.* Who can take his place?

Love, Papa and Mama

✍ ✍

My niece, Frume Altusky, lived on the East River Drive in a building whose courtyard adjoined the building Rabbi Feinstein lived in. From her porch, she often saw Rabbi Feinstein returning from the Yeshivah. Children were usually playing in the courtyard at that time, she told me, and she often saw him stop to tie the shoelaces of one youngster, button the coat of another in cold weather, and affectionately pat the others who ran over to him.

A friend told me that once, while Rabbi Feinstein was walking from his home on the East River Drive to the Yeshivah, which was quite a distance, a young man drove up and offered him a ride to the Yeshivah. Rabbi Feinstein accepted, and climbed into the front seat of the car. The back of the car was filled with other passengers. As the car drove along, the driver's little son, who was seated between his father and Rabbi Feinstein, whispered to his father, "Daddy, I'm getting squished." Rabbi Feinstein then asked the driver to stop the car. He opened the door, got out, turned to the child and said, "Forgive me for squishing you." (These stories were so popular that they were later included in the biography of Rabbi Moshe Feinstein that was published by Artscroll.)

✍ ✍

I became aware of some interesting facts after Rabbi Feinstein's funeral. A few weeks before his passing, there was a drought, and rain was vitally needed in Eretz Yisrael. The farmers were very concerned about their produce with summer approaching, when there is no rain.

There is a known *segulah* in Yerushalayim that when a great man passes on, and rain is needed, a wet towel is wrapped around the *niftar*'s hand and buried with him. This was done with Reb Moshe Feinstein, and a day or so later, rain fell. I was told that when the great *gaon*, Reb Aaron Kotler, passed away, there had been hardly any rain although it was already Kislev, and the same *segulah* was applied. Rain poured down the night after his funeral.

Another interesting story was widely circulated at the time. For days after Rabbi Feinstein's funeral, a certain man suffered excruciating headaches. His doctor could not find any physical cause, and he sought the advice of a *Gadol*, who suggested using the *goral* of the Vilna Gaon to find the answer.* The following verse showed up: "Why did you not fear to speak against my servant Moshe?" [*Bemidbar* 12:8]. When the *Gadol* prodded him to look for a connection, he recalled that at Reb Moshe Feinstein's funeral, he had been

* This is a tradition attributed to the Vilna Gaon, in which the answer to a problem can be found by taking a certain edition of the *Tanach* and arriving at a specific verse by a random process, following a formula of "seven times seven."

annoyed that it was taking so much time away from the joy of Purim, which would be diminished, and he had mentioned this to a few people who stood near him. Upon hearing this, the *Gadol* advised him to gather a minyan and go to Reb Moshe Feinstein's grave and ask him for forgiveness. He immediately obeyed, and the headaches left him as suddenly as they had appeared.

The "Strains" of Pesach

PESACH IN ERETZ YISRAEL gladdens the heart. Fruit trees are blossoming; wildflowers are in bloom everywhere; the winter's rains have brought a carpet of lush green from the Golan to the Negev. The days are sunny and warm; the nights are starry and cool. Spring, in all her glory, has made her grand debut.

Since Pesach is one of the three *Regalim*, the pilgrimage Festivals when the Jews went up to Yerushalayim, today too Jews from all over Israel, as well as tourists, flock to Yerushalayim. Visiting the *Kosel* is an essential part of this. Buses bursting with men, women, and children dressed in their holiday best (including many *shtreimlach*) make their slow way to the *Kosel* through throngs of people. (It is interesting to note that Pesach was the only one of the three pilgrimage Festivals in which women were also commanded to go up to Yerushalayim.)

At the Pesach Seder, families gather together. The Haggadah states: "Whoever is hungry — let him come and eat! Whoever is needy — let him come and celebrate Pesach!" The homes in Yerushalayim are open to all who need a place to spend their Seder night.

Visiting with relatives and friends occupies much of *Chol Ha-Mo'ed.* The streets of Yerushalayim are filled with entire families out for the day, going here and there. There is a festive atmosphere which makes the whole week of Pesach a family *Yom Tov* of great joy.

As we know, the spiritual and the physical are closely related. And when it comes to Pesach preparations, the physical is much in evidence!

Dearest Children,

Erev Pesach is in the air, in the streets, in the houses, in the closets, on the ceilings, and under the beds. You walk with it, talk with it, go to sleep with it, and wake up with it.

It really started some months ago, when I overheard the women in our neighborhood talking about the Pesach cleaning they had already begun. Why so early, I thought, when it will surely need redoing? But since I couldn't fight this *erev Pesach* hysteria, I, too, joined the brigade, and I am busy cleaning out closets already — even though we've hardly digested our Purim goodies!

Last week I made a remarkable discovery. Walking along the streets of Yerushalayim, I noticed the women standing on their balconies and beating their mattresses, rugs, clothes, couch cushions, and anything else that could be beaten. They use something I had never seen before, a bamboo carpet-beater with a long handle and an artistically woven head.

Until now I never felt the need for such a thing, as I clean all our things the American way, with an electric vacuum cleaner. But I suddenly developed an overwhelming desire to be an Israeli housewife and beat something — so on the spur of the moment, I rushed into a store and bought such a beater.

I hurried home carrying my prize, and right away looked for something to beat. I spied the two throw rugs that lie on either side of our beds — just the thing! I took them out to the balcony, hung them over the railing, and beat them with all the strength I could muster.

Guess what? As the dust flew, and I beat away steadily, I felt all my petty frustrations dissolving: the constant drip from our bathroom faucet, the interminable wait for the plumber to arrive as he promised weeks ago, the often out-of-order elevator that makes me carry my heavy packages up the two-and-a-half flights of stairs to our apartment, the sudden increased electric bill that I cannot understand, and a host of other little grievances that were lodged in my mind.

As I produced that wonderful, hollow, rhythmic beat that so characterizes the sounds of Yerushalayim on a pre-Pesach morning, I finally solved the enigma of why the local women are so easygoing and accepting of all situations. They just beat everything out of their systems! In addition, I have discovered that it is an excellent antidote for insomnia, tones up flaccid muscles, and gives one a general sense of well-being.

In fact, when Papa returned from the Yeshivah and noticed the sparkle in my eyes, he remarked, "You look relaxed today; there is nothing like a good rest to do that for you."

I firmly recommend that all psychiatrists and psychologists prescribe this treatment for their patients. It "beats" tranquilizers and sleeping pills.

More about *erev Pesach* in another letter. I must go now — the winter quilts need beating.

Love, Papa and Mama

Dearest Children,

As you know, Papa and I have a very happy marriage, *baruch Hashem,* and we agree on most things. However, we have never been able to come to terms on the subject of pre-Pesach cleaning. Papa simply cannot understand why I must clean every clothes closet thoroughly, since we never go there with any *chametz.* I rationalize, explaining that there are crumbs all over, but deep down I know that it is for the sake of a general spring cleaning. Papa feels that all this extra cleaning could, and should, be done after Pesach. But I explain to him, "What I don't do before Pesach will not be done afterwards."

I also get a compulsion to get rid of things that I hoard carefully the entire year. This compulsion lasts only through the *erev Pesach* cleaning. Now, if I did not give away all these clothes, etc., every year, we would be living in a storage warehouse by now and not a home.

But the above are the minor disagreements. It is when I clean the stove and refrigerator that Papa and I really tangle. For instance, I keep my bread and cake in the freezer section of my refrigerator throughout the year. Naturally, crumbs accumulate in the rubber gaskets around the doors of the freezer and the refrigerator. Well, I wash, scrub, and then — with toothpicks — pry the crumbs free. It is fortunate that refrigerators are so very expensive here, otherwise I would have surely been less careful and "blown a gasket by now!"

After working away for hours, I hear Papa's "call of the wild": "Racoma, enough is enough!" "Moshe," I yell back desperately, "just see for yourself — there are still some crumbs left." Papa stalks in with his determined look, and I brace myself for what's coming. He checks the freezer and refrigerator carefully and then asks the usual question which determines whether something is sufficiently free of *chametz.* "Would a dog eat it? If a dog wouldn't eat it, you have nothing to worry about. Racoma, this is absolutely kosher."

In exasperation I cry out, "We never owned a dog, so how can I know if a dog would eat it? All I know is what I see. And I see crumbs!" Of course, Papa does not take "No" for an answer, and I capitulate out of sheer exhaustion, as I don't have the strength to argue the point. He has another way of getting me to stop, too — he appeals to my emotions: "It's time for lunch, and I'm very hungry."

I recall hearing that the Brisker Rav, Reb Yehoshua Leib Diskin, *zt"l* once said to his wife, as she was washing down her walls before Pesach, "This is not necessary for Pesach." Her answer was, "If I relied upon *you,* we'd have *chametz* in our house."

It comforts me to know that this argument between husband and wife has come down through the ages.

Love, Papa and Mama

Dearest Children,

With every additional *erev Pesach,* I become more convinced that during this period we must actually go through the experience of being slaves, and then Pesach finally liberates us.

Let me give you a play-by-play description of the unforeseen events that have plagued us during the last few weeks:

It started with our boiler. This was the first catastrophe — no hot water would be a real disaster during the days of washing and scrubbing. We would need a new one!

Then our Shabbos clock "blacked out," leaving us with a bright, light Shabbos as the electricity did not shut off at the scheduled time. Since I keep a lamp on near my bed, the large-watt bulb shone straight into my eyes the entire night. I caught up with all my special reading, which made me spiritually "high," but physically "low," for lack of sleep. Hashem created the world with day and night — light and dark — and we need both. So we had to buy a new Shabbos clock.

A third mishap was the breaking of the sliding glass door of our china closet, which slipped out of the groove as I was cleaning it, and shattered into myriad pieces all over our living room floor. You can imagine that Papa and I did a real "*bedikas* glass" trying to gather all the tiny shards together.

Then we ordered a new glass door.

I am now on the last leg of my *erev Pesach* work, and thank Hashem, I am still on *my* legs. I mentioned to Papa that each *erev Pesach* it becomes more of a strain, and in a few years, we shall have to consider a senior citizen's home. Papa humored me, saying, "It's an excellent idea to consider — in about thirty years or so." At least I don't have to make any snap decisions right now.

Love, Papa and Mama

✍ ✍

Dearest Children,

What with a heat wave the week before Pesach, and a cold wave with stormy weather two days before Pesach, a burn on my right hand and a cut on my left hand, bones that ached from work I could not ignore, we thought we'd never make it, but — finally — we greeted the great and wonderful *Chag Ha-Pesach.*

Let me share with you an awful experience our neighbors had to endure, of which we were inadvertently the cause. Rivky, Yehudis's sister, who is studying in Bnei Brak Seminary for the year, asked if she and her friend could sleep in our house for the first two nights of Pesach. Since Papa and I were going to Uncle Nochum Dovid and Aunt Chaye Dube's for those two days, we were happy to give Rivky access to our home.

At 1:00 P.M., I turned our living room radio up to its highest volume, so that I could hear the news while I packed our clothes in the bedroom. Just then Rivky and her friend arrived from Bnei Brak. I called out to Papa to be sure to prepare the Shabbos clock for them: to set it to go on right after candlelighting, and off an hour after midnight, when I assumed that Rivky and her friend would have returned from their Seder.

Papa set the Shabbos clock accordingly, and bade Rivky and her friend "Happy *Yom Tov,*" and off we went. What we did not realize was that Papa had neglected to turn off the radio, as it went off automatically when he switched the "off" button of our Shabbos clock.

Well, as soon as the Shabbos clock turned our lights on after candlelighting, the radio also went on full blast, blaring Arabic music (the Hebrew program had gone off for *Yom Tov*). The piercing, raucous music resounded through every part of our building, from the ground floor all the way to the sixth floor. Rivky and her friend had left, with the keys to our door, before the lights went on; they had no idea what was happening.

The neighbors tried to discover where the booming, blasting music — if you can call it that — was coming from, and traced it to our apartment. We received a blow-by-blow description when we returned. It seems the strains of Middle Eastern melodies accompanied every neighbor throughout the Seder, and they were ready to have us evicted! However, by the time we returned, they were taking it good-humoredly, but as one neighbor said to me, "It was a Seder we shall never forget."

Love, Papa and Mama

P.S. I thought that I would miss not having two Seders, as we do in the States, for the first time in my life. But it wasn't so. On the contrary, knowing that there would be only one, and "that this is it," made a great impact on me. I concentrated much more on each part of the Seder, which became very significant.

Bonfires and Blintzes

LAG BA-OMER IS the 33rd day in the 49-day period of semi-mourning between Pesach and Shavuos. It is a day of rejoicing because on this day the plague that killed Rabbi Akiva's 24,000 *talmidim* ceased. This day, the 18th of Iyar, is also the yahrtzeit of the great Rabbi Shimon Bar Yochai, who is buried in the city of Meron, in the Galilee. Since ancient times it has been a custom to travel to his tomb in Meron on Lag Ba-Omer, to pray there, light great fires, and give the day a festive character. Thousands make the trek up north, with many people spending the night on the mountainside near his grave.

Weddings and celebrations are celebrated on this day, and haircutting is permitted. In fact, it is customary to give three-year-old boys their first haircut on this day, and to make it a joyous occasion. Many parents take their little sons to Meron to observe this custom. Those who cannot make the trip often take their three-year-olds to the *kever* of Shimon

Ha-Tzaddik, in Yerushalayim.

Lag Ba-Omer is an exciting day with its varied aspects. Many families are out en masse, going on trips and picnics. But the eve of Lag Ba-Omer is what the children wait for all year, for it is then that great bonfires blaze throughout our Land. A visitor who flew into Eretz Yisrael on the night of Lag Ba-Omer commented, "It was a most thrilling sight to see the entire Land alight with thousands of bonfires."

Dearest Children,

Days before Lag Ba-Omer, the neighborhood boys started collecting every sort of inflammable object they could lay their hands on. Wooden crates, broken chairs, dead tree branches, and a great variety of unidentified wooden objects are piled up in strategic locations. Finally, the great night arrives, the bonfires burst into flame, and the children frolic wildly around them, with the parents keeping a nervous and watchful eye on them.

All of Yerushalayim is ablaze. The smoke penetrates every room of our house, and this is no time to leave laundry on the line. Papa and I bear it patiently.

For us, Lag Ba-Omer has personal significance as well. It is the yahrtzeit of Papa's mother, your Bubbie Gneshe, *a"h.* Do you know that she was married to Zaidie Shimon at 3:00 P.M. on Lag Ba-Omer, and fifty-three years later — on the same day and at the same hour — she passed away suddenly!

From the time I became a bride, Bubbie Gneshe welcomed me as one of her own. I dropped the "in-law" from "mother-in-law," as she was a devoted, loving mother to me. Although she had a large family, as you know, and your Papa was the oldest of ten children, she always found time for each of her children and her grandchildren.

Zaidie and Bubbie Shain had an exceptional, loving marriage. Though their home was filled with lively children, I always felt a great sense of inner peace when I was there. She was the true "*Yiddishe Mama.*" She looked with disdain at a can opener! Her homemade challahs and cakes, her delicious and healthful food, would be rated A-plus by any nutritionist today.

Whenever we came to visit, her warm greeting and delicious hot meal awaited us. She understood all of her children and accepted each one as an individual. I cannot recall ever hearing her raise her voice in anger. I think that Bubbie Gneshe's "old-fashioned" psychology could compete with some of the modern theories on child-rearing.

May she rest peacefully in her very special place in Heaven.

Love, Papa and Mama

✍ ✍

After finishing the counting of the omer, the great Festival of Shavuos is welcomed by *Klal Yisrael.* In Yerushalayim, this Festival, which marks the giving of the Torah on Mount Sinai, takes on a special aura of holiness. Many men stay awake the entire night studying Torah. From our open windows, I can hear the sound of learning that fills the air. At dawn, the men's voices are raised in *Yom Tov* prayers.

Much before dawn, thousands of men and women begin to stream toward the *Kosel* to recite morning prayers at first light. The streets of Yerushalayim are alive and as crowded as if it were the middle of the day.

Because it would have been difficult for Reb Moshe and me to walk that distance, we never went, but a friend described the scene that took place. As the huge crowd of men neared the steps descending to the *Kosel,* they joined hands and danced their way closer and closer, continuing their dancing until prayers were started. It was a most captivating sight as the dark of night slowly departed, and the first light of dawn entered, growing brighter and brighter until the sun broke through in all her splendor. The *Kosel* was enveloped in a blaze of sunshine that danced around each stone and joined the throngs in the joy of Shavuos.

Dearest Children,

Papa and I had an inspiring Shavuos. I decorated our house with greenery, and a few friends sent us sweet-smelling bouquets of flowers. Papa stayed up until late in the night learning, and I read the English translation of *Megillas Ruth* from start to finish. Of course, I prepared special cheese blintzes and other dairy dishes for our *Yom Tov* meal after the morning Kiddush.

You know, children, whenever we eat blintzes, I am reminded of what happened to Raphael Yitzchok on Shavuos many years ago, when he was just past bar mitzvah. Raphael Yitzchok will remember this well, but I don't know if all the rest of you ever heard about it.

Well, he decided to spend the entire night learning in the Yeshivah. As he left, he called out, "I'll return in the morning right after *Shacharis.*" I ran after him and called out, "I'll have some very good blintzes and cheesecake ready for you when you get home."

A very tired Raphael Yitzchok came home early in the morning. As he ate his blintzes, he told me: "In the middle of the night, Mama, I felt so sleepy that I just couldn't keep my eyes open anymore. I decided I must go home and get to bed, although I was so tired I didn't know how I would be able to walk the twelve blocks home.

"But the thought that I would soon be able to go to sleep gave me the energy to go on, and I finally made it. I climbed the four flights of stairs to our apartment and — found the door locked! I knocked gently, hoping and praying that you would hear me, but all remained quiet. I was really very tempted to bang loudly until you woke up and opened the door, but, somehow, I couldn't bring myself to wake you and I held back.

"I walked the twelve blocks back to the Yeshivah, and by

that time I was wide awake and contined my learning until the early morning prayers.''

When he finished telling me of his experience, I was so proud of him that I gave him a double portion of cheesecake! Papa also shared my pride in him when I told him about the incident.

Raphael Yitzchok was certainly fulfilling the mitzvah of honoring one's father and mother, one of the Ten Commandments that are part of the Torah reading on Shavuos.

You know, children, it is really only after Shavuos that summer in its golden glory comes to settle down in Yerushalayim. Although winter seems officially over at Pesach, when the children trade their boots for sandals, the weather remains unsettled. Rain, hail, blazing *chamsins*, sandstorms, and the occasional nice day characterize this period.

Perhaps between celebrating the exodus from Egypt and the receiving of the Torah at Mount Sinai, *Am Yisrael* is a little uneasy too. But with Shavuos, the summer in Yerushalayim is here to stay, with its clear, dry, radiant days and cool, dewy nights.

Love, Papa and Mama

Reliving History

TO BE IN YERUSHALAYIM on the days preceding Tisha B'Av, and on Tisha B'Av itself, makes the pain, sorrow, and despair of the Destruction of our *Beis Ha-Mikdash* and of the Exile come alive.

During the first eight days of the month of Av every form of rejoicing is diminished. We do not eat meat or drink wine, except on Shabbos or at a *seudas mitzvah,* such as a bris. We do not listen to music. We limit washing of clothes, cleaning our homes, sewing, and shopping for new garments. In general, we try to recreate the sense of the disaster that befell our Jewish Nation almost two thousand years ago. And the very fact that we are witnessing in our time the return of the Jewish People to our homeland highlights even more the enormity of the event and its significance for us. For when we live in Yerushalayim and stand at the *Kosel* we feel the reality of the absence of the *Beis Ha-Mikdash.*

On *erev Tisha B'Av,* as sunset nears, the signs of mourning increase. We remove our shoes and replace them with non-leather ones. We sit on low stools, and eat our *seudah mafsekes*, the meal before the fast, which usually includes a hard-boiled egg dipped in ashes.

When we enter the shul on the night of Tisha B'Av to listen to the reading of *Megillas Eichah*, the lights are dimmed, people are seated either on very low benches or on the floor, and even the blue velvet *paroches* covering the Ark has been removed, making one feel that the *sifrei Torah* themselves join in our deep mourning. In fact, learning Torah on Tisha B'Av is forbidden.

Dearest Children,

The blazing sun is finally setting, and a wisp of welcome cool air fans me, as I sit typing this letter to you. The fast of Tisha B'Av will soon be over. Though it has been a day of weeping, yet, mingled with our tears, there is a fervent hope that soon, very soon, this day will become transformed into one of joy for *Klal Yisrael*.

For the first few years after Papa and I settled in Yerushalayim, on every Tisha B'Av we would go to the *Kosel* for early-morning prayers and *Kinos*. When it became increasingly difficult for Papa, he began to attend the Isbee minyan and he would recite the *Kinos* there. However, Mollie Isbee and I have continued to go every year.

Today, once again, Mollie and I headed for the *Kosel*. Though it was early in the morning, a little after 7:00 A.M., the sun was already waxing hot in the cloudless sky. The Egged bus company provided extra buses to transport the thousands of people who flocked to the *Kosel* on the night of Tisha B'Av and throughout the day. The bus we boarded was crowded, but many people would not sit down because of the custom to sit only on low stools until midday. For Mollie and me, it would have been too much of a strain to stand the entire way, so we were thankful to get seats.

When we arrived, the women's section was almost filled to capacity. We finally found a shady spot, and I spread out the blanket I had brought with me. Many women were already waiting for Mollie, as she comes each year to the *Kosel* to read about the Destruction in Yiddish.

With Mollie's sad and tearful voice recounting the tragic happenings of Tisha B'Av, we all cried together. There were a number of small children seated near us, but they sensed the somber mood, and were quiet. Although the *churban* happened almost two thousand years ago, I could feel sharply the anguish and despair of our Jewish Nation. I could hear the heart-rending cries of the starving people, and I could see the burning ruins and desolation of the *Beis Ha-Mikdash.* It was all happening right here and now....

The *Kosel,* which stands as a testimony to that calamitous period, seemed to lift up her voice and cry out in desperation, "Hashem, I have stood alone for almost two thousand years, and have listened to the pleas and prayers of your beloved Children. When, oh when, will you return and rebuild Your Sanctuary?" Her valid question remained suspended in air for a few moments, and then slowly wafted its way toward the Heavens and disappeared Above.

I was told to look for a pair of mourning doves, one black and one white, which are usually seen in the crevices of the *Kosel* on Tisha B'Av. Sure enough, I looked up and there they were, perched high above us. What tidings did each one come to tell us, I wondered?

It was almost noon when we got back to Kiryat Mattersdorf. I was very tired, but it was worth all the effort to be at the *Kosel* today, the actual place where the enormous tragedy had struck our Jewish Nation.

May we be *zocheh* on Tisha B'Av to hear the sound of joy and dancing in the streets of Yerushalayim, as *Am Yisrael* flocks to the rebuilt *Beis Ha-Mikdash.* AMEN!

Love, Papa and Mama

PART THREE:

Only in Israel

A Visit to Rachel Immenu

RACHEL'S TOMB, located on the Jerusalem-Hebron road at the entrance to Bethlehem, is ten kilometers (six and a half miles) from Jaffa Gate in Jerusalem. Although it is very close to Yerushalayim, the Jews had no access to this very holy site for almost twenty years, as it was in Jordanian hands from 1948 until 1967 when Bethlehem and the surrounding areas were recaptured by Israel during the Six-Day War.

We read in *Bereshis* that when Yaakov *Avinu* and his family left Lavan's house after twenty years, to come back to Eretz Yisrael, Rachel was expecting her second child. As they neared Bethlehem, she gave birth to her son Binyamin and passed away. Yaakov buried his beloved wife Rachel there, as it is written: "And Rachel died, and was buried on the way to Efras, which is Bethlehem" [*Bereshis* 35:19].

It was by Divine commandment that Rachel lies there, we are taught, for Yaakov was told that in the future when Nevuchadnetzar would exile the Jews, they would pass

Rachel's tomb, and she would plead to Hashem to have mercy on her children. We read in *Yirmeyahu* 31:14 the well-known, moving words: "A voice was heard in Ramah, lamentation and bitter weeping; Rachel, weeping for her children."

Hashem answered her prayers: "Thus says the Lord, 'Restrain your voice from weeping, and your eyes from tears, for your good work shall be rewarded.' Says the Lord, 'And they shall return again from the land of the enemy...and your children shall come back again to their own border' " [*Yirmeyahu* 31:15-16].

Dearest Children,

As it is customary in Eretz Yisrael to visit the graves of great *tzaddikim* on their yahrtzeits, Papa and I were really looking forward to our first visit to the *kever* of Rachel *Immenu.* Although there were special buses leaving every half hour from the central bus station, so we had no problem with transportation, the bus we boarded was nevertheless very crowded with men, women, and even little children, but two young girls were courteous enough to give Papa and me seats.

When we arrived, we could hardly squeeze into the little room where her tomb stands bedecked with a blue velvet cover on which is inscribed: "A voice was heard in Ramah, lamentation and bitter weeping; Rachel, weeping for her children."

Cries were emanating from the throng of people gathered there, which echoed and re-echoed into our heart. Even older men cried like babies, calling to Mother Rachel in Yiddish, "*Muter Rochel, Muter Rochel,*" as they stood near her *kever.* Rachel *Immenu* was so very young when she passed away, and yet she has become the symbol of the Jewish mother, who weeps and pleads for her children, *Klal Yisrael.*

As I stood there reciting *Tehillim* with the tears flowing freely down my cheeks, it was difficult to believe that only a year and a half ago, Papa and I could not even contemplate our having the *zechus* to be standing in this holy place, because it was under Jordanian rule.

As we left Rachel *Immenu*'s *kever,* Papa turned to me. "In America we learn Torah," he said to me. "Here, we actually live it." He was deeply moved.

Since it was *erev Shabbos* and we were in a hurry to get home, and our Egged bus was due only in twenty minutes, we took the first available bus that stopped at the bus stop across from Rachel's Tomb: an Arab bus. The bus driver drove off taking a different route from the Egged bus we had come with. He raced along the mountainside, on narrow, twisting roads barely wide enough for a donkey, at such speed that Papa and I had to hold on for dear life. The view was breathtaking — when we could catch our breath.

We fervently prayed that the *tefillas ha-derech* we had recited when we set out would continue to protect us. It reminded me of the wild "loop-the-loop" rides in Steeple Chase that I used to go on when I was a little girl. Miraculously, we arrived in one piece at Sha'ar Shechem, in the Old City, about twenty minutes later. The ride cost each of us half a pound — the equivalent of fifteen cents, and it certainly was a bargain.

Since we were not too far from the *Kosel,* Papa and I decided to go there to daven *Minchah.* We walked through the teeming Arab marketplace, and from the narrow, dark alleys filled with shops, suddenly we were out in an open sunny expanse, with a full view of the *Kosel.* It was a delightful and spiritually uplifting moment.

From the *Kosel,* we caught a bus that took us home. I had cooked most of the Shabbos meal before we left, so I had only the cholent to prepare, and the water to boil in the large samovar. I had enough time to light the candles as the siren announced the coming of Shabbos.

May Rachel *Immenu*'s pleas be heard by Hashem, and bring the *geulah shelemah* very soon.

Love, Papa and Mama

P.S. Let me explain the red ribbon I am enclosing in this letter. When Bubbie Aidel's parents, my Zaidie and Bubbie Andron, sailed for Israel in 1921 (it was then "Palestine"), I was a very young child. Bubbie Aidel took us children to the boat to say goodbye to them.

One of Bubbie Andron's first actions in Eretz Yisrael was to visit Rachel's Tomb and measure its width seven times with the traditional red ribbon. She then sent Bubbie Aidel the ribbon and wrote her that each of us children should wear a piece of it attached to our clothing, as protection against *ayin ha-ra,* the evil eye. Bubbie Aidel impressed upon us the importance of it, and I guarded that piece of ribbon as if it were a great treasure.

Now, almost half a century later, as I myself planned a visit to Rachel's Tomb, I found out that this custom is still prevalent, so I bought yards of red ribbon before Papa and I started out on our trip. Though it was not a simple matter to walk around and measure Rachel *Immenu*'s tomb on her yahrtzeit because of the crowds of people gathered near it, a kind young man offered to do it for me. It gave me great satisfaction to be able to follow in the footsteps of my Bubbie Fruma Rochel Andron. Please give a piece of the red ribbon to each of the grandchildren for us.

A Shabbos for the Land

THERE ARE CERTAIN mitzvos that can only be performed when one lives in Eretz Yisrael. One of them is the mitzvah of observing *shemittah,* in which we are commanded by Hashem to allow the Land to lie fallow every seventh year, thereby making a Shabbos for the holy soil.

It was spiritually uplifting for Reb Moshe and me to have the *zechus* to keep this great mitzvah for the first time, when we settled in Eretz Yisrael. I recall our first *shemittah* clearly, when we were only fledglings and faced with what seemed innumerable and complicated halachos that became part of our daily lives for more than a year.

Winter, 1986

Dearest Children,

Years fly by, and it is our third *shemittah* year in Yerushalayim. It is unbelievable what a difference there is between this *shemittah* year and our first, way back in 1972, and even our second one, in 1979.

Now we can buy an abundance of fruits and vegetables, of good quality too, although we pay higher prices for them than we would for produce which does not meet the halachic requirements of *shemittah.* There are many places to shop, and few shortages.

I remember that before the beginning of our first *shemittah* year, I attended classes on this subject especially for women. A rabbi discussed the many halachos of *shemittah,* and I was completely confused. I had a difficult time trying to digest all the "do's and don't's."

For certain fruits and vegetables, there were different periods when *shemittah* regulations went into effect — depending on when they ripened, when they were harvested, etc. In this respect, we also had to be watchful of canned foods and be able to read the different dating codes printed on the bottom of the cans.

My first trip into town to buy *shemittah* foods was a preview of what to expect during that year. I walked through the aisles of a large produce store which displayed luscious fruits and vegetables, until I came to a small room at the back of the store set aside for *shemittah* ones — products that were grown either outside the Biblical boundaries of Eretz Yisrael or under other halachically permissible conditions.

There I was met with a sorry sight. Most of the fruits and vegetables were fourth- or fifth-rate, and in short supply as well. The prices were exorbitant. I managed to choose just a few wilted celery stalks, soft, wrinkled carrots and bruised tiny tomatoes, and left with a half-empty basket.

I decided to concentrate instead on preparing meals from starchy foods like rice and cereals, for many of them were imported from other countries, and thus not subject to the laws of *shemittah.* Fortunately Papa liked rice, but we certainly gained weight that year!

Once, when I could not get into town, I set out very early and hurried up the hill to a local vegetable stand which sold *shemittah* foods. After foraging through a pile of half-rotten potatoes and onions, I finally bought a small quantity and returned home. I placed the "valuable package" on my kitchen counter, and busied myself with other things, like preparing Papa's breakfast.

A short while after he left for the Yeshivah, I decided to prepare dinner and make some sort of vegetable soup from my precious purchase. Though I searched high and low for the bag, it was simply nowhere to be found. I went back to my rice-cooking.

When Papa returned from the Yeshivah, I asked him, "Moshe, did you perhaps see a bag of potatoes and onions on the kitchen counter?"

Papa thought for a few moments and answered, "I do remember seeing a bag on the counter, but I checked it, and I thought it was garbage, so on my way out I took it down to the garbage room and threw it away."

"That bag of garbage was supposed to be part of our dinner! But I don't blame you — they *did* look like nothing more than garbage, and anyway they were probably not edible," I soothed Papa. Now, looking back, we can laugh it off, but at that time, it posed a problem for us.

We are carefully observing the halachos of *shemittah,* which give us much "food" (*first*-rate) for thought and bring us closer to Hashem. Observing these special mitzvos which apply only to Eretz Yisrael, just as our ancestors did here in ancient times, is a wonderful feeling. It is as if our days are truly being "renewed as of old," as we say in our Shabbos prayers.

May Papa and I be blessed with many more healthy years to live, and to observe more *shemittah* years.

Love, Papa and Mama

✍ ✍

Over the years, I have heard many interesting stories that were related to *shemittah* in Eretz Yisrael. Of these, I heard of some truly miraculous events that happened on Moshav Komemiut, going back to the days before Israel became a State.

From its inception, this agricultural settlement observed the laws of *shemittah* stringently. Once, they say, this moshav and the neighboring ones planted orchards before the *shemittah* year. Of course, the farmers of Komemiut did not cultivate their orchards for the entire year, while their neighbors continued to prune, and water, and tend theirs. After the *shemittah* year had ended, the Komemiut orchards had blossomed to their fullest, while the neighboring orchards had withered away.

During another *shemittah* year, a locust plague affected a large area of farmland and left destruction in its wake. When the swarms of locust reached the borders of Moshav Komemiut, they suddenly swerved, changing their course and leaving its fields untouched.

It reminds me of what our Sages say in connection with the locust plague in Egypt, the eighth of the ten plagues with which Hashem punished the Egyptians for their cruelty to *Bnei Yisrael.* When the locusts invaded, they stopped exactly at "all the borders of Egypt" [*Shemos* 10:14], and did not cross over to neighboring Cush.

In a third incident concerning this moshav, the farmers could not get suitable seeds for planting before the beginning of the *shemittah* year, but they decided to plant anyway, using the defective seeds they were able to purchase. The surrounding farms waited to receive perfect seeds, and planted after the start of the *shemittah* year. Moshav Komemiut's poor-quality seeds sprouted and yielded a bumper crop, while the other farms were not that fortunate, and suffered an unsuccessful year.

These Israeli farmers were rewarded by Hashem for their steadfast faith and trust in Him.

Money Madness

IN 1985, INFLATION had reached such proportions that instead of our being concerned with the "basket of currency in the world financial market," it looked as if we would need a "basket to carry the currency to the market," just to buy a few groceries. Money seemed to lose all meaning when one paid thousands of shekels for simple household items!

Loss of the public's confidence in the legal tender of a country causes unrest, and so the government of Israel scrapped the old shekel and introduced the new one, which was worth one thousand old ones. This change was accompanied by chaos, for now everything appeared to be ridiculously cheap. And of course many Israelis, including shopkeepers, continued to think, and do business, in old shekels while *using* the new ones. "That will be two thousand shekels," the shopkeeper would say, and the customer would hand him two tiny new shekel coins.

Yes, confusion reigned, but so did our sense of humor.

Dearest Children,

Although we now have a new shekel, we can still use the old one through the end of December — which means that we have two currencies — the old and the new — in use at the same time! This has lead to utter confusion.

When I went shopping at the local grocery store this morning, there was pandemonium. Some of the shoppers had new shekels, and some the old ones. The customers were so mixed up, and the grocer as well, that many of them asked if they could pay their bills in a few days. The grocer himself seemed relieved that he would not have to figure out the charges, and happily wrote everything down in his book — in the old currency.

To give you an idea of what's what: our old one-thousand-shekel banknote is now one new shekel — a tiny coin no larger than a U.S. dime. The shock of seeing one thousand shekels reduced to a minuscule coin is difficult for most of us to absorb.

This morning a poor man came to my door asking for charity. When I offered him the new half-shekel (which is larger in size than the new shekel), the equivalent of the old 500-shekel banknote, he looked at the coin with disdain and refused to accept it!

A friend of ours bought an expensive wedding gift, paying with the new currency. Later on, when she thought it over, she sensed that something was wrong and that she had been overcharged. When she returned to the store, the owner realized he had made a mistake and immediately reimbursed her. Asking for her forgiveness, he explained that he was still not sure how to figure out the new shekel prices. Had she not noticed the error, that wedding gift might have been a lot more expensive than my friend had intended!

As you know, children, I have always been very good at math, and I even took some accounting courses at university, but the new currency has me befuddled. Every time I buy something I have to make several calculations to be sure that I have paid the correct amount.

I guess in time we'll all get used to it, but "currently" the currency is causing considerable commotion.

Love, Papa and Mama

P.S. I am enclosing a leaflet that the Bank of Israel has distributed to help the bewildered public in converting from the old shekel to the new.

You will notice that toward the bottom of the leaflet is a photo of the new fifty-shekel banknote. Now, we never had a fifty-thousand-shekel banknote in old shekels, so this is an entirely new number. You will also notice that the well-known author, Shmuel Yosef (Shai) Agnon, is pictured on it, with his head bent and his hand on his forehead, looking very perturbed. This is an excellent portrayal of how the public is being affected by the new currency!

בנק ישראל

שקל חדש בישראל

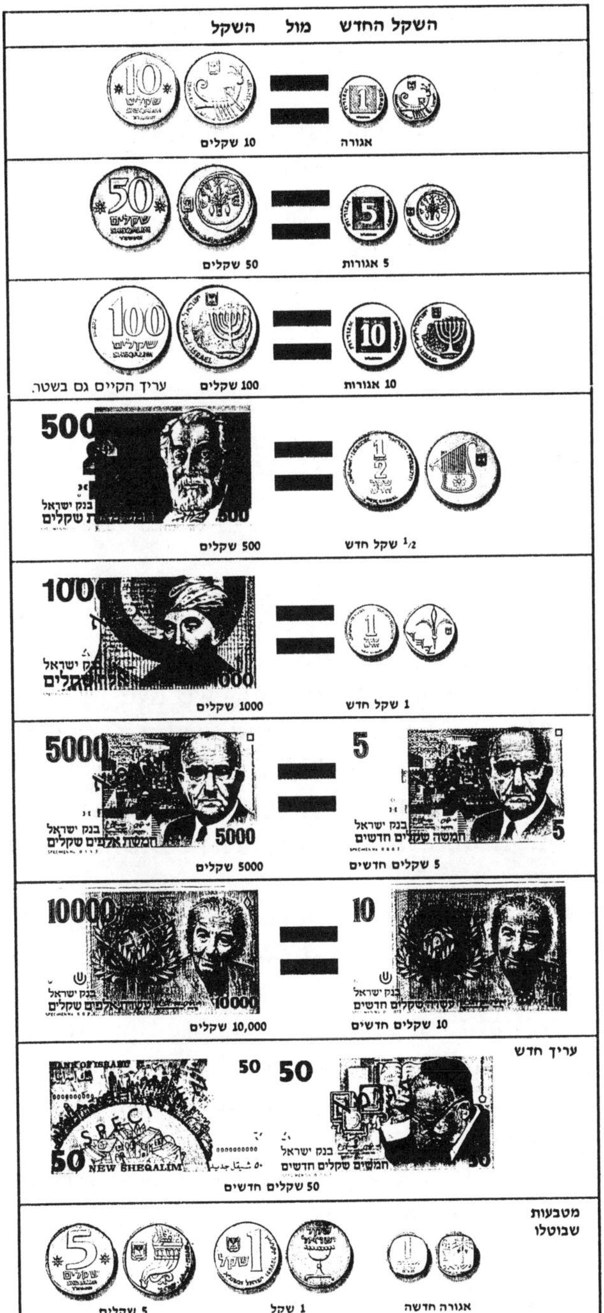

גודל המטבעות והשטרות אינו הגודל המקורי.

"Patience, Patients!"

ISRAEL IS A LAND OF striking contrasts — geographical and human. At one and the same time, we live in an ethereal realm and in a practical, mundane realm — a "Heavenly Yerushalayim" and an "earthly Yerushalayim." Ever since our *aliyah,* one of the most "striking" contrasts for me has been the notion of striking workers in the holiest city on earth.

Here in tiny Eretz Yisrael a workers' strike affects everyone personally, and unfortunately there have been many such job actions and walkouts that made life difficult, to say the least. Police and firefighters' strikes can be life-threatening. Even the threat of a mail strike "strikes" terror in our hearts, because it means the letters from our children will be delayed. A bus strike caused losses of time and money, too, as we had to resort to taking taxis. The worst strike for us, however, was the doctors' strike.

Dearest Children,

We are in the midst of a prolonged doctors' strike. I will not take sides between our finance minister, who refuses to break the wage scale, and the doctors, who refuse to give up their demand for higher wages and shorter working hours. They both have justifiable claims. For us, however, it poses a major problem. Papa and I have had several "trying" experiences trying to receive adequate medical attention during this strike.

Papa developed a cough recently, which normally would have sent us hurrying to our local kupat cholim [health fund] doctor. I called to find out the procedure during the strike. It turned out that I had to go to the Histadrut building in town and pay a fee of six hundred and fifty [old] shekels for a *petek* — a slip of paper giving us permission to take two buses to our doctor's home, where he had set up practice temporarily.

I decided to doctor Papa myself.

Our medicine chest contains a variety of medications which every good Israeli household stocks. I found a bottle of cough medicine and gave Papa a tablespoon every four hours. That, together with a regimen of hot drinks, the vaporizer, and plenty of vitamin C, improved his cough, thank Hashem.

I hope that we won't require the services of any doctor (aside from me) while the strike continues.

Love, Papa and Mama

Dearest Children,

My optimism has taken a tailspin. The doctors' strike is continuing, and when Papa's eyes started to tear and redden, I felt inadequate to the task, my medical specialties not including ophthalmology. I searched the list of local doctors who belong to our health fund and found the names of two eye specialists. When we tried the first, we discovered a sign tacked to his door announcing that his fee was eight hundred and fifty (old) shekels! When I called the second one, he told me that he would accept Papa without any charges, and he gave us a 4:15 P.M. appointment.

By 3:00 P.M. we were already on our way, and we arrived at the doctor's office half an hour early. The secretary took Papa's name and some basic information, and told us that there would be about an hour's wait. Her optimism was admirable.

We entered a packed waiting room, and two young people courteously stood up and offered us seats. The doctor had not arrived at his office yet. I was told that he had been attending patients the entire morning, and had escaped for a needed rest. Fortunately, I had taken my easy-Hebrew newspaper along with me, and I was pleased to have the opportunity to work on improving my language skills. At least that is what I thought!

Four lively small children of various ages were playing, whooping, crawling, and crying. A teenager decided he needed air and opened all the windows, which made the room chilly and drafty. Some of the other patients were engaged in loud and animated conversation, so I could not concentrate. Papa tried to doze, as this was usually his nap time, but to no avail.

At 4:40 P.M. the doctor strode in, and everyone surged forward. The secretary called out the name of the first patient, who jumped up eagerly — she had been waiting for over two hours. It seemed to take ages until she left the office and another patient was called.

At 5:30 I asked the secretary when Papa's turn would come. She checked her list and said calmly, "Please be patient. There are nine others ahead of you."

I did not know if we should give up and just go home, or sit it out. I felt that it was a strain for Papa to wait for such a long time, and I, too, was feeling the tension, but Papa decided we should wait.

At 6:45 P.M. I threw all caution to the wind and did what another desperate patient had done before me: As soon as the doctor's office door opened and a patient walked out, I leaped up, rushed in and called for Papa to follow. "We have been waiting our turn for almost three hours, and my husband has a heart condition. Please see him now." The doctor looked up wearily and nodded his head. He examined Papa's eyes quickly, and wrote a prescription for eye drops. His diagnosis was that Papa was suffering from an allergy.

This was something I had surmised, because all the pollen-laden flowers were starting to bloom. We staggered out of his office at 7:00 P.M., and I apologized to the other patients for my discourteous behavior. They seemed to understand, as I guess they had respect for Papa and for our age. We wanted to take a taxi, but no vacant ones appeared, so we made our way to the bus stop. We waited half an hour for our bus, because some of the bus drivers were also on strike and arrived home after 8:00 P.M. — hungry, exhausted, bleary-eyed, and allergic to all doctors.

Love, Papa and Mama

Dearest Children,

The strike goes on! A special unit — a *moked* — has been set up to receive patients during the strike. Papa had to have his routine heart examination, something that we could not put off. We paid seven hundred [old] shekels for the service. This time, though, we came amply prepared. I brought a day's mending, all my correspondence that needed answering, two books that I have been anxious to read, and a good supply of food to keep us from starving. Papa took along some *sefarim.* We have learned to become "patient" patients.

Miracles! After waiting for "only" two and a half hours, Papa's name was called. Thank Hashem, he was examined and given a favorable report — which I considered another miracle, with all the strain that we had to endure in order to see the cardiologist.

Love, Papa and Mama

Sunrise Service

IN ADDITION TO the numerous daily blessings, there are other blessings that we recite for special occasions, thanking Hashem when we witness certain aspects of His bountiful Creation: the mighty oceans, thunder and lightning, the colorful hues of the rainbow reminding us of Hashem's covenant to never again destroy the world through flood. There is also the beautiful once-a-year blessing that we recite in the month of Nisan upon seeing two fruit trees in bloom.

There is another blessing, rarer yet, that can only be said in Nisan: *birkas ha-chamah* — the blessing of the sun. This blessing is recited only once in twenty-eight years, when the sun returns to the precise position where Hashem placed it on the day of its Creation.

The excitement surrounding this occasion had a most profound impact on me. For days beforehand, we had been alerted that on Wednesday, the fourth day of Nisan 5741 (1981), the mitzvah of *birkas ha-chamah* would be observed.

The day before, loudspeakers mounted on trucks blared forth announcements that people should congregate at the *Kosel* at dawn to recite this blessing. This was the first time since the Destruction of the Temple that thousands of Jews would gather to recite this *berachah* together at the *Kosel.* (Twenty-eight years before, the *Kosel* had been in Jordanian hands.)

Before dawn, the streets of our Kiryah were crowded with men, women, and children, including entire families with infants, all trying to get to the *Kosel.* Loudspeakers kept announcing through the streets, "Arise, arise for *Avodas Hashem.*"

Dearest Children,

If we had settled in Yerushalayim just for the *zechus* of being part of the spiritual experience of *birkas ha-chamah,* then *dayenu* — it would have been sufficient!

For Papa, it would have been too much of a strain to ride to the *Kosel.* He stayed home and would recite the blessing from our balcony, but he encouraged me to go. I made arrangements with Rivky (Yehudis's sister) to meet her at the Mattersdorf bus stop at 3:45 A.M! As you can imagine, I did not get too much sleep, and before the set time I was already standing at the bus stop. Rivky arrived a few minutes later, and we waited impatiently to board a bus to get us to the *Kosel.*

Bus after bus already packed with passengers passed us by, and I suggested that we walk over to Kiryat Itri, several streets away, and try to catch a bus there. Once we got there, however, the same problem awaited us. Just when we were getting panicky about not getting to the *Kosel* in time, our prayers were answered, and an empty bus pulled up and stopped in front of us. We were shoved onto the bus by the crowds waiting near us, and within a few minutes it was filled to capacity.

The bus parked several blocks from the *Kosel,* as it was

impossible to get near it. We squeezed ourselves into a spot where we could see and hear what was going on. I heard that there were about 120,000 people gathered there.

Though we understood the holiness of this mitzvah, the atmosphere was far from solemn. There was an air of festivity, and a band was playing music. Over the loudspeaker, it was announced that we would be told the exact moment to recite the blessing. With our heads turned upwards and our eyes glued to the sky above Har Hazeisim, we waited impatiently for her appearance.

Precious moments flew by as gray clouds covered the sun, which peeked out for a second, teasingly, only to disappear again. Tension mounted, and we became concerned that the sun would not show itself in time for the blessing.

As the sun darted in and out of the clouds, I thought, "Does Hashem perhaps not want us to perform this mitzvah?" There was an announcement that *Tehillim* would be recited and everyone should join in. Psalm 130 was recited, sentence by sentence, with great emotion.

Suddenly the clouds parted, and the sun in all its glory shone through. From the loudspeaker came an emotional, "Now!" With our voices raised triumphantly, we recited the *berachah*: "Blessed be you, O God, our God, King of the Universe, *oseh ma'aseh Bereshis* — Who created the work of the Beginning." It echoed and re-echoed through the hills and valleys of Yerushalayim. We were one People, with one thought: to pay homage to Hashem and His Creation. This moment will remain in my memory forever.

With the release of tension, people greeted each other with elation. The band played, men danced and clapped their hands to the music. Then the throng paraded all the way from the *Kosel* down Jaffa Road, dancing and singing.

The next time *birkas ha-chamah* is to be recited will be in the year 2009, when I will be 94 years old, and Papa a few years older. May we live to perform this great mitzvah once again.

Love, Papa and Mama

A week after the unforgettable experience of *birkas ha-chamah,* I still felt an inner stirring when I awakened at dawn, and watched the rising of the sun.

Many of us take for granted Hashem's creations, until we are prodded by a special event such as *birkas ha-chamah.* The poem, "All Things Bright and Beautiful," by Cecil Francis Alexander, a favorite of mine, describes with eloquence the beauty that surrounds us. I have taken a few stanzas to share with you:

All things bright and beautiful,
All creatures great and small,
All things wise and wonderful,
God, He made them all.

The purple-headed mountain,
The river running by,
The sunset and the morning,
That brightens up the sky.

He gave us eyes to see them,
And lips that we might tell,
How great is God — All Mighty,
Who has made all things well.

Counting Our Blessings

IN *THE MIDRASH SAYS,* Rabbi Moshe Weisman relates the following:

Hashem told Moshe to command the *Kohanim*: "Thus shall you bless the *Bnei Yisrael...*" *Thus* denotes that the *Kohanim* are required to bestow their blessings in the following manner: standing, and raising their hands — with their raised hands pointed Heavenward. The *Kohanim* are further required to face the community, to pronounce the blessings in *lashon ha-kodesh,* and, in the *Beis Ha-mikdash,* to enunciate Hashem's Four-Letter-Name as it is written.

When the Jews were told that the *Kohanim* would bless them, they protested. "Master of the Universe," they said, "why do You bless us through *Kohanim*? We desire that You bless us directly."

Hashem replied: "Although I commanded the *Kohanim* to bless you, I shall be present, too."

Outside of Eretz Yisrael, the Priestly Blessing — *Birkas Kohanim* — is recited only on Rosh Hashanah, Yom Kippur, Sukkos, Pesach and Shavuous. In Eretz Yisrael, however, it is recited daily during *Shacharis* and twice on *Shabbosim* and *Yamim Tovim*, during *Shacharis* and *Musaf.*

During *Chol Ha-Mo'ed* of Pesach and Sukkos, hundreds of *Kohanim* congregate at the *Kosel* to bless the nation en masse. In our first year in Israel, there was a public *Birkas Kohanim* held in the month of Sivan as well. I was told that the date, the third day of the third week of the third month (counting from Nisan), held special significance as *Birkas Kohanim* is a threefold blessing. Signs were posted all over Yerushalayim announcing the event.

Dearest Children,

As soon as I found out that today there would be public *Birkas Kohanim* at the *Kosel,* I decided to go. I could hardly sleep last night, out of anticipation of witnessing this awe-inspiring event for the first time in my life.

I left Kiryat Mattersdorf on the 6:45 bus and arrived at the *Kosel* to find thousands of people already waiting there. I found a bit of space on the parapet between the men's and the women's section and sat down. *Shacharis* had already begun, and I heard the voice of the *ba'al tefillah* over the loudspeaker, raised in prayer.

The early summer morning was cool, and the blue sky was covered with fleecy clouds which gave me protection from the bright sun. I watched for a moment as people streamed toward the *Kosel* from every possible direction, filling all available space. They stood in massive clusters near the *Kosel,* on the mountainside overlooking it, and on the roofs of adjoining buildings.

Praying near the *Kosel* together with thousands of other people has an impact as emotional as davening *Ne'ilah* on Yom Kippur. When we were through with *Shemoneh Esreh,* and the *ba'al tefillah* started *chazaras ha-shatz*, there was an intense feeling of expectancy, as we awaited the moment we would hear *Birkas Kohanim* from the hundreds, if not thousands, of *Kohanim* who had come from all parts of Israel to bless *Klal Yisrael*.

There was sudden hushed silence, broken only by the flapping wings of pigeons who flew round and round above us.

Then, loud and clear, as everyone held his breath, came the word "*Yevarechecha*..." Even infants became as still as little statues as the *Kohanim* continued in their ringing voices until they finished with the last of the blessings.

There was such palpable religious fervor in the air that I was praying for miracles and wondrous occurrences to take place then and there. I remained standing for a few moments without moving, as I visualized the glory of the rebuilt *Beis Ha-Mikdash* in all its splendor.

Love, Papa and Mama

P.S. Since there were thousands of people at the *Kosel* you can imagine how difficult it was trying to get on a bus afterwards. I finally squeezed myself *near* one, but when the doors of the bus opened, there was so much pushing and shoving that I was almost trampled by a crowd of men.

I became exasperated and called out loudly in Yiddish, "You've just come from prayers at the *Kosel*, and here you are pushing and shoving a woman." There was a moment of silence, and then a bearded man called out, "Let the women go first." Like the parting of the Red Sea, the men made way for me and the other women to board the bus.

The men certainly deserved a note of praise for their quick response to the rebuke.

Peace or Piece?

THROUGHOUT THE FIFTY YEARS that I lived in the United States, politics never affected me as deeply as they do here in Israel. Here, every occurrence touches me personally and emotionally. The hourly news bulletins become topics of discussion. Somehow, each event is everyone's concern.

For example, in May 1977, awaiting the results of the exciting elections kept me up half the night. The Likud party, with Menachem Begin as Prime Minister, was swept into power after being on the opposition bench for many years. The Labor party, which had enjoyed a twenty-eight-year monopoly, was defeated with a resounding crash.

Small as our country is, it is beset with many big problems. At that time, the economy was hard hit with rising inflation and strikes galore. Then, as now, there seemed no end in sight to the enmity of our Arab neighbors. The terrorist organizations continued to escalate their hatred and hostility, with continued attacks on civilians.

Dearest Children,

We need fresh, stimulating leadership, and I hope Menachem Begin and his Likud party will be able to resolve some of our problems. Of course, if we had a government based on Torah, Eretz Yisrael could be a Garden of Eden, but I guess the time has not come yet.

Your mother has become a seasoned political analyst, children. In fact, every morning the girls in my office await my personal commentary on the latest events.

Love, Papa and Mama

✍ ✍

November 1977

Dearest Children,

Egypt's President Anwar Sadat has arrived! Yerushalayim has become topsy-turvy, with many streets closed to traffic and buses rerouted. Security is very tight, and the police are patrolling everywhere.

This is certainly a historic event — who would have imagined such a thing would happen? The abnormal — an unending state of hostility with all our neighbors — has become normal, and what *should* be normal — a visit from a neighboring head of state — is an unbelievable event. Every radio broadcast blares the news, and it is the main topic of conversation. Most people are glued to their television sets, which, of course, we do not have in Kiryat Mattersdorf.

There is a general mood of enthusiasm and anticipation, and the beginning of a glimmer of hope that at long last we shall have peace with our Arab neighbors. I hope the bubble won't burst.

Love, Papa and Mama

Dearest Children,

I imagine that you too heard President Sadat's address to

the Knesset. I have the impression that he does want peace — but only on his terms, which means a "piece" of our land.

You know, when I taught vocabulary to the elementary grades, I used homonyms, and one of the examples was: peace — piece. Little did I know then that someday these words would have serious connotations for Eretz Yisrael. The sense of euphoria that peace is at hand is quickly dissipating, and there is a feeling of disillusionment.

Love, Papa and Mama

When I heard that Camp David was to be the site chosen for the peace negotiations between Israel and Egypt, I thought that the name was quite appropriate — however, many feared that this time Goliath would not be downed by a single stone from David's slingshot.

Many quips were circulating: "Hopefully the presidential resort won't turn out to be our last resort!" And, "President Jimmy Carter would like to carve out a place for himself in history as the President who brought peace to the Middle East. May he not carve Israel up in the process!"

The peace talks seemed to be dragging on, with a lot of rhetoric, but nothing concrete. Although Prime Minister Begin had a very strong character, many feared that the pressure would cause him to capitulate and surrender a lot, for nothing in return.

Dearest Children,

I just heard the news that Prime Minister Begin and President Sadat, with the "assistance" (a better word would be "arm-twisting") of President Carter, have reached a comprehensive agreement at Camp David. This agreement is supposed to resolve the problem of the Palestinian Arabs as well — which remains to be seen.

I have grave doubts about this peace treaty. Israel has committed herself to returning Sinai, which means that we shall give up the oil fields, and then, most probably, have to buy the oil back from Egypt. There are also military bases in the Sinai, and thriving towns and settlements that will be given up as part of this deal. However, who knows? If even one Jewish soldier's life is spared as a result of all this, then all the concessions will have been worth it. Let us hope that we shall not have any more bloodshed in our Land.

Love, Papa and Mama

✍ ✍

Dearest Children,

I feel the need to continue sharing with you all the dramatic events that are taking place.

You have read that the Camp David accord spelled out a five-year autonomy period for the Arabs of the Territories. At this point everyone is conjecturing and giving his opinion of what autonomy means — what exactly will take place. From the grocer to the bus driver, we are all authorities!

This reminds me of the story that was told about the meeting between President Truman and Prime Minister Ben-Gurion. When Ben-Gurion referred to the many problems that he was facing in his country, Truman reportedly answered something to the effect of, "How many problems can such a tiny nation have? There are almost two hundred million citizens in my country, while yours doesn't even have two million."

"You may have almost two hundred million citizens Mr. President," Ben-Gurion replied, "but I have two million prime ministers!"

Love, Papa and Mama

March 1979

Dearest Children,

When I saw the newspaper photograph of President Carter,

President Sadat, and Prime Minister Begin clasping hands, with delighted smiles on their faces after signing the peace treaty amid much fanfare, I thought to myself: I can understand President Carter and President Sadat feeling elated at this ceremony, because they both received all they had hoped for. But I wonder what the true feelings of Prime Minister Begin are, and if his broad smile is just a mask he wears for the world.

It is true that he has accomplished no small feat by signing a peace treaty with the most prominent of our Arab neighbors, but the concessions have all been on our side. President Sadat has only agreed not to wage war against us, and to establish diplomatic relations. I guess this is a courageous step for him, as he has been ostracized and is held in disrepute by the other Arab countries, merely for recognizing the existence of Israel.

And so, while there is cause to be happy and grateful, nevertheless there remain a lot of unanswered questions. In *Mishlei,* we read that: "Like water courses is the king's heart in the Hand of Hashem"[21:1]. I guess this is the answer to all the questions, as He is determining the course of events "Upstairs."

Love, Papa and Mama

✍ ✍

The assassination of President Anwar Sadat appeared to be a death blow to the peace process, and it was a relief to hear his successor, President Hosni Mubarak, declare that he would continue Sadat's policies. To this day, we do have some sort of diplomatic relations with Egypt, with mutual embassies in both countries. There are lots of Israeli tourists going to visit Egypt, but very few Egyptian tourists coming our way. As for the Arabs and the autonomy plan, I don't think we can ever attain real peace with them, as their hatred for us is well-established and ingrained.

✍ ✍

1982

Dearest Children,

Although I was well aware that the beautiful town of Yamit on the Sinai coast was to be given up to Egypt under the terms of the peace treaty, I was not prepared emotionally for the scenes of destruction that took place.

I had never visited Yamit, but some of my friends who had been there described it as a most beautiful town, a gem gleaming in the desert sands. Its many beautiful homes, shopping centers, parks and gardens were a dream come true for the first settlers who struggled to build this city on the sand dunes. The ones who followed felt that this was home to them, and each one who lived there took pride in this lush and vibrant city.

There was great controversy regarding Yamit. Many of her residents, and a large segment of our population, felt that Yamit was an integral part of Eretz Yisrael, and should never have been included in the peace treaty in the first place. Nevertheless, since Prime Minister Begin had committed himself to giving it up, he adhered carefully to the agreement.

The Begin government decided to raze the town and return to Egypt just the site, the sand and gravel. Although the townspeople were promised full financial compensation for their losses, can any amount of money really compensate them for the loss of their cherished homes and gardens, for the destruction of the town they had built and loved with all their hearts?

Most of Yamit's families evacuated their homes when they were ordered to do so. Although it was with utter sadness, it was done peacefully. There were a few families, however, who refused to leave. They, in turn, were joined by supporters from many parts of Israel, who moved into some of the vacated homes to demonstrate their support.

To witness our own Israeli soldiers dragging their fellow Jews from the rooftops, amid cries of anguish and despair, has left a deep emotional scar. It hurts to see Jew battling Jew. For the soldiers it was heartbreaking, but they had no recourse but to do their duty. For the settlers it was no less heartbreaking: the soldiers were in some cases boys and men they knew personally.

The bulldozers plowed their way through the town, demolishing it house by house and uprooting the beautiful parks and flowering gardens.

As I heard the radio broadcasts and saw the newspaper pictures of the tragic scenes, I felt much empathy for the residents who had to vacate their homes. Our People has known so much destruction and rebuilding, so many uprootings and new beginnings throughout our long history. To see it happen here, in our own Land, to people who thought their wanderings had come to an end, was very painful.

Yamit lies in ruins. The sand and rubble sigh in the desert wind, and bear witness to a town that once had been a vibrant, thriving community. Can a garden that has been planted with loving hands be replanted in different soil and still blossom?

Can such destruction really be the road to peace?

Love, Papa and Mama

✍ ✍

My uncle Yonkev Leib Andron, my mother's oldest brother, used to visit us quite often when my family lived on Division Street in New York. He was a brilliant man, a *ben Torah*, an experienced educator and orator, and a well-known personality in the Torah world. In fact, he helped his father, Reb Shmuel Yitzchok Andron, found the Rabbi Jacob Joseph Yeshivah. "RJJ" was called the "mother yeshivah," because it was the very first yeshivah in America to have a full program of both religious and secular studies, and my uncle Yonkev Leib was principal there for some years.

Besides his many other talents, he was a creative writer. Shortly after the destruction of Yamit, I found tucked away among some of my own writings that I had brought with me when we settled in Yerushalayim, a poem he wrote many years ago. The paper was yellow with age and half-torn, but his handwriting was still legible.

My uncle's poem helped to lift my spirits, which had been on the gloomy side. I will share it with you:

Have faith and trust, ye wavering,
God's ways we may not see.
What may seem chaos in our view,
To Him is Harmony.
And when deep anguish fills our hearts,
And tears well from our eyes,
The ill that causes them may be
A blessing in disguise.
The noisome, poisonous weed,
Which grows without a single charm
May hold in its obnoxious stem,
A medical balm.
And tempests that overwhelm us,
And fill us with dismay
May render pure the fetid air,
And drive disease away.
Then faint not when reverses come,
Have faith, and hope and trust
That all is ordered for the best,
That God is kind and just.
Dwell not on evils that may come,
Nor mourn over evils past
But nurse the precious hope that God
Will comfort you at last.

May Hashem Avenge Their Blood

EVERY MORNING I listen to the 7:00 A.M. English news broadcast on the radio. When I hear the time signal which precedes the news, I wait with trepidation for what I will hear. Were there any terrorist attacks? Were any rocks thrown at Israeli cars, with dire consequences? Did any of our soldiers fall in action? When the first item of the news is only about in-fighting among the political parties, I sigh with relief!

Since 1968, when Reb Moshe and I settled in Yerushalayim, we have lived through wars, terrorist attacks, and during the last few years, the *Intifada.* These things are part of our everyday life. Every hour the radio blares the news, and all of *am Yisrael* — shopping in the grocery store, riding on a bus or doing housework — hold their breath, hoping for the best and expecting the worst.

When will there be an end to the bloodshed in our beloved land, and each of us sit "under his grapevine and his fig tree" in peace and security?

June 1978

Dearest Children,

I am sure you heard about the terrible tragedy that struck Yerushalayim last *erev Shabbos,* and left us all in shock and sorrow. At 1:15 P.M., bus number 12, on its way to Bayit Vegan, was attacked by Arab terrorists. You can imagine that the bus was crowded at that hour on a Friday afternoon with many schoolchildren on their way home. Several were killed and others wounded critically.

The neighborhood of Bayit Vegan is mourning, and we grieve along with them. May Hashem comfort the bereaved families and send a *refuah shelemah* to the wounded.

This senseless spilling of young Jewish blood is another chapter in our Nation's suffering. The victims were attacked for no other reason than that they were Jews. Since this tragedy occurred *erev Shabbos* afternoon, does it carry a message to us? Hopefully, we stand on the brink of the *geulah,* as we await the Shabbos at the End of Days. We must prepare ourselves for that special Shabbos when peace will reign in our land and over the entire world, may it come speedily and in our time.

Love, Papa and Mama

✍ ✍

1982

Dearest Children,

Although we signed a peace treaty with Egypt and had hoped that there would be peace in our land, once again we are faced with war and bloodshed.

It is already several months since we've been embroiled in the war in Lebanon. So many of our soldiers have been killed and wounded, leaving us all with a sense of sorrow and heartache. At first, it seemed as if this war would be a short and quick action, getting rid of the terrorist enclaves and eliminating the source of danger to the north of Israel. But the war continues as we dig deeper into Lebanon and casualties mount.

May we see an end to the fighting, peace to the northern border, and the return of our soldiers to their families.

Love, Papa and Mama

✍ ✍

When there is wanton murder of Jews by terrorists, all of *Klal Yisrael* shares the sorrow. But the brutal murder of yeshivah student Asher Aaron Gross in Hebron touched us even more deeply, as we know the family personally, and they live near Kiryat Mattersdorf.

July 1983

Dearest Children,

Asher Aaron Gross was attacked by knife-wielding Arabs in the streets of Hebron, and then left to die. It is hard to believe the words as I write them. He had been waiting for a bus of kindergarten children whom he had volunteered to accompany home to Kiryat Arba, where he was studying in Yeshivas Shavei Chevron.

Papa and I went to the Grosses' home during *shivah.* Asher Aaron, *z"l,* was the oldest of Alex and Arlene's eight children. The loss of their brother is a trauma for the younger children. When we were there, Arlene was holding her five-month-old baby son, who was cooing in her arms, oblivious to the disaster that had befallen his family, the loss of his eldest brother whom he would never know.

I sat near Arlene, who did not once question, "Why?" Instead, she spoke about her son and his exceptional talents and fine *middos.* "Asher Aaron was always ready to help wherever he was needed," she said softly. "He was a gentle soul, devoted to studying Torah." We all cried with her.

We truly long for peace with our neighbors, but when we witness the unprovoked, cold-blooded murder of an innocent young man, just because he was a Jew, we wonder if they will ever want peace with us.

May Hashem avenge his innocent blood.

Love, Papa and Mama

✍ ✍

December 1987

Dearest Children,

I am becoming quite fluent in foreign languages. I can speak about *glasnost* and *perestroika* as if I really knew Russian. And now a new word has entered my vocabulary, this time in Arabic: *Intifada* — which means uprising.

The habitual hostility of the Arabs in Judea, Samaria, and the Gaza Strip apparently needed only a spark to be ignited. I had never thought twice about going to the *Kosel* or to Har Hazeisim, or to Hebron and Bethlehem, but now there is fear of being struck by stones and attacked with knives. A large rock thrown with force from a distance can indeed be a murder weapon.

May Hashem guard us and protect us from our enemies who seek our destruction, and guide us toward a lasting peace in our precious Land.

Love, Papa and Mama

Snowed In and Snowed Under

GROWING UP IN NEW YORK CITY, winter snows were a regular part of my life. Even when we had snowfalls of twenty-five inches or more, we always took them in stride: schools were open, store-owners sold their wares, people went to work, and life went on.

When I was a young girl, New York City did not have the modern snow-clearing equipment that it has today. Then, snowplows would pile the snow high near the curbs, and there it would remain for several days, much to the delight of all the children. Returning from school, we would scamper happily over these snow mountains, often looking like snowmen ourselves by the time we reached home.

When Reb Moshe and I lived in Mir, as soon as winter set in and the snowstorms descended at a fast pace, our tiny city was bedecked with a mantle of snow that became a permanent part of our winter landscape and our lives. It was the spring sunshine, months later, that finally vied with the snow and turned it into mounds of mud. There was only one adjustment we had to make during the winter months: If one had to travel out of the city, he used a horse-drawn sled instead of a horse and wagon!

In Yerushalayim, we encountered a new phenomenon. Here, where sunshine reigns supreme for at least eight months of the year, even a three-inch snow disrupts our lives. The city grinds to a halt, schools are closed, roads are blocked. Despite our discomfort, we still delight in the sight of the white, dancing snowflakes.

Dearest Children,

We awoke yesterday to see snow gently falling. The streets were already covered with it. This is our first real snow in Yerushalayim, and it was an exciting event. I told Papa not to go to the Yeshivah in this weather, and I would go to the office and try to get back early in time for lunch.

We davened, ate breakfast, and off I went, not realizing what I would have to contend with. The buses were still running, but I had to wait a long time until my bus arrived, and there were few passengers aboard. When I walked into the Orphan Home, the housemother and the children stared at me in shock. "You mean you came to work in such a heavy snowstorm!" they said in wonder. Of course, none of the other secretaries even attempted to come, and even the directors were not to be seen.

I waited for about an hour to see if the snow would abate, but it continued to fall. The radio warned that there might be up to *five* inches of snow, and all transportation had been halted. It seems that neither the city buses nor private cars are equipped with snow tires or chains, and there was no equipment in evidence to clear the snow from the streets.

I realized that there would be no way for me to reach home within the next few hours, so I telephoned Papa and told him to go up to Aunt Bessie's for lunch, and I would try to get home as soon as possible. Papa sounded forlorn, and was worried about how I would get home. I tried to comfort him as best as I could, reassuring him that it would not pose that much of a problem. Little did I know then how difficult it would be!

I decided I would walk to Uncle Nochum Dovid and Aunt Chaye Dube, who live about ten blocks away from the Home. I trudged along through the soft snow, which was still falling thickly, only this time it was accompanied by strong gusts of wind.

Yerushalayim was beautiful in the snow. Instead of its usual colorful red tile roofs, pale golden stone, and dark green pine trees, now the city was all white. Yerushalayim appeared heavenly, bathed in light.

The only ones who seemed to be actually enjoying the snow were the children, who were out en masse, whooping it up and reveling in their transformed white world. A snowfall worthy of the name is rare here.

It took me almost an hour to reach my destination, and I arrived frozen and out of breath. I knocked at the door, and Uncle Nochum Dovid opened it gingerly, wondering who could be visiting in this kind of weather. When he saw me, he exclaimed loudly, "Chaye Dube, look who the snow brought in!" She took one look at me, and said, "Racoma, I have hot soup for you." Uncle Nochum Dovid added, "I'll give her some *shnapps* to warm her up."

Though I received V.I.P. treatment in their home, I was worried about Papa being alone. I kept calling him, and he was very upset that I would not be able to get back in the foreseeable future! We made many attempts to get some sort of transportation for me to Kiryat Mattersdorf, but all proved futile.

Finally a solution was found. It seemed some of the Rebbes who lived in my vicinity were stranded in Itri (Reb Mordechai Elefant's yeshivah) and they needed to get home too. Someone found a soldier with a half-track who was willing to brave the storm, and I was picked up on the way.

Slowly the half-track chugged through the snow, with all of us praying we should not get stuck like the many abandoned snow-covered cars which were blocking our path. I reached home at about 9:00 P.M. and was greeted enthusiastically by Papa. What was usually a ten-minute trip had taken almost an hour. It had been a long, long day for both of us, and it taught me a valuable lesson: When it snows in Yerushalayim, STAY HOME!

Love, Papa and Mama

✍ ✍

Dearest Children,

A few years ago, I wrote you about our first snowstorm in Yerushalayim, and how I was stranded in the city. Over the years, there have been other snowfalls, but usually the snow either turns to drizzle, or the sun appears and melts what little of it there is, much to the disappointment of the children.

Yesterday, however, we had a *real* snowstorm, by any standards — a ten-inch one! We awoke to a bright, white wonderland of snow. As I gazed out the window at the snow-laden trees in our garden, each one seemed to have its own new snow-personality. One was bent forward, in acceptance of the burden which Heaven had placed on her boughs. Another stood straight and stalwart with the snow piled high on her branches, showing off her weight-lifting prowess.

There on a bush a snowy polar bear seemed to lie, its paws outstretched. Next to it, a soft, white cuddly pajama-sleeper lay ready for an infant to crawl inside. As I stood there watching the many fascinating shapes and patterns the snow had formed in our garden, I recalled teaching my first-graders about snow, and explaining how every snowflake is unique. It was difficult, I told them, to see each snowflake as a separate entity when they were all bunched together. We can learn a valuable lesson from snowflakes, I mused.

Although each of us is unique, we are also all part of a whole and can live together in harmony.

Then a lone bird flew onto our balcony, the snow having usurped her place in her nest. I hoped she would find another spot to rest until the snow melts and allows her to fly back to her rightful home.

Now, back to the practical considerations of how we fared in this "big" snowstorm. First of all, after the initial excitement, we discovered that there was a power failure — most probably because of the strong winds that had struck the outside electric cables. Our house was freezing, since the central heating system needs electricity to operate. I dragged out the kerosene stove and the supply of kerosene we had bought years ago for such an eventuality and shoved and pushed the heavy can into our living room.

Then Papa and I got to work trying to get the heater started. We poured the kerosene into the small tank, and waited until the wick was saturated. We tried to light it, but it proved obstinate. Finally, after using almost an entire box of matches, it lit. But the smell of kerosene was so strong that we had to open the window to get the smoky fumes out. The house naturally remained very cold, and we had to sit right next to the heater to get any benefit from it at all.

The radio let us know that due to the "major" snowstorm there would be no deliveries of bread or milk products. In fact, the roads were closed and Yerushalayim was snowed in and isolated from the rest of Israel. Fortunately, I did have a supply of food in the house, but I was not sure how long it would last if the snow kept up. I heard that there was panic-buying in our local grocery store, and most of the staples were removed from the shelves, almost like in the Yom Kippur War.

One of our neighbors generously asked if I needed any food. She had baked her own bread, and brought us half a loaf, which was delicious. The halls were filled with the aroma of baking and cooking, as most of the neighbors took the opportunity to keep themselves busy in this manner and warm up their apartments a bit at the same time. During the day, while Papa learned with his *chavrusa,* who had braved the snow and walked from his house, I caught up with my correspondence.

As night set in, and the electricity had still not come on, I lit some candles. Papa and I filled the kerosene heater again, but our house was far from comfortable, to say the least. Papa and I looked like Eskimos, dressed in layers upon layers of clothing. I can't understand how many people in Yerushalayim use only kerosene heating the entire winter. Not only did the fumes make our house reek, they seemed to waft into our food too — everything we ate tasted like kerosene.

Suddenly — unannounced — the power came back on. Children, you cannot imagine our joy. It was as if we were witnessing the Creation, and Hashem said, "Let there be light!" The house glowed and the refrigerator hummed and we felt warmer already just *seeing* the electricity. We immediately turned off the smelly kerosene heater and turned on the electric one. Soon the steam heat came up too, our house became warm, and our lives returned to normal.

Today the sun came out and most of the snow melted. The only reminders of the snowstorm are the few puddles and the overstocked pantries. I packed the kerosene stove back into our storage room, hoping that we won't have to use it again.

Love, Papa and Mama

P.S. Israel is known for its innovative and advanced technology. However, it seems she cannot cope with one little snow that Hashem sprinkles from Heaven. It shows that no matter how advanced society becomes, man is still vulnerable...

Beware! Wet Paint!

OUR HOUSE HAD FINALLY been painted, and everything put back into place. But what would have been a routine painting job in the States took on tremendous proportions in Yerushalayim.

I hoped the weather would be sunny and mild for the painting job, as I had scheduled it for some time after Purim — but it was not to be. The weather forecast was for temperatures below normal, rain, sleet, and high winds. I tried to cancel the whole thing, but the painter had already arranged for an assistant, and had no way to contact him.

And so, promptly at 7:00 A.M., a damp wind blew them in, along with ladders, cans of paint, brushes, and other equipment.

Since our apartment had not been painted for fifteen years, there was a lot of preparation to do before they could get down to the actual painting. Finally, the scraping, patching and plastering was completed, and they applied the first coat of paint in our smaller bedroom. But it needed a second coat, and the paint would not dry. The steady rain outside, the dripping windowsill and steamy windows, and the cold damp walls were not the best conditions for paint to dry in.

I turned on our small electric heater, as the building's central heating was not turned on during the day, but it did not help at all. I watched with growing desperation as the fresh paint slowly crept down the walls and reached the floor, staining it and leaving the walls streaked in colors of varied and unusual hues.

The paint job that was supposed to take two days at the most dragged on for over a week.

Our house became a virtual refrigerator. The painters removed all our doors and windows from their frames in order to paint the woodwork, so we were exposed constantly to the bitter, freezing weather.

Despite the fact that I wore lined boots, a winter coat, scarf, and gloves, I still shook like a *lulav.*

This taught me a good lesson: Painting in Yerushalayim should be done in the heat of the summer! I hope the *Mashiach* comes before our next painting job!

Dearest Children,

Now that I have had a chance to recuperate from the painting job, I am enjoying our fresh, clean walls and I can look back on the experience from a different perspective. Zaidie Herman once said to me, "Yerushalayim is the city where the *churban Beis Ha-Mikdash* took place, and we must always be reminded of it." We did follow tradition and leave a large area on the wall over the doorway unpainted, as a reminder. And I have seen time and time again that, as our Sages said, "Eretz Yisrael is acquired with hardships." I doubt if the paint job qualifies as *yissurim,* but believe me it was no picnic.

I tried my best to keep Papa from suffering during the

painting, so I bundled him off to our dear friends, the Mandels, where he received lots of warmth and nourishing meals.

There was one experience during the painting that gave Papa and me not only *chizzuk,* but also a good laugh. In order to have the house ready for the painters, we asked Aaron Dovid to take all the *sefarim* out of the bookcases, which had to be moved, and also to move the heavy furniture onto the balcony. Knowing it would be a big strain for him to do it all by himself, I asked one of our neighbors if he could help too.

Whenever Aaron Dovid is with us for Shabbos, he goes to Torah Ore Yeshivah right after *shaleshudes* to hear Uncle Chaim's shmooze. And so this time too, he left, saying, "I'll be back right after *Ma'ariv,* and it should only take a little while to have everything moved. Don't worry, Bubbie." Well, after *Havdalah,* our neighbor appeared, as planned, to help Aaron Dovid — but he had not yet returned from the Yeshivah, so our neighbor proceeded to tackle the job himself.

Finally, when he had finished all the shlepping, and the books were taken down and the heavy furniture moved, in marched Aaron Dovid ready for action — just in time for me to serve him his usual *melaveh malkah:* French toast, coffee and cake. Before he rushed off to study with a young man who lives in the Ezrat Torah neighborhood, I told him to be sure to return after the paint job, to put everything back in place. He assured me that he would call and added, "Don't worry, I'll take care of it, Bubbie."

He did call, but of course the paint job was not finished, so he said he would call again. When the painting was finally done, I tried to call him, but could not reach him. My neighbor came over and asked if he could help put things back together. I did not want him to strain himself, so I said, "My grandson should be calling, and he will take care of it. Really, you've done more than your share already." An hour later, my neighbor returned, bringing along a friend, and both young men finished all the work.

Sure enough, the next day Aaron Dovid called. "Well,

Bubbie, is the painting finished? Can I come today?" I did not tell him that everything had been taken care of! "Please do," I replied, and told him to come for lunch. "I'll come straight after our morning session, grab a bite, and get down to work," he assured me.

He walked in with gusto, ready to pitch in; however, he was quite surprised to find everything in order and nothing left for him to do.

During lunch, when he expressed remorse that he hadn't helped, I told him that he proved what we read in *Pirkei Avos* 3:6 — "Rabbi Nechunyah ben Hakanah says: He who takes upon himself the yoke of Torah, from him the yoke of government and the yoke of secular life will be removed."

Love, Papa and Mama

PART FOUR:
A Book Is Born

The "Ups and Ups" of Writing a Book

EVERYONE — children, grandchildren, relatives, friends, and even the secretaries in my office — knew that I intended, someday, to write a book about my father's life. But no one really took me seriously. Perhaps for me too, at the beginning, it was only a fantasy, a far-off dream.

I felt that it was important not only for my children and grandchildren personally, but also for Jews in general to read about my father's sacrifice and dedication in bringing Torah and Yiddishkeit to America during a period when it was sorely lacking — the early twentieth century.

Dearest Children,

The time has come! I awoke at dawn with an urgent desire: I must start writing the book — now or never!

I poured out my feelings to Papa. "I just have to get the book out of my system, Moshe, and the only way that I could really get started would be to give up my job and concentrate all my efforts on writing."

Although Papa was of course fully aware of my compulsion to write the book, he, too, had thought of it as part of some far-away future. But now he listened attentively. "If you are serious about writing your book," he replied, "then I'm all for it."

With his backing, when I got to work I proudly announced to the secretaries in my office that I intended to resign and start writing my book. Of course they still did not take me seriously, and they smiled with an "Oh, sure" look in their eyes.

In order to show them that I meant "business," I knocked at the door of our senior director, Rabbi Rosenfeld, and went into his office. Sitting on the edge of my chair, I blurted out, "I want to hand in my letter of resignation —"

Before I had a chance to explain, he asked sharply, "What happened? Why do you want to leave all of a sudden? Do you want a raise?"

"Oh, it has nothing at all to do with my work here," I assured him. "In fact, I feel very much a part of Bayit Lepletot — after all, I've worked here for thirteen years. The reason I am leaving is that I want to write a book about my father, Reb Yaakov Yosef."

Rabbi Rosenfeld looked relieved. "Well, it is certainly a noble idea, Mrs. Shain. You know that I knew your father, and he was indeed a great *tzaddik*. But what has this got to do with your leaving Bayit Lepletot? Surely in the afternoons, when you get home from work, you can write as much as you want."

I pointed out to him that I needed the mornings when I was fresh and energetic and could concentrate, but my explanation did not impress him at all.

"But Mrs. Shain, you must understand that you are needed here. I am certain you will find time to write your book in your spare time. Think it over, and you will surely realize that it would be unwise for you to leave at this time."

The secretaries were waiting impatiently for me to come

out of his office. "I don't think Rabbi Rosenfeld took me seriously either," I told them. "He wants me to think it over. He is sure I'll change my mind." The girls gave me a look that said "We knew it..."

I came home from work very confused. As you know, children, I enjoy my work in the Orphan Home, and the very close relationship with the other secretaries. The salary is of course also a consideration. However, writing the book has become almost an obsession with me. At least Papa understands my feelings.

I hope I have the courage to stick to my convictions.

Love, Papa and Mama

A few days later, I handed in my letter of resignation to Rabbi Rosenfeld. I gave six weeks notice, instead of the usual two weeks, for I wanted to leave in a responsible way and make sure that all the letters piling up on my desk were answered. He read my resignation slowly, and looked at me skeptically as he shoved the letter into his desk drawer. "I am sure you will change your mind, Mrs. Shain. It is important for you to be busy, you know, especially, *at your age.*"

When my nephew Shmuel Yitzchok Stern, who is a director at the Orphan Home, heard the news, he asked me, "Are you really serious about this, Aunt Ruchoma?" He then added, "I would like to see Zaidie Herman's life story written too, but I'm sure you can work it into your schedule without leaving the Orphan Home." Then, as an afterthought, he asked, "Have you any idea who would sponsor you? You know, it is an expensive proposition to publish a book."

"I haven't even thought that far," I answered, "but once the book is completed, I'll try to find a publisher."

"I know Mr. Feldheim from Feldheim Publishers personally," he said. "I could call him up and ask him if he would be interested in your book."

I was very grateful. "Give it a try," I told him, "but I don't hold out too much hope. After all, I have never written a book before, and he doesn't know who I am." Shmuel Yitzchok's offer gave me a good feeling — at least someone besides Reb Moshe was taking my writing the book seriously.

Shmuel Yitzchok kindly called Mr. Feldheim, who suggested that I send him some samples of my writing. I felt it would be a waste of time and effort, but my nephew kept after me. "What have you got to lose?" he asked. But somehow I kept putting it off.

One day I was waiting at the bus stop when I happened to meet my friend Judy Weil, who also lived in Kiryat Mattersdorf. Since she was a free-lance writer who had published articles in newspapers both here and abroad, I confided in her. "Judy, I am thinking seriously about writing the story of my father's life. What chance do you think I have that Feldheim Publishers might be interested?"

She thought for a few moments, and then answered, "Mrs. Shain — nothing ventured, nothing gained." Both Judy and Shmuel Yitzchok had expressed the same sentiment: What did I have to lose?

I therefore chose two stories that I had written about my father, which had been published a few years before in *The Light* magazine (which is now defunct), and mailed them to Feldheim Publishers. Although I had always been an optimist, this time I had few illusions that I would receive a positive answer from Feldheim.

✍ ✍

A few days before what I called my "lifeline" (I like to stress the positive, so I don't use the word "deadline"), the directors and staff finally realized that I was actually leaving. They got busy and prepared a very elaborate farewell party, with lots of delicious food, including home-baked cakes.

Each of the secretaries spoke, and it was quite emotional

for all of us. The directors joined us also, and Shmuel Yitzchok gave a speech on behalf of the staff. He ended his remarks with the words, "The doors of Bayit Lepletot will always remain open to you." I got the message that all those present still thought that after a few weeks of my "fling" at writing, I would be happy to return. The secretaries gave me a beautiful set of leather-bound *machzorim* for all the *Yamim Tovim,* and the directors presented me with a small filing cabinet filled with all kinds of writing paper and other items a writer would need. On the cabinet was a small plaque, which read:

To Mrs. R. Shain
in appreciation
for 13 years of tireless and devoted work
Bayit Lepletot

In the top drawer of the cabinet was the following poem:

We all know, and we all agree,
That with the English language you feel quite free.
Coupled with your knack of easy storytelling,
You'll have no problems with your book's quick selling.
Your departure from here leaves us in distress,
The letters will pile up; the office will be a mess.
Our heartfelt blessings go with you nonetheless,
For good health, good fortune, and tremendous success.

Dearest Children,

It is now more than two weeks since I left Bayit Lepletot. I am sorry to say that I have not really gotten any serious writing done — just a page here and there. One reason is that I am having a problem: Now that the word is out that I am "free as a bird" and have time on my hands, many people are stopping by or calling with requests for me to do volunteer work, to help them with their personal needs, to socialize more, and a host of other suggestions.

Finally I posted a sign on our front door saying that I was not to be disturbed between 9:00 A.M. and 2:00 P.M. What can I tell you? It was mostly disregarded, and my doorbell rang incessantly. Papa told me not to answer and pretend I was away at work. I tried to do that, but sometimes the ringing just wouldn't stop, so I would run to the door thinking it must be an emergency. Sure enough, it usually turned out to be someone who *had* to tell me something of great importance — *for her* — that could easily have waited until after 2:00 P.M.

I didn't want to disconnect the telephone, because Papa might try to reach me from the Yeshivah, so we arranged a signal between us — he would let the phone ring twice and then hang up, and I would call him back. But the other day, the telephone just rang and rang and rang. It was not Papa's signal, but it made me nervous. I wondered if it was someone who was trying to test me to see if I could hold out without answering, for I have let it be known to *friend and foe alike* that I am not available in the morning hours. At any rate, none of this has been conducive to my creativity and concentration, and I feel frustrated at not making any progress.

But there are other problems too. Even when the house is quiet and the phone isn't ringing, I sit down at my desk, stare at the empty page in the typewriter and tell myself: "Write!" Then I get so nervous I can't think of how to begin.

Papa returns from Yeshivah every day with a questioning look that seems to say: How did your writing go today? I have many thoughts and ideas in my head, but I just can't seem to express them properly. When I type one page and read it afterwards, I am not satisfied and tear it up. And speaking about thoughts, I am having second thoughts about my decision to stop working. Perhaps I should have kept my job, and written the book in the afternoons after work, as my bosses advised me.

Love, Papa and Mama

> P.S. Papa just brought up your letters with our mail. They certainly gave me the emotional injection I needed. I hope and pray to live up to your high expectations, and, someday, be the author of a BOOK!

It had been over a month since I submitted my writing samples to Mr. Feldheim, and I really did not have "great expectations" of hearing from him. This was especially so after I ran into an acquaintance of mine who was involved in writing, and I mentioned that I had submitted something to Feldheim Publishers. His reaction was swift in coming: "Mrs. Shain, I hate to discourage you," he said, "but Feldheim Publishers are *big time.* Most probably, they have dozens of people like you asking to be published. Why not go to some small, lesser known publishing house. Perhaps they might undertake it."

Though he did not intend to put a damper on my writing efforts, his advice certainly did nothing to lift my spirits. But I remembered the following poem and it provided the encouragement that I needed at this time:

Don't Quit!!

When things go wrong, as they sometimes will,
When the road you're trudging seems all uphill,
When care is pressing you down a bit,
Rest if you must, but don't you quit.

Life is queer with its twists and turns,
As every one of us sometimes learns.
Don't give up though the pace seems slow,
You may succeed with another blow.

Success is failure turned inside out,
So try your best for another bout.
Stick to the fight when you're hardest hit,
It's when things seem worst that you mustn't quit.

Kiryat Mattersdorf, in the beginning — a few buildings and lots of rocky mountainside.

How I loved sitting in our little *sukkah* with Reb Moshe. It was a *mechayeh* having it right outside our kitchen.

Rabbi Shmuel Ehrenfeld, *zt"l*, founder of Kiryat Mattersdorf, a dream that came true.

The bare hills were soon bursting with new buildings, and Kiryat Mattersdorf continued to grow.

Rabbi Chaim Scheinberg, and near him Rabbi Simcha Bunim Klein, the administrator of Kiryat Mattersdorf, at the groundbreaking ceremonies of Yeshivah Torah Ore in October 1965.

Yeshivah Torah Ore, still growing up, almost thirty years later, in 1992.

My grandniece, Chana, all dressed up and ready for Purim in Yerushalayim.

Rabbi Moshe Feinstein, *zt"l*, holding the cup of wine and conducting the wedding ceremony of my children Elimelech and Mashi. My brother, Reb Nochum Dovid, is holding a slip of paper with the names of those to be honored by saying the *berachos* under the *chuppah*. My father-in-law, Reb Shimon Shain, can be seen in the background, to the right.

Like all good Israelis, Reb Moshe and I went visiting friends and family on *Chol Ha-Mo'ed*. It was a special treat to visit the Levitts in Gilo. Here we are with our dear adopted granddaughter, Chana.

In addition to going to Rachel's Tomb, at the first opportunity, Reb Moshe and I also visited the Cave of the Patriarchs in Hebron, now once again in Jewish hands after the Six Day War. Left to right, my sister-in-law, Chaye Dube, and my sisters, Esther and Bessie.

"Jerusalem of Gold" is quickly transformed into "Jerusalem of White," during a rare snowstorm. Here the trees are showing off their winter finery.

This beautiful baby girl is one of my "Ruchomaleh"s, named in my honor by readers who were moved by my book.

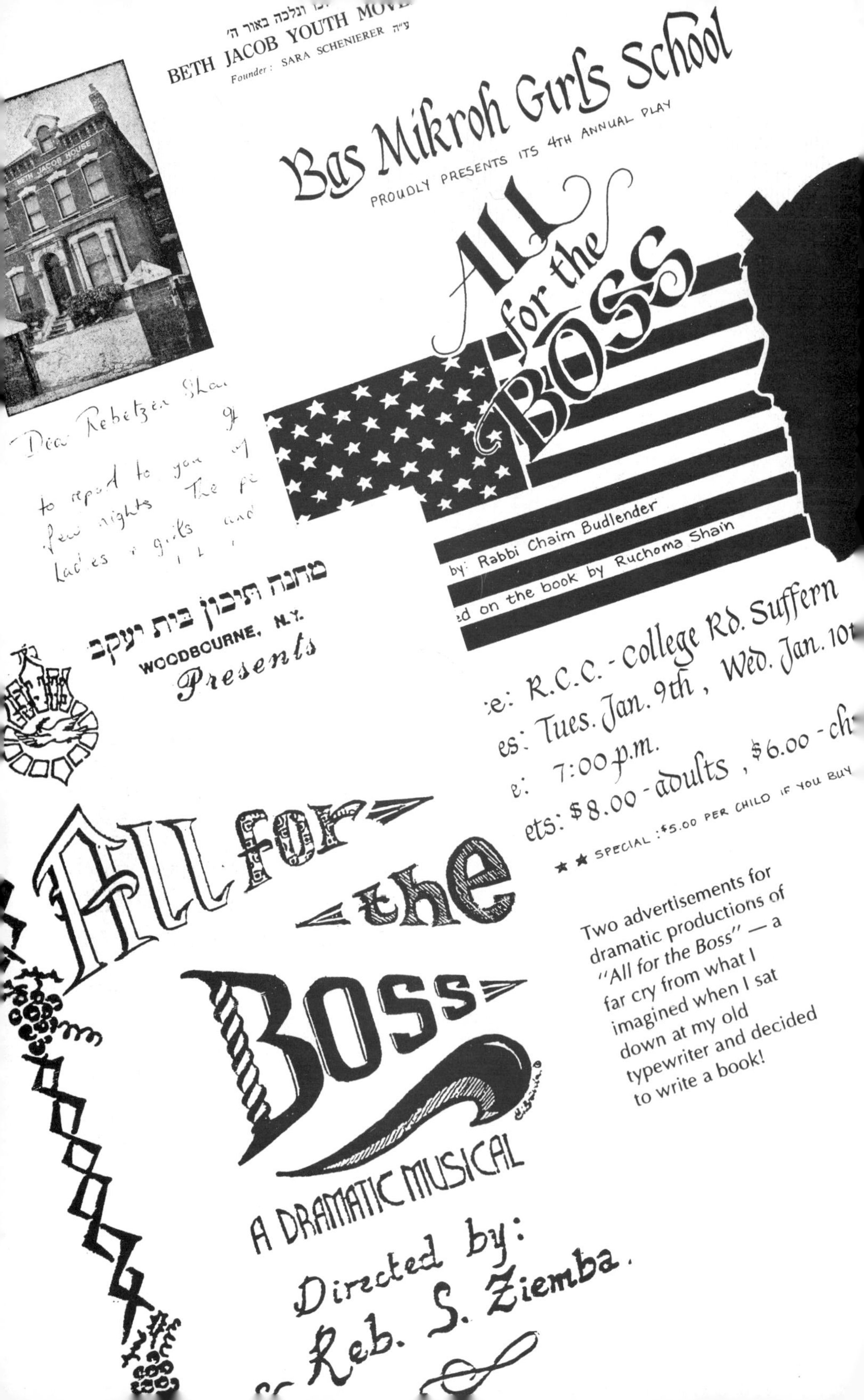

Two advertisements for dramatic productions of "All for the Boss" — a far cry from what I imagined when I sat down at my old typewriter and decided to write a book!

An exciting 70th
birthday, surrounded by
flowers from
well-wishers...with our
famous air conditioner
in the background.

One of the miracle *minyanim* that materialized for us, this time for my Zaidie Shmuel Yitzchok Andron's yahrtzeit.

My Zaidie's grave, next to my mother's, on Har Hazeisim. The tombstones are covered with small stones, traditionally placed there by visitors to the gravesite.

✍ ✍

Dearest Children,

Today is DECEMBER 6! I am sure you are aware that it is my birthday, and I didn't have to capitalize the date for you to take note, but something very special happened today. I received a very exciting present on my sixty-seventh birthday. Thank Hashem! HURRAH! HURRAH! HURRAH!

At about noon today, the telephone rang. I was tempted not to answer it, as I wanted to prove my self-discipline and keep to my determination of not answering the phone during my "working hours," but I did not have much fight left in me, and I picked it up. Who do you think was on the other end of the line? Mr. Feldheim!!

I tried to remember every single word of the telephone conversation, so that I could repeat it to Papa and write it to you. Here goes: "Mrs. Shain, this is Yaakov Feldheim speaking. Please forgive the delay in getting in touch with you, but my editor has been very busy, and I wanted her to read your writing before I got back to you. We both like your style and feel the book has a lot to offer our readers, so I will be happy to publish it. By the way, what are you going to call it?"

Though I certainly did not expect his call, I was able to answer that question without hesitating. Ever since I dreamed of writing the book, I knew that I wanted it to be called *"All for the Boss"*. I am sure you recall the story about Zaidie Herman, which I must have told you many times — how he was willing to lose all his belongings in Haifa Port, so as not to desecrate the Shabbos. That Shabbos he said to Bubbie Herman, "The Boss does everything for me. Now I've given away everything I own, ALL FOR THE BOSS!"

Now, to go on to the rest of the telephone conversation. "I like the title," Mr. Feldheim said. "Now, I expect the book to have at least two hundred pages, and I will give you nine months to complete it." He then briefly discussed the financial arrangement, and said, "I will send you a contract which will have all the details in it. Please sign it and return it to me, and I will be in touch with you. *B'hatzlachah.*"

Throughout the conversation, I had remained mum, too stunned to respond. I had clutched the telephone so tightly that I could hardly unclasp my hand.

When Papa returned from the Yeshivah, he took one look at me and asked anxiously, "Is everything all right?" In one gulp, I told him the entire conversation. Papa was elated and gave me one of his special smiles. "It is a very wonderful birthday present for you," he said, and then added, "And for me as well. Now I am sure you will finally write the book."

May Hashem guide me!

Love, Papa and Mama

Dearest Children,

I am flying down from "cloud nine," which means that I have sobered up from the overwhelming elation and initial shock of having my book accepted by Feldheim Publishers. All I have to do now is write it.

I realize that I am facing one of the greatest challenges of my life. You know, children, that I have always welcomed challenges. I married at seventeen, and left my family behind, going to Mir where life was a constant challenge. I started university when I was already a grandmother, and jumped into teaching without prior experience. And then Papa and I left our children, grandchildren, our home and our positions to settle in Eretz Yisrael.

But, somehow, I feel the challenge of writing this book makes all the others pale in comparison. Perhaps it is because I am older now. Although everyone tells me, "You are young in spirit," I have to face the reality of my chronological age.

Where will I accumulate enough material to fill up two hundred pages or more? How can I complete it in nine months, when I feel that I need unlimited time? How much of my personal life can I include, if this is for the general public? I am getting emotional cold feet! And since winter is setting in, my feet are getting physically cold, as well, especially since I sit in one place all morning at my desk, and our apartment is not very warm.

Papa is a bulwark of strength, but I can't muster the confidence that he has. Have I bitten off more than I can chew?

Love, Papa and Mama

Every day, with Reb Moshe's blessings spurring me on, I would sit down at my typewriter. On the first day, I slipped a sheet of paper in, and in capital letters typed "ALL FOR THE BOSS," and under it: Page 1. That was as far as I got. I thought the words would flow, but there was not even a trickle. I just didn't know where to begin.

Reb Moshe returned from Yeshivah to find me in a panic. I poured out my woes to him, and he calmed me down, saying, "First let's eat lunch and then we'll discuss it." I served him, but I could hardly get any food down myself. Reb Moshe's advice was logical: "Don't feel pressured. Just relax and enjoy your writing." How could I enjoy my writing when I had a time limit and had to produce and make progress?

Rivky, a close friend of mine, came to visit and to hear how I was faring. One look at me told her more than my words did. I had lost weight, and there were dark circles under my eyes, from sleepless nights filled with tossing and turning. She was, of course, very concerned.

"You know what," she advised, "don't worry about starting at the beginning. Just write whatever comes to mind, without worrying where it will fit in or what should follow it. Afterwards, you will fit it all together like a jigsaw puzzle."

I followed her excellent advice, and as my typewriter clicked away, the pages started to fill up. The dark night that had enveloped me began to fade, and with the light of day, I could see the road ahead.

✍ ✍

Dearest Children,

Our letters must have crossed in the mail, and by now you surely have received my letter on a much more optimistic note. I realize how very worried you were, as I was indeed distraught. For a while I felt overwhelmed and could not cope with the responsibility of writing this book. I almost wanted to quit, which is not like me.

Mashi, I am glad that your advice came *after* I had begun to make real progress with the book! Otherwise I would have been tempted to succumb to your persuasion. You were correct that I sounded terrible, and that nothing warranted losing my physical and emotional health — even this most important project. However, your suggestion to stop in my tracks and take time off from writing until I felt more relaxed would not have worked in any case. For just as you cannot tell a fetus to stop growing for a while so that the mother can have some respite from nausea, heartburn, and other discomforts of pregnancy, I cannot tell myself to stop my writing until I "give birth" to this book.

As I wrote in my last letter, I am making progress, and that is the most important way to keep my spirits up.

Love, Papa and Mama

P.S. When Papa returns from the Yeshivah every day, he can tell immediately what I've been writing about. The other day he found me with puffy, bloodshot eyes. I had written about Zaidie Yonkev Yosef's passing away, and I had cried so much that the paper was soaked with tears. This was the first time that Papa showed no alarm at my tears! He just "cheered" me on.

Dearest Children,

Your Papa is a great help to me in my writing, as he is a whiz with vocabulary. Since he majored in Latin and Greek, he knows the etymology of many English words. Although I was an English teacher, and have a command of the language, sometimes a word eludes me, and I call out to Papa for help. We have all our reference works handy: *Webster's World Dictionary*, *Roget's Thesaurus*, and *Webster's Dictionary of Synonyms*. Papa's always had a yen for dictionaries, and he enjoys finding the exact word for me.

I don't think I ever told you the following story, that happened before Mashi and Raphael Yitzchok were born. When we returned from Mir, Papa began to learn in a *Kollel* and was receiving a pittance of a stipend. We were hard-pressed to meet our daily expenses, and had few luxuries in our life. The only thing that Papa "splurged" on was buying *sefarim*, for which we tightened our belts to save every available penny.

I wanted very much to get Papa a nice present for his birthday, so five months earlier, I started to put aside twenty-five cents from our weekly budget. By the time his birthday arrived, I had saved the princely sum of five dollars, a lot of money in those days.

On Papa's birthday, I handed him a birthday card, and tucked inside was the five-dollar bill. I wanted him to have the pleasure of choosing his own present.

Off he went, and I envisioned him returning with a luxurious bathrobe with satin lapels, or, perhaps, two white-on-white shirts. He returned shortly, carrying a very large package, his eyes glowing. He opened the package, and there was...the largest dictionary I had ever seen: *Webster's Encyclopedic Dictionary — A Library of Essential Knowledge.*

Of course, I did not express any disappointment over his choice, and I shared Papa's joy with his birthday present. In fact, when I was packing my books for our lift before we came to Yerushalayim, I included the old dictionary even though it was falling apart, since I did not have the heart to leave it behind. It still occupies a place of honor on our bookshelf.

Love, Papa and Mama

✍ ✍

I became so engrossed in writing my book that I essentially lived with it all day and most of the night. In fact, every night I kept a pad and pen handy near my bed, and as soon as a thought popped into my mind, I turned on my bedside lamp and made a note of it. Many a time when I couldn't sleep, my note pad became filled with my thoughts.

Friday night had always been the most relaxing time of the week. Right after our Shabbos meal, I would hurry to bed with the various *sefarim* I always saved for my Shabbos reading. Reb Moshe usually learned for a while and then dozed off. A dramatic change took place now. My most creative thoughts plagued me on Friday nights, when I could not write them down!

I tried to repeat them to myself, so that I should not forget them before *Havdalah*, after which I would make a mad dash for my pen and pad. Most of the time I did remember them, but sometimes they disappeared into the depths of my mind, and I couldn't dig them out again.

Dearest Children,

Last Friday night a very special thought came to mind, and I wanted to make sure I would not forget it. I looked to see if Papa was asleep, and it seemed to me that he was only *slightly* drowsing. I called him softly once or twice, and then raised my voice a little. He opened his eyes, and I said, "Moshe, I've just thought of something important that will fit into one of the chapters I'm in the middle of. Let me tell you what it is, because I'm afraid I'll forget it." Papa listened intently to every word, and then went back to sleep.

Knowing that I had shared it with him eased my anxiety, and I, too, was finally able to fall asleep. Early Shabbos morning, I asked Papa if he remembered what I had told him the night before. He looked at me blankly, and said: "Just repeat it to me, and I'm sure I'll remember."

Thank Hashem, I did not forget it!

Love, Papa and Mama

Sometimes I just couldn't find the right word for what I wanted to express. Once, when I had the frustrating experience of having a word on the tip of my tongue all morning, I waited anxiously for Reb Moshe to return from the Yeshivah. I tried to explain the word I was looking for: "It means a word that is used to make something sound nicer than it really is." Even Reb Moshe could not think of it then, so I left a blank space to be filled in later when the word would come to mind, and I went on with my writing.

But the elusive word did not let me rest for two days, and my concentration suffered. Suddenly, like a flash of light, it came to me: "euphemism." (Later, when my manuscript had all been turned in, the editor at Feldheim's, in one stroke of her pen, casually deleted that word, not realizing the hours and hours that I had suffered and the great energy I had expended trying to find it!)

✍ ✍

Dearest Children,

Guess what! Papa and I are going away for the whole week of Pesach. It will be the first time that we have left home for *Yom Tov*. Uncle Nochum Dovid suggested it, to ease Aunt Chayẹ Dube's burden, and since we always spend the Seder with them, naturally, we are going together. It will be a boon for me too, as I will have more time to spend with my writing. No Pesach dishes to take down, no shopping, no cooking, no baking. I certainly can use the rest, as I am very tired and tense.

The writing is progressing, and the more I write, the more I have to write. The book has become such an integral part of my life, or I should say our lives, that I'm practically a recluse.

The only time I go out is when we have a wedding or other family *simchah* to attend. Last week I made an exception and attended the wedding of a neighbor's son: During the meal, everyone was busy talking and I sat oblivious to them, thinking about my book. Our relatives and friends eyed me with a mixture of pride and pity — mostly pity!!

We are receiving your encouraging letters, and appreciate your continuing to write weekly letters and not waiting for mine. A happy, kosher Pesach to all of you.

Love, Papa and Mama

P.S. Please send me at least 6 typewriter ribbons at the earliest opportunity. The ribbons I bought here are not exactly what I need. I hope my old Smith Corona will survive until I complete the book. For every page I write, I retype it at least four times. By the end of the day my arms are so sore that I can hardly move them. I should really treat myself to an electric typewriter, but I have grown attached to this one.

We came home from our Pesach vacation refreshed. I could not wait to get back to my writing, which had occupied a good deal of my thoughts during the entire week of Pesach. I decided that Part 2 of my book would be about our life in Mir, Poland. I had written many letters to my parents during the six years we were living there, but since I did not have the originals, I had to reconstruct them from memory. It was amazing how, once I put my mind to it, I began to recall even the smallest details, although fifty years had gone by since then.

Reliving this part of our lives gave me much joy, because Reb Moshe and I had spent productive, satisfying years in the Mir Yeshivah, and our firstborn son, Yisroel Meyer, was born in Mir. However, the memories also brought with them a flood of tears and a great deal of sadness. I could still visualize our parting, when many Yeshivah boys and most of the townspeople came to bid us farewell. Their cries still echoed in my heart...

It was difficult to believe that our close friends, and most of the townspeople, were gone — killed in the Holocaust. Mir is now only a ghost town, where a vibrant center of Torah had once thrived.

✍ ✍

Dearest Children,

Papa is the only one who is reading my manuscript, besides Yaakov Feldheim and the editor. I realize that you are very anxious to read what I have written, but somehow, I would like you to wait until the book is completed.

I hope to hand in the entire manuscript before Rosh Hashanah. It is very important to me that I do, so I will be able to concentrate on my prayers for a happy, healthy, successful year. Now that it is nearing, I will miss my writing, which has become part of my life.

Thank you, children, for your understanding and patience. I know you will be relieved when the book is completed and Mama will be Mama again.

Love, Papa and Mama

P.S. I alternate between feeling optimistic — telling myself that the readers will like it, to feeling depressed — fearing that they won't...

✍ ✍

Dearest Children,

MAZAL TOV! MAZAL TOV! The book was born today. I "delivered" a few days earlier than expected. I have a great sense of accomplishment, having actually produced a complete manuscript — and a very large one at that — but I am suffering conflicting emotions. First of all, I shall be waiting anxiously for the editor's reaction, as the book has to undergo her scrutiny. I'm sure she will go through it with a fine-tooth comb. And second of all, I will have to be a "lady-in-waiting" until the book is finally published, which will be a period of great tension for me.

Of course Papa is delighted that I finally handed in the manuscript. Although I did not neglect him in any way, he did accompany me through all the "ups and ups" of writing my book. He told me last night, "Your dream has at last been realized. Now it is time for you to relax. I'm sure the book will be successful." I wish I had his confidence.

May the New Year bring with it peace for our Jewish Nation and peace of mind for all of us.

Love, Papa and Mama

I decided that I would try not to think about my book throughout the *Yamim Tovim*, and I was able to control myself somewhat. But afterwards it invaded my thoughts full force once again. I called the editor to find out how the book was moving along — and found out that it wasn't. During the holidays, little work had been done. Besides, the editor had another book to edit before she tackled mine.

I learned that it might take months, or even a year, until it was finally published. I had to make peace with myself and stop counting the days. For a start, I decided to stop calling Feldheim's, as I did not want to *nudge*. Then I decided to take the wise advice that Shlomo *Ha-Melech* gives us in *Koheles*: "Everything has its season, and there is a time for everything under Heaven." Whenever Hashem designates the time for my book to be published, it will be.

✍ ✍

Dearest Children,

Hashem has answered my prayers. You know how much I've needed some kind of activity outside the house to keep me busy. Well, I am now giving weekly talks in a women's seminary. Most of the students are mature and not only knowledgeable in religious studies, but also have secular degrees in various fields. I usually have a large turnout.

This keeps me on my toes, and requires my full concentration. My weekly sessions, "Topics for Discussion," are both challenging and rewarding. We discuss various subjects in class: In my last talk, I discussed "rationalization," and how we try to make our actions justified from our point of view. It led to a lively discussion with many innovative thoughts.

I always try to inject a light note into these talks, and one day I read the students the following saying by Mark Twain: "When I was a boy of fourteen, my father was so ignorant I could hardly stand to have the old man around. But when I got to be twenty-one, I was amazed how much he had learned in seven years."

This not only brought laughter from my students, but also a animated discussion on parent-child relationships.

Love, Papa and Mama

P.S. It is now over a year since I handed in my manuscript. Though I would like to see my book published, it is remarkable the way my attitude has changed. I feel that this waiting period is a prelude to that special day. In a sense, I am enjoying the anticipation of the great event, allowing my imagination free rein.

In the Afterglow of Writing My Book

Dearest Children,

Today I experienced one of the most precious moments of my life. Yitzchak Isbee, who is part of the staff at Feldheim's, hurried to bring me my book straight from the bookbinder.

I took it with trembling fingers, and without even opening it, I clasped it to my heart, saying over and over again, "My book — my book!" The only comparable emotion I have ever felt was when my babies were born and I held them close to me for the first time. Papa's eyes filled with tears, and my tears flowed down my cheeks unchecked — tears of thankfulness to Hashem.

Children, this book is not only the realization of a dream I had for many years, but also the culmination of months of almost super-human effort. It is just a few weeks short of two years since I turned in my completed manuscript. As I wrote you at that time, I had made peace with myself, and stopped worrying about when it would be out. I got engrossed in teaching again. Of course, from time to time the book occupied some of my thoughts, with the nagging question, "When?" However, I did not allow it to become central in my life. Now, however, the book has returned full force, invading my thoughts again.

The next few weeks will be tense, as I await the verdict of the readers. As I told you on the phone, I will send you your copies at the first opportunity. I can well imagine your impatience.

Love, Papa and Mama

When I heard that a young woman who lives in Kiryat Mattersdorf was planning to go to New York, I phoned and asked her exactly when she was leaving, as I was very anxious to send copies of my book to my children and grandchildren. She told me that her flight was scheduled for the following night.

"I would like to ask a special favor of you," I said, "but please let me know if it won't be too difficult." I paused and then asked, "Are you overweight?"

There was a silence at the other end of the line, and then a hesitant,"Um...well, to be perfectly honest, I am."

I questioned her further. "Are you very much overweight?"

This time there was a longer pause. "Well, I'm not sure how much, but I guess I must be at least five or six kilos overweight."

"Oh, in that case, I won't trouble you," I said.

"Mrs. Shain, I would be happy to help you in any way I can," she said, "and whatever it is, I'm sure the weight will not be a problem."

"I appreciate that very much," I replied, "but books weigh quite a bit, and you are already over the weight allowance for your luggage," I replied. For a moment there was silence again, and then a sudden burst of hysterical laughter.

"Oh, Mrs. Shain! I though you were referring to my

personal weight."

This time, I was the one who could not control my laughter. When we both were able to calm down, she said kindly, "My suitcases are only half full, and you can send as many books as you wish. I would consider it a privilege to have your books in my luggage." She then added, "And you know, Mrs. Shain, I really should lose weight. Thanks for bringing it to my attention!"

Dearest Children,

Your enthusiastic telephone call was music to my ears. You told me what I longed to hear. I am also receiving calls and visits from many readers, telling me how much they enjoyed the book. Thank Hashem!

Love, Papa and Mama

✍ ✍

The annual Jewish Book Fair in Yerushalayim is a very popular event, and all book lovers flock to Liberty Bell Park to buy books at discount prices.

As I said earlier, I was not worried about when my book would be published for I drew comfort from Shlomo *Ha-melech's* words: "There is a time for everything under Heaven." Well, my book came out at the most optimum time, just when the Fair opened. "*All for the Boss*" was receiving publicity, and was being snatched up as quickly as it could be stocked and restocked at the Feldheim booth.

A neighbor told me that her husband had bought it and was up half the night reading the book. He could hardly open his eyes the next morning, but he leapt out of bed when she said, "Reb Yaakov Yosef Herman, *z"l*, took a plane to catch a minyan."

I have always stressed the importance of *shalom bayis*, but when I heard that a certain couple were arguing about who would read the book first, it didn't bother me a bit!

When people told me, "I laughed and cried as I was reading the book," I certainly could understand that, as I had laughed and cried all through the writing of it. My book had reached foreign shores, too, and it was most gratifying to receive letters from all over the world. I was kept very busy answering all those who had written to tell me how much encouragement the book had given them.

Yaakov Feldheim told me that *"All for the Boss"* was the most successful English book that Feldheim Publishers had put out since their beginnings forty years earlier. In fact, the word was out: "Reb Yaakov Yosef Herman is promoting *"All for the Boss"* from Heaven!" I could visualize my beloved father "living it up," and reaching new spiritual heights.

After all the self-doubt, hesitation, and often painful effort, I could now say with a happy heart, "Those who sow in tears will reap in joy" [*Tehillim* 126:5].

✍ ✍

Dearest Children,

A new dimension has been added to our lives since the publication of my book. There is never a dull moment!

Last Friday morning, when I was in the midst of doing my *sponja,* my doorbell rang. I hoped it would not be visitors, since I was wearing an old housedress, and a kerchief on my head. When I opened the door, there stood an elegantly dressed, middle-aged woman.

"Is it possible to see Ruchoma Shain?" she asked in a clipped English accent. I invited her in and offered her a chair. She explained, "I am visiting relatives in Yerushalayim, and was given the book *"All for the Boss"* as a gift. I read it, and was so impressed with it that I would appreciate it if Mrs. Shain would kindly autograph my book. I really do not like to bother her, especially on *erev Shabbos,* but I will not be in

Yerushalayim again before leaving for London."

By that time I was certain of what I had suspected at the start: she had mistaken me for the *ozeret,* the cleaning lady, dressed as I was in my floor-washing getup. She kept looking around, waiting for the "grand entrance" of Ruchoma Shain herself. What could I do, but introduce myself! "I... I...," I stammered almost apologetically, "I'm Ruchoma Shain."

For a moment she just stared at me in disbelief, from my mop to my kerchief, and then blurted out, "My dear, *you,* an author, are doing such menial labor?" I explained that I did not think washing floors was beneath my dignity, and that it was excellent physical exercise as well. It took her a while to accept the fact that I was who I was, and she calmed down. By the time I had autographed her book, we were enjoying each other's company. She left, promising to keep up a correspondence with me. I can't get used to all the fuss and fame of being a public figure. I guess at my age, I can only be myself.

Love, Papa and Mama

P.S. By the way, many people come to ask me to autograph their books, and also books that they are giving as gifts. It's fun!

✍ ✍

I wanted my book to be reviewed in a certain English magazine that was widely read, not only in Israel but also in English-speaking countries. At that time, the author Hanoch Teller often wrote articles for that magazine, and I decided to ask him to do the review, even though I did not know him personally. Through extensive inquiries I learned that he and his wife and children were living at the time with his grandmother in Yerushalayim.

When I phoned, his grandmother answered the phone. I introduced myself and she recognized my name right away.

She had enjoyed my book, she told me, and mentioned that *her* father, Rabbi Shapiro of Atlantic City, had often spoken of my father. I asked her to please give her grandson the message that I would appreciate his reviewing my book. She graciously agreed.

Two days later, Hanoch Teller called and said with mock annoyance, "You know, my grandmother is giving me a rough time because of you! She is threatening to dispossess me, and my wife is threatening even worse, unless I review your book."

"Your wife?" I asked, taken aback. "Do I know her?"

"Aidel says she is very close to you and owes you a great deal for your devotion to her when she worked in Bayit Lepletot. The least she can do is to repay you in some measure by *my* writing your book review!"

"What?!" I cried incredulously. "Do you mean to say that *my Aidel* is *your wife*?" Then it all came back to me.

When I was executive secretary in the Orphan Home, I used to interview applicants for any job opening in our office. One day, after we had advertised for a switchboard operator, a pretty young newlywed came in to inquire about the position.

"May I please see Mrs. Shain?" she asked the receptionist politely. I called the young woman over to my desk and asked her name. As soon as she said "Aidel," I did not question her further about her qualifications, and did not ask her any personal questions. "You're hired," I said. She looked a little puzzled, and I explained. "My mother's name was Aidel, you see, and with such a name, I'm sure you will be just right for the position."

So Aidel came to Bayit Lepletot and into my life. We had a close relationship, and I sort of mothered her. One day she confided in me that she was expecting her first baby. Of course, I was overjoyed for her. As the months went by, she asked my advice about whether she should return to her job after her three-month maternity leave was up, or, perhaps, do babysitting at home, so she could be with her infant while she continued to contribute to the family's livelihood.

Although I knew I would miss Aidel very much, I advised her to stay home with her baby, and she did. We continued to keep in touch, but somehow I never connected her with the writer Hanoch Teller.

Hanoch Teller wrote an excellent review of my book! "Cast your bread upon the waters..."

✍ ✍

It is customary in our circles that if a newborn infant is named for someone, the name given is that of a departed one. A few months ago, a woman who had just read my book called to tell me the "good news" that if the baby she was expecting was a girl, she would name her "Ruchoma" after me.

This startled and upset me quite a bit, until she explained that she was Sephardic, and their custom was to name an infant for a *living* person. She did give birth to a girl, and since then, there have been several more little "Ruchomas" born. I feel like an honorary Sephardi.

✍ ✍

One day I had a visit from a young man who wanted to share an interesting experience with me. Lance had come to Israel from the States and was studying in a yeshivah. Although he was on his way to becoming a *ba'al teshuvah*, he was still not certain that he had found what he was seeking. A friend gave him a copy of *"All for the Boss"* and, as he told me, "The story was so inspiring that my conflicts were somehow resolved, and I knew I was on the right path."

Shortly afterwards Lance had met Sharon, who was a

ba'alas teshuvah herself and also studying Judaism in Yerushalayim. They got married, settled here, and have a little girl named — "Ruchoma."

"I just wanted you to know how much your book has influenced our lives," Lance concluded.

✍ ✍

Dearest Children,

This morning, my friend Debbie, called to share the exciting news that her daughter had become engaged. I was overjoyed, since I knew she had been waiting for quite a while for this happy event.

She went on to explain. "When I read *"All for the Boss"*, I decided to go to your father's grave on his yahrtzeit, and ask him to intercede for me with "the Boss" about three specific problems which were troubling me very much."

As she spoke, I recalled that when we had come to Zaidie's grave that day, I had seen Debbie standing at a distance, weeping.

"After leaving the cemetery," she continued, "I already felt a stone had been lifted from my heart. The first two problems were resolved shortly afterwards, and the third — my daughter becoming a *kallah* — was granted me now. I can see that your father was a great *tzaddik*, and truly close to 'the Boss' — thank Hashem."

When we were last at Zaidie's grave, I had noticed many little scraps of paper weighted down with pebbles. Apparently many people come with requests. May they all be answered.

Love, Papa and Mama

✍ ✍

December 6, 1984

Dearest Children,

Your early phone calls this morning with your loving wishes

for my seventieth birthday started off this special day with joy and thankfulness. Three score and ten years are considered a lifespan, and each additional year a special blessing from Hashem. May He bless me with many more years in which to serve Him with joy, and may I continue to accomplish things to my fullest capacity.

I received many gifts and good wishes from our relatives and friends, and even from unexpected quarters. A number of people who had read *"All for the Boss"* remembered my birth date from the book, and called me or sent birthday cards. I certainly basked in all the excitement.

I composed the following poem for the occasion:

Morning greeted me bright and clear,
Cheerily announcing my 70th year.
"Oh, my!" It sounded so old and staid.
I ran to the mirror and was afraid.
I suddenly snatched the zero and hid it away.
And then pretended it was my seventh birthday.
I jumped for joy, and clapped my hands in glee,
As all the gifts were presented to me.

Throughout the day, Papa's eyes glistened with pride in me, which was my most precious gift of all.

May we always share happy birthdays with each other.

Love, Papa and Mama

✍ ✍

"All for the Boss" is still being widely read, more than seven years since its publication. It has been translated into Hebrew and French, and it may be translated into Spanish and Russian as well. I am happy seeing it translated into so many languages, but I am especially excited about the Russian edition. One of the reasons my father fasted for forty years was for the Russian Jews, who, at that time, were trapped behind the Iron Curtain.

✍ ✍

One afternoon when I visited my sister, I found a young couple there waiting to see her husband, Rabbi Scheinberg. Bessie introduced me to them. "This is my sister, Ruchoma Shain, who wrote the book, *All for the Boss.*" They seemed to be familiar with my book, and the young man said, "It's a pleasure to meet you. And you may be interested in hearing our story, as it is clear from your writings that you like inspiring stories." This was certainly true, and I invited them to come down to our apartment when they finished at the Scheinbergs.

About half an hour later, they knocked at the door. The young man, Dr. Stephen, was a dermatologist. His wife, Leah, was an optometrist. They had come to Israel recently, to study for a year in a *ba'al teshuvah* yeshivah and women's seminary. I am always interested in what has brought *ba'alei teshuvah* to Torah and mitzvos, and I asked this lovely couple that question. Dr. Stephen replied, "After I received my medical degree, I somehow felt unsatisfied. There was a vacuum in my life, and turning to my Jewish roots was my answer. But ask Leah for *her* story, as it is well worth hearing."

Reb Moshe and I sat entranced as Leah unfolded her moving experience. "I was at college, studying optometry. I guess I chose that field because I was always blessed (whatever that meant to me) with exceptionally good eyesight, and I wanted to help others gain good vision.

"It was then that I met Stephen, and we started to date. Despite the fact that we had a lot in common and enjoyed each other's company, we had one basic problem: He was well on the road toward religion, and I was an atheist and not at all interested in any aspect of religion.

"As our relationship deepened and became more serious, Stephen asked me if I would be willing to keep a kosher home, and not allow our children to marry out of our faith.

I thought it over and told him that I would not mind keeping a kosher home for him, but I could not promise that I would oppose our children's intermarrying, if they met fine partners who were not Jewish.

"I was in complete turmoil, as I liked Stephen very much, but the conflict over religion was a barrier that separated us. Stephen went out of his way to have me meet his religious friends, and I was invited to their homes for Shabbos. I enjoyed their company, but that was all.

"The Jewish New Year was approaching, and this usually held no special meaning for me. That year, however, I felt I needed direction. But to where was I to turn? I did a lot of soul-searching, and on Yom Kippur, I decided to fast. I didn't go to synagogue, but I did sit at home all day, asking God, if there was a God, to send me a sign. I waited the entire day, but no sign came, and I felt a deep sense of despair.

"A few days later, I awoke to a sudden frightening discovery. The vision in my left eye was blurred. I could not understand it, as there had been no previous symptoms. As the day progressed, it became much worse, and I could hardly see. I went to an ophthamologist whom I knew, and after examining me, he told me that he could not find a cause for the blurred vision.

"Well, Mrs. Shain, I was examined by four ophthamologists that same day, and my condition was finally diagnosed as AMPPPE — Acute Multifocal Posterior Placquiod Pigmentary Epitheliopathy." (Leah wrote this out for me, as I certainly could not remember it.) "The disease is rare and has been known for only about ten years. I was prescribed steroid eye drops and cortisone tablets.

"A few days later, I started to lose vision in my right eye. By that time, I realized that God was sending me the sign I had asked Him for. I began to pray and asked Him to cure me. I promised I would become a believing, religious Jew.

"I kept my promise, Mrs. Shain! It took several weeks until

my vision slowly returned to normal. I see clearly now, but more important is *what* I see. I see *God* clearly now. Stephen and I were married several months ago, and we decided to spend a year in Yerushalayim becoming closer to God."

✍ ✍

One day I received a phone call from a woman who told me her name was Batya and asked if she and her husband could visit us. She had read my book, *"Ha-Kol l'Adon Ha-Kol"* (the Hebrew translation of *"All for the Boss"*) while she was recently hospitalized, and was anxious to meet me. "I am sure you will be interested in meeting us and hearing our story," she added. I invited them to come the next afternoon.

When they walked in, I was quite surprised to notice that although Batya looked to be well into middle age, she was in the last months of pregnancy. Her husband, Akiva, looked considerably older than his wife.

Akiva, who was an American, began to tell us their story. Batya was a single girl who immigrated to Israel from Russia at the age of thirty-six. She decided to become a *ba'alas teshuvah* and hoped to meet a fine, religious man to marry, but the years went by and she remained single.

Akiva had come from the States and had left behind married children and grandchildren from a previous marriage. When they met, Batya was forty-four years old, and he was in his late fifties. They got married, and found companionship in each other, but, understandably, longed to have a child.

The doctor they consulted was very discouraging, but they did not give up hope. Four years later, at the age of forty-eight, Batya became pregnant, much to their joy. Because having a baby — and all the more so, a first baby — at this age is problematic, her obstetrician kept a watchful eye on her and for most of the pregnancy, Batya was hospitalized.

Now that she had entered the ninth month, and the baby was developing normally, she was released from the hospital.

We were indeed interested and thrilled at this story, and waited eagerly for the upcoming birth.

Dearest Children,

Mazal tov! Akiva just called and told us that Batya gave birth to a beautiful, healthy baby boy. Papa and I are very excited. May his parents have much nachas from him.

Their story reminds me of Bubbie Basha. She was Zaide Yonkev Yosef's grandmother, Bubbie Minna Rivka's mother, and Aunt Bessie is named after her. Did I ever tell you this?

Bubbie Basha was anxious for her oldest daughter, Minna Rivka, to become a *kallah.* She was of age, but there were few suitable young men available for a girl from a poor family. They traveled to Slutsk to ask the great rabbi, Reb Yaakov David ben Ze'ev (the Ridbaz) for a blessing. Somehow, he did not hear her request clearly, and instead of giving her a blessing for her daughter to become a bride, he gave her a blessing that *she* should have a baby!

Well, the great rabbi's blessing brought results. His entreaty was answered, and a year later, at the age of fifty, Bubbie Basha gave birth to my great aunt Mollie, who lived until the age of ninety-two. And in time, Minna Rivka indeed became a *kallah* and married Zaidie Yitzchok Isaac. I remember the standard joke that was repeated in our house: "Bubbie Basha wanted a *chasan* for her daughter, and instead was blessed with another daughter!"

Love, Papa and Mama

PART FIVE:

Simchahs and Sorrows

Upon the Mount of Olives

ABOUT TEN YEARS AGO, I had a very disturbing dream in which my father appeared to me. Looking very troubled, he said, "It is nineteen years already, and it has still not been taken care of." As soon as I awoke, I told Reb Moshe about the dream, and we racked our brains trying to figure out the significance of the number nineteen, and what could be bothering my father, but we could not figure it out. I turned to my brother, Reb Nochum Dovid, and to my brother-in-law, Reb Chaim Scheinberg, but they were as puzzled as we were. We even tried out various *gematrias* of the number nineteen, but we could not come up with an interpretation of the dream.

After several sleepness nights, I finally recalled a request that my father had made of me nineteen years before, when I had visited him in Yerushalayim in 1963.

One morning, when I entered his store in Meah Shearim, where I spent a lot of time with him, he had said to me,

"Ruchoma, something has been troubling me, and I need your help. When Mama and I left the States for Yerushalayim in 1939, there was an unspoken understanding between Zaidie and me that as soon as we had settled, I would send for him and his wife." (My grandfather had remarried a few years after my grandmother had passed away.)

"Well, as soon as we arrived, the Second World War broke out, and there was no way to bring my father and his wife here, to what was then called Palestine. Eight months later, Zaidie passed away and you children took care of his funeral and burial in New York."

Papa sighed and went on. "Lately, I have been disturbed by the thought that I was unable to bring him here to Eretz Yisrael when he was still living. Ruchoma, as soon as you return to New York, speak to the *chevrah kadisha* about bringing my father to Yerushalayim for reburial. It would be a great *chesed* for him, and for me."

I assured my father that I would take care of it, and would let him know all the particulars.

I recalled that when I was a young girl, my grandfather, Reb Yitzchok Isaac, had spent a year in Yerushalayim. He had hoped that my grandmother would join him, but she would not leave her children and grandchildren, so my grandfather gave up his dream and returned to the States. However, he never lost hope that he would someday live here.

Of course, I attended to my father's request immediately. I called the *chevrah kadisha* which was responsible for the area in the cemetery where my grandfather was buried, and asked about having him disinterred for reburial in Yerushalayim. I gave them all the pertinent information, and was told they would get back to me in a few days.

A week later they called back with an answer: it was not feasible. They explained that since he had passed away over twenty-three years before, and the area where he was buried was very swampy, there would be few remains to rebury.

I wrote to my father telling him what the *chevrah kadisha* had told me, and I assumed that he had accepted the decision, since he never mentioned it to me again. Now, however, after my dream, I wondered: Could this be what my father was trying to tell me?

Reb Moshe realized how much the dream was still bothering me, and said, "Ruchoma, calm down. You've always given your father *kibbud av,* and you did take care of his request, so try not to get carried away by this."

That summer, our son, Raphael Yitzchok, wrote that he wanted very much to visit us, and we encouraged him to come. One afternoon during his visit, I told him about the dream that was still plaguing me, and what had occurred over nineteen years before. He thought for a few minutes, and then said, "Mama, since I am named after Zaidie Yitzchok Isaac, I think I should make further inquiries about bringing him to Yerushalayim for reburial." I was very relieved when he suggested it, as the thought had never left me. Reb Moshe and I told him to go ahead.

He returned to the States in late August, and contacted a rabbi who was known for his expertise in bringing the deceased here for reburial. The rabbi was also quite hesitant. He, too, felt that there would be few remains, if any, to rebury, since it was now over forty-three years since my grandfather had passed away. However, by that time, the family here was backing me up, and we had made the decision that at all cost we would bring my grandfather to Yerushalayim for reburial.

It was no simple matter. Permission had to be granted by the United States government, and there were many documents to fill out and to be signed and notarized by all the living grandchildren.

We also received from the rabbi an itemized bill of all the expenses, which came to a very great sum. In the meantime, we bought a plot on Har Hazeisim for him and engaged the *chevrah kadisha* to be on hand when his remains would be brought here.

Months passed and finally Raphael Yitzchok called to tell us that he had received word from the rabbi to meet him at the cemetery on the day before *erev Chanukah*, when the workers would dig up the grave. Raphael Yitzchok asked my son-in-law, Elimelech, to be there. My nephew, Shmuel Yitzchok Stern, who was then visiting the States, said he would join them also.

It was a very cold, drizzly, windy morning when Raphael Yitzchok and the others gathered at the cemetery. The rabbi warned Raphael Yitzchok, once again, that the remains might be in terrible condition. He also advised them to keep their distance, as witnessing a disinterment can be a traumatic experience, especially after so many years.

As the workers continued their laborious digging, suddenly the rabbi shouted, and motioned to Raphael Yitzchok and the others to come closer. Lo and behold! My grandfather's entire skeleton, from head to toe, was intact. They were all astounded, as they stood witnessing this extraordinary occurrence. "What a *tzaddik*!" the rabbi exclaimed. "What a *tzaddik*! In all my experience, I have never witnessed such a phenomenon." This was echoed over and over again by the *chevrah kadisha* in Yerushalayim as well. As one of them said, "He was surely an *ish emes* to have merited such a miracle."

Dearest Children,

We have spent a good part of the day at Har Hazeisim. This morning we were there for Bubbie Aidel's yahrtzeit, and tonight, the first light of Chanukah, the grandchildren and great-grandchildren of Zaidie Yitzchok Isaac gathered at Uncle Nochum Dovid's house and from there we proceeded to Har Hazeisim for the reburial.

The funeral was an emotional one, as Uncle Nochum Dovid spoke about Zaidie and the sacrifices he had made to uphold Torah and Yiddishkeit for himself and his family, when he had come to America in 1888. He ended his talk with the following heartfelt words: "Zaidie Yitzchok Isaac, we have finally granted your wish, after 44 years, and brought you to Yerushalayim, where you always wanted to be. Rest peacefully in your new home."

Love, Papa and Mama

P.S. After we returned from the funeral, Aunt Bessie told the family a story about Zaidie Yitzchok Isaac which I don't think you ever heard.

When she was in the middle of her pregnancy with Simcha, Zaidie Yitzchok Isaac came to visit her, and told her that he had dreamt she would give birth to a son. He then added, "I would like to be the *sandek* at the bris."

Of course Aunt Bessie was delighted at the idea that she would have a son, especially since she already had three daughters. When she related the dream to Uncle Chaim, and mentioned Zaidie's wish to be the *sandek* at the bris, Uncle Chaim said, "That presents a problem. If it's a boy, I think I would have to give my *Rosh Yeshivah* the honor of being *sandek.*" (At the time, Uncle Chaim was a *mashgiach* in a yeshivah in the States.)

Well, Aunt Bessie did give birth to a boy, just as Zaidie had dreamt. And as the bris approached, she was very troubled at the thought that she would have to tell her grandfather that he would not be the *sandek,* but would receive another *kibbud* instead.

The night before the bris, something unforeseen happened that made it impossible for the *Rosh Yeshivah* to be present at the bris. Of course, Zaidie Yitzchok Isaac was *sandek*!

"A *tzaddik* decrees, and Hashem fulfills his wish!"

Love again,
Papa and Mama

✍ ✍

My father once told me that someone who makes sacrifices for Torah is awarded a special insurance policy from Heaven. Perhaps it is because my grandfather founded the Rabbi Jacob Joseph School, the first yeshivah in America, with such great difficulty, that he has great *zechuyos*.

Dearest Children,

Yesterday was Zaidie Shmuel Yitzchok Andron's yahrtzeit and we visited his grave as we do every year. He passed away on the 28th of Shevat and Bubbie Fruma Rochel one year later on the 24th, four days before her husband's first yahrtzeit. For the twenty years we have been in Yerushalayim, we have tried to go to his grave every year with a minyan, and we also keep in mind that it is for Bubbie's yahrtzeit too.

Only three times in twenty years did it happen that we could not assemble a minyan beforehand, and each time, through *hashgachah pratis*, Hashem provided us with one. The first time occurred many years ago, when the day fell on a Friday. We just could not get ten men together, but Uncle Nochum Dovid, Aunt Chaye Dube, Aunt Esther and I decided to go to the cemetery anyway. Aunt Bessie was not feeling well that day.

I recall feeling very upset that since we could not get a minyan together, Uncle Nochum Dovid would not be able to recite Kaddish. The taxi stopped at the top of Har Hazeisim, and we slowly made our way towards Zaidie's *kever*, down a steep incline. [At that time there were no steps there.]

As we drew nearer, it seemed to me that there were a lot of people near the grave, but I told myself it must be a mirage. It was not! The large group of men were not at Zaidie's grave, but at another one a short distance away. The mystery was solved when we recognized many of those gathered there.

It turned out that the yahrtzeit of Reb Noson Zvi Finkel (*Der Alter* of Slobodka) was one day later, on Shabbos that year, so many of his relatives and students and teachers from the Mir Yeshivah had come on Friday. We caught them minutes before they were about to leave. Of course they came over to Zaidie Andron's *kever,* and so we ended up with not one but several *minyanim* of *bnei Torah* who participated in Zaidie's yahrtzeit. Uncle Nochum Dovid recited the Kaddish.

The second time we had no minyan was a few years later, when we had *almost* a minyan: nine men. We were in a quandary when we arrived at Har Hazeisim. Your cousin Gershon Kaufman said jokingly, "Don't worry — I'll get a tenth even if I have to dig one up!"

Off he went up the mountain, skipping and hopping over the graves. Suddenly, from afar, we saw him stop, peer down into an open grave, and appear to engage in conversation with someone! Then, much to our astonishment, we watched as a man climbed out of the grave, and followed Gershon. As Gershon approached, and saw the expressions on our faces he said, laughing, "I told you that I'd get a tenth, didn't I?"

Of course, there was a simple explanation. The man worked for the *chevrah kadisha,* and was preparing a grave. He naturally was willing to complete our minyan.

Yesterday, children, was the third time that we witnessed *hashgachah pratis,* which makes it a *chazakah.* Again we had only nine men, and as we drove toward Har Hazeisim, Ephraim Shrage [my grandson, who was studying in a yeshivah in Yerushalayim] said, "I'm sure there will be another miracle, and we'll have a minyan." Sure enough, there was! It was the *sheloshim* for a great *tzaddik,* who was buried not too far from Zaidie Shmuel Yitzchok, and a huge crowd had gathered. So again we had a minyan for Zaidie's yahrtzeit. You know, in all the years, whenever we went with a minyan, there was never a "living soul" in sight. The whole cemetery was silent and empty, in wind-swept isolation. And it was only the three times when we had no minyan that there were other people around.

Love, Papa and Mama

My beloved brother and sister-in-law, Reb Nochum Dovid and Chaye Dube.

Reb Moshe and I visited the *Kosel* with my brother and sister-in-law soon after we arrived. Then, only two years after its liberation in the Six Day War, the little palm tree was still there, and today's broad plaza had not yet been developed.

Reb Moshe and me with our grandson, Yonkev Yosef (Elimelech and Mashi's). Right behind him is a portrait of my father, after whom he is named.

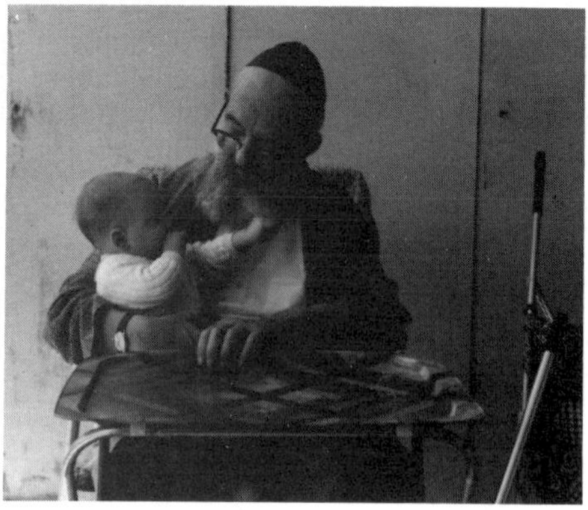

On our balcony, with Kiryat Mattersdorf's buildings, topped with water tanks, in the background. Little Yonkev Yosef is holding fast to his Zaidie's beard.

Raphael Yitzchok and Yehudis's little girls, Aidel and Yocheved (in high chair), livening things up and enjoying one of their first licks of Israeli ice cream.

My grandson Shimon (Willner) delivering his bar mitzvah speech in Yerushalayim. His uncle Reb Chaim Scheinberg is at his right, Reb Moshe and his uncle Reb Nochum Dovid are at his left, his brother Avrohom Yitzchok is in the foreground.

Our grandsons Aaron Dovid, Shimon and Avrohom Yitzchok, the "little" Willner boys, who, to Reb Moshe's surprise, would not need his help in crossing the street! They had grown a bit since we'd seen them last!

Reb Moshe learning with our grandson Avrohom Yitzchok, with his little sister Esther Gitel vying for attention. Reb Moshe doesn't seem to mind the interruption!

At the *Kosel* with our children, Elimelech and Mashi, and our grandsons Shimon and Avrohom Yitzchok.

Reb Moshe and me with grandson Motti (Yisroel Meyer and Chaya's son). It was a source of joy to get to know more and more of our grandchildren as they visited us in turn.

Yisroel Meyer at the *Kosel*, during his visit to us for our 48th wedding anniversary.

My brother-in-law, Rabbi Chaim Scheinberg. Here he is surrounded by *sefarim*, wearing his *tefillin* as he does all day, and clothed in his many pairs of *tzitzis*.

The morning after a Yerushalayim blizzard: Reb Chaim Scheinberg, outside his Yeshivah Torah Ore right after *Shacharis*. To his right, his nephew Abba Miller; to his left, two of his *talmidim*.

I was thankful to Hashem that I could attend my first grandchild's wedding. The *kallah* was Aidel, Yisroel Meyer and Chaya's daughter.

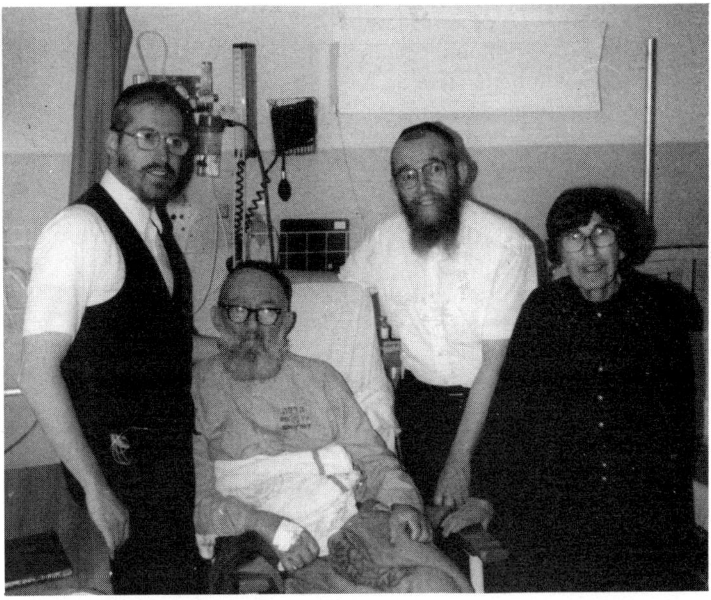

Our two sons, Yisroel Meyer and Raphael Yitzchok, came to visit in April 1988 when Reb Moshe was in Hadassah Hospital. To have his loving sons at his side was truly the best medicine in the world.

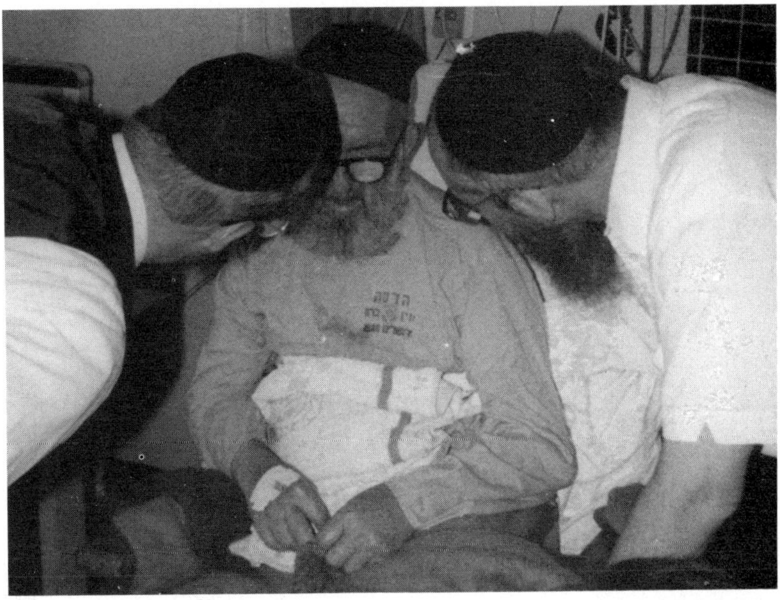

Yisroel Meyer and Raphael Yitzchok, devoted sons who wanted to hear every word their father said.

My beloved Reb Moshe's *kever* on the Mount of Olives, overlooking the site of the Holy Temple.

The view from Reb Moshe's *kever*: the Old City, the Temple Mount, and modern Yerushalayim rising beyond it.

Reb Moshe and me standing in front of the bookcase which he designed to hold our *sefer Torah*. This bookcase made *aliyah* with us.

Surrounded by my loving children (at the wedding of my grandson Aaron Dovid, Elimelech and Mashi's oldest son). Standing, left to right: Elimelech, Raphael Yitzchok, Yehudis, Chaya, Yisroel Meyer. Mashi is seated next to me.

January 15, 1991. Wearing my gas mask, a *sefer Tehillim* in my hand and a prayer in my heart, I was in the sealed room and ready for war.

My grandnephews and grandniece, Reuven, Yehuda and Chana (my niece Mindy's children), didn't have *these* masks in mind when they looked forward to Purim. Fortunately, on Purim, they were able to pack these away and put on masks they liked better.

✍ ✍

There is an apt saying: "Behind every great man stands a woman." My grandfather indeed reached great spiritual heights in his lifetime, but it was the support and encouragement of my grandmother, Fruma Rochel, that made it possible for him to attain his lofty goals.

The following poem was written by my uncle, Rabbi Yisroel Isser Andron (my mother's younger brother, a talented, brilliant orator and educator) on the yahrtzeit of his mother:

24 Shevat 5701

To the Memory of my Revered Mother

AT LONG LAST

And each according to his worth,
Is laid to rest in humble earth.
Strange is the tale of the cemetery!
One flies! The others float on Hades' ferry.
No meaning mile-high monument,
Though marble might it be!
One kind deed towards Heaven bent,
Merits G-d's eternity!

✍ ✍

Dearest Children,

As you know, Papa and I have always looked for *hashgachah pratis* in our daily lives. Sometimes, we see it only in retrospect. Let me share with you yesterday's happenings on Bubbie Aidel's yahrtzeit.

We have been going to her *kever* with a minyan every year from the time we settled here. This was the first time that it was difficult to get ten men together. Since the *Intifada* erupted, and Har Hazeisim is in East Yerushalayim, many people hesitate to go there for fear of being struck by rocks thrown by the Arabs. There have been serious injuries as a result of all the rocks thrown at Jewish vehicles.

Simcha Kaufman said he would go, and would even borrow a friend's station wagon to get us there. Finally, nine other courageous men offered to be part of the minyan. Our good friend, Reb Yosi Brown, who has a car, was one of them. Though Aunt Esther and Aunt Chaya Dube also wanted to be there, they were not feeling well. And as you know, Aunt Bessie is in the States. Chana Levitt, whom I can always depend upon, was to accompany me. I needed her support, as it was difficult for me to walk over the stony path from the parking lot to Bubbie Aidel's grave. I asked Chana to buy me a large whistle, so that if we were attacked by Arabs, God forbid, I would bravely blow the whistle to alert the police!

I had arranged for us to start out from our house at 8:30 A.M. I hardly slept the night before, because of my anxiety about taking people to Har Hazeisim now, during the height of the *Intifada.* I prayed to Hashem to watch over us.

At 6:30 A.M. the telephone rang. It was Julie Brown. "Mrs. Shain, I'm so sorry, but Yosi will not be able to make it. He has come down with a stomach virus." Of course, I wished her husband a *refuah shelemah.* When I finished the conversation, I realized that not only had I lost one man for the minyan, but also the use of Yosi's car.

A few minutes later the telephone rang again. This time it was Simcha Kaufman. "Tante, the station wagon that my friend was going to lend me broke down, so I will be coming without a car."

By this time I was desperate. "Simcha, please try your best to hire a van that can accommodate twelve people. And we also need another man for the minyan." He promised to do his best. I sat near the telephone tensely awaiting his return call.

About half an hour later, his brother Gershon called me. "Tante, we've called company after company trying to hire a van, but the drivers don't want to make the trip to Har Hazeisim. Finally, *baruch Hashem,* I got one who was willing, but it will cost us fifty shekels an hour. Also, I'm not working today, so I'll be able to come — you needn't worry about having a minyan." I sighed with relief.

At 8:10, I was already pacing in front of our house awaiting the minyan. As they gathered, what should pull up but a large, modern tour bus. Parking in front of our house, the driver opened the door and called out, "Shain — Har Hazeisim?"

I went over to him, quite surprised. "My nephew ordered a simple van, not a tour bus!"

The driver explained. "My company did not have a van available right now, and since there are no tourists anyway, the boss sent me with this."

"But how much will this cost us per hour?" I expected to hear an exhorbitant fee for such a luxurious coach. I had with me only 100 shekels.

"It will cost you 50 shekels per hour, as you agreed," he said. This was very fair.

The ten men, Chana and I boarded the huge bus, sank into the velvety, cushioned seats, and off we rode. We drove by the Old City and through East Yerushalayim, and though there were many Arabs milling around, none of them paid any attention to the large vehicle with the words "Tour Bus" prominently displayed on both sides. Had they seen Israeli cars with bearded, Jewish drivers, they might have been tempted to throw rocks.

We arrived at Bubbie Aidel's *kever* and recited the appropriate *Tehillim*, and Simcha said the Kaddish. Once again, we boarded the enormous, luxurious tour bus, sank into the wonderful seats, watched in comfort from our big windows as we sped smoothly through East Yerushalayim, and alighted from the bus in our own familiar neighborhood. I asked the driver how much I owed him, and he glanced at his watch. "It was just two hours, so it comes to 100 shekels." I paid him, and felt grateful to Hashem that I had the *zechus* to be at my beloved mother's *kever* on her yahrtzeit, and that we had come back safely.

But wait, I'm not finished yet! A short while after I came home, there was a knock at the door. In answer to my "Come in," two couples entered. They were visiting from England, they explained, and since they had read *"All for the Boss"*, they decided to take a chance and see if they could meet me.

During the course of our conversation, I mentioned that my book had just been published in Hebrew. They asked if I had any copies on hand that they could purchase, because they had several Israeli relatives who would appreciate the Hebrew book as a gift. I was happy to oblige.

When they left, there were exactly 100 shekels on our living-room table. I saw clearly that the various problems that I had encountered, that had distressed me so much, were all resolved, and that this was clearly Hashem's *hashgachah pratis* watching over us.

Love, Papa and Mama

✍ ✍

My niece and nephew, Mindy and Yisroel Mayer Stern, came to see me. They had come from the States for two weeks to visit their mother, my sister Esther. I told them that their mitzvah of *kibbud em*, coming to be with their mother, was a very great deed, and Hashem would repay them.

When I mentioned that I was in the midst of writing my third book, and had just finished a chapter on Har Hazeisim, Mindy said to me, "Aunt Racoma, I know of an experience that has to do with *kibbud em* and Har Hazeisim, and I think it might fit right into this chapter." She told me some of the details, and then advised me to contact Shmuel Yitzchok Stern, who knew the entire story.

This goes back almost twenty years. Ben, a very close friend of the Stern family, came to Israel from the States to visit his mother's grave on Har Hazeisim for the first time. He telephoned Shmuel Yitzchok and asked him if he would drive him to the grave site, as he had no idea where his mother was buried. (His sister was also buried there.) They went to Har Hazeisim, and Shmuel Yitzchok took him to the two graves. Both women were known as very righteous souls.

While they were standing at his mother's grave, Ben — a man in his early seventies — broke down and cried like a baby. Suddenly, he announced to Shmuel Yitzchok, "I've just made a decision. When my time is up, I want to be buried right here, near my mother." He pointed to an empty plot near her grave. "Let's get this settled right away."

Shmuel Yitzchok was quite hesitant, as Ben was not an observant Jew, and he did not think that the *chevrah kadisha* would allow him to be buried in this particular section, where the policy was to bury only observant Jews.

However, at Ben's insistence, he drove him to the office of the *chevrah kadisha.* When Shmuel Yitzchok explained Ben's request, and mentioned that Ben was not an observant Jew, the *chevrah kadisha* flatly refused to sell him the plot. Ben, who was a multi-millionaire, whispered to Shmuel Yitzchok, "Let's not beat around the bush. Everything has a price. Just get that grave near my mother, and I will pay them any amount they ask."

But the *chevrah kadisha* would not be swayed from their stand, and no amount of money would change their principles. As the two men left the office, Shmuel Yitzchok said gently, "Ben, this time, with all your money, you cannot buy what a poor man can."

Ben was sorely troubled, as they drove back to the hotel where he was staying. "Shmuel Yitzchok, what do I have to do to get that grave?"

"The only way you could buy that grave would be if you became a completely observant Jew."

Ben was silent for a few minutes. "Okay," he said. "They win. Tell me — how do I go about it?" Shmuel Yitzchok was astounded. Ben was an elderly man and this would mean a complete metamorphosis for him.

"When you return to the States," Shmuel Yitzchok advised him, "contact the Orthodox rabbi from your community, whom I know very well, and ask him for guidance. I will be in touch with him and with you. May Hashem guide you in this holy undertaking."

With the rabbi's directions and encouragement, Ben had his kitchen made kosher, began to put on *tefillin* every morning, went to the synagogue for daily prayers, and became a Sabbath observer — so much so, that when he entered a hotel or a building on Shabbos that had a Sabbath elevator that he was permitted to use, he would refrain from using it, and instead would trudge up the many flights of stairs.

A year later, the rabbi confirmed in writing to the *chevrah kadisha* in Yerushalayim that Ben was a truly observant Jew in every sense of the word, and they could sell him the plot near his mother.

When Ben passed away in the States, several years later, the rabbi delivered a moving *hesped* to the overflowing crowd. "All of us," he exclaimed, "can learn an important lesson about the great mitzvah of *kibbud em*, from our deceased."

Ben was brought to Yerushalayim and laid to rest near his mother. May His soul rest in eternal peace!

My "Big" Brother

MY BELOVED BROTHER, Reb Nochum Dovid, *zt"l,* passed away during Chanukah 1984 after a sudden heart attack. He left a vacuum in all our lives that can never be filled.

During the week of *shivah,* hundreds of relatives and friends came to comfort the family. They spoke about his sterling qualities: he was a great *ben Torah,* an excellent teacher, a witty orator. But above all, what endeared him to everyone was his manner of bringing joy wherever he went.

He always entered our home with a contagious smile and a good joke. Once, a great-nephew of ours was visiting us when my brother walked in. Reb Nochum Dovid greeted the young man cheerfully and quipped in Yiddish, "Ich bin dine *elter fetter* (a great-uncle), because I am *older* and *fatter* than you!" He had the remarkable attribute of being able to laugh at himself.

Dearest Children,

From our telephone conversations while I was sitting *shivah*, I could sense your shock at Uncle Nochum Dovid's passing. I myself am still reeling from the blow of his death, and can't seem to get back to earth. The *shivah* period was characterized by a mixture of anguish over our sudden loss, and consolation from the many who came to comfort us.

I realize you are anxious to hear all the details, so I'll try my best to describe what happened. In short, what Nochum Dovid thought was a little stomach upset turned out to be a sudden major heart attack. Somehow, when he first mentioned his symptoms, the thought of heart trouble occurred to me and I suggested that he see a cardiologist. He "pooh-poohed" the idea. However, with Aunt Chaye Dube's coaxing, he did go to the doctor, a geriatric specialist, who examined him, took a cardiogram, and saw no cause for alarm.

The doctor advised Uncle Nochum Dovid to take it easy for a few days. Now, "taking it easy" for Uncle Nochum Dovid meant going to shul three times a day, attending a bris in the morning and a bar mitzvah at night, and various other activities in cold, windy weather.

When I telephoned him a few days later, on a Sunday morning, he said, "*Baruch Hashem,* I feel much better." I was relieved but advised him not to overdo it. Aaron Dovid, who visited him during lunch break from the Yeshivah, mentioned that I was worried about him. He answered, "Tell your Bubbie to stop making a fuss over me."

That same evening, while eating his dinner, he slumped over in his chair, lost consciousness, and was rushed by ambulance to the hospital. He had suffered a major heart attack.

We were all informed, and in no time we gathered outside the intensive care unit, where Aunt Chaye Dube and her children, Reb Mordechai and Goldie, were waiting. Shmuel Yitzchok, who lives in Migdal Ha-Emek, joined us a few hours later. We stood in the corridor of the intensive care unit reciting *Tehillim* with quaking hearts.

It is hard for me to continue now, children, so I will write you more later.

Love, Papa and Mama

Dearest Children,

A kind of exhaustion that comes with grief and mourning overcame me as I was writing last night. This morning I feel that I can go on with my letter.

The next few days were very tense ones, as Papa and I awaited each bulletin from the hospital. Finally we were told the good news that Uncle Nochum Dovid was making a remarkable recovery, and we could visit him. The cloud of impending doom that had descended upon all of us was lifted.

We hurried to the hospital, and were allowed to go in one at a time. When I walked over to him, he seemed his old jolly self, and said, "This time you were right, but don't forget, I'm still your *big* brother."

Yes, children, he was my big and only brother, whom I adored from the time I was a tiny tot. Since I was the youngest of his four sisters, and the baby of the family, I felt I had a unique place in his heart. He was the "shining star" of our family, with Bubbie Aidel and the four of us girls doting on him. Of course, Zaidie Yonkev Yosef gave his only son special attention in his fatherly way.

Papa and I always had a close, loving relationship with him and Aunt Chaye Dube, but it became much closer from the time we settled in Yerushalayim. Especially when we first came here, Uncle Nochum Dovid was always ready to help us in every way. He and Aunt Chaye Dube understood very well our lonesomeness for all of you.

We were often invited to them for Shabbos. One Friday night when Aunt Chaye Dube finished serving the meal, Uncle Nochum Dovid took a bite and said to her, "You know, you must have forgotten to salt the food." "Oh, no I didn't," she replied. "Racoma told me that Moshe's cardiologist advised him to be on a salt-free diet, so I cooked everything without salt. You can use the saltshaker for *your* food.'' Uncle Nochum Dovid took it good-naturedly.

When I fractured my femur and could not ready our house for Pesach, it was to their house I was taken, and Papa and I received the loving care we needed. These acts of devotion have become embedded in our hearts.

I thought that I would be able to write it all in one letter, then in two, but I realize now that it will take several letters to express my feelings.

Love, Papa and Mama

✍ ✍

Dearest Children,

On *erev Chanukah,* on Bubbie Aidel's yahrtzeit, we went to her *kever* on Har Hazeisim with a minyan, as we always do. It was the first time that Uncle Nochum Dovid was not with us, and would not be saying Kaddish. All our thoughts and prayers were centered around him, and a *mi-sheberach* was said for his *refuah shelemah.* I went over to Bubbie Aidel's grave and silently asked her to use her holy influence with Hashem that her beloved son should have a complete recovery.

From there we went directly to the hospital, and were given the good tidings that he had been transferred from the intensive care unit to a regular ward. One of the attending cardiologists told me that Uncle Nochum Dovid had kept up the spirits of all the doctors and nurses in the intensive care unit, and whenever they had the chance, they went over to him just to hear his interesting comments.

When they were taking his medical history and asked about his childhood illnesses, he had answered that he had contracted pneumonia as a young boy. ''Would you remember on what side?'' the doctor asked. ''Of course, I remember,'' he chuckled. ''It was on the Lower East Side!''

When we spoke to him, he was relaxed and told us that he had asked to be taken by wheelchair to the shul in the hospital so that he could say Kaddish for Bubbie Aidel on her yahrtzeit. His condition seemed so good that there was even talk that he might be released in time to go home for Shabbos Chanukah. Aunt Chaye Dube was already planning a gala *melaveh malkah* for this joyous event. For the first time since he fell ill, I thought to myself, "We'll have a happy Chanukah after all."

The next day, while putting on his *Rabbenu Tam tefillin,* which was his daily custom for *Minchah,* he suffered another major heart attack. His grandson, Aaron, was at his bedside. Despite the life-saving efforts of the chief cardiologist and a team of doctors, Uncle Nochum Dovid's holy soul departed and was taken to Heaven. He passed away just as the second light of Chanukah was about to be kindled.

The very large, emotional funeral was that same night, as there is a custom in Yerushalayim not to keep the deceased overnight without burial. Everyone was in a state of shock. As one close relative remarked wryly, "I can't believe that Nochum Dovid, who was so full of life, would allow himself to be buried." However, the decree was handed down from Above.

While we were on Har Hamenuchos, and Uncle Nochum Dovid was being lowered into his grave, a most unusual phenomenon occurred: for a few moments there was a sudden glow of light in the sky. Later, one of the men from the *chevrah kadisha* explained excitedly, "We witnessed an *amuda d'nura* — a pillar of light — which sometimes appears when a great *tzaddik* passes on." Uncle Nochum Dovid, *zt"l,* was just that, and we were privileged to have him as our brother.

Uncle Nochum Dovid is buried near his father, Zaidie Yonkev Yosef, his father-in-law, Reb Avrohom Horowitz, and Uncle Yom Tov Lipman Stern. His mother-in-law, Sarah Leah Horowitz, is buried nearby. The area is *chelkas ha-rabbanim,* where some of the greatest *talmidei chachamim* are buried. Reb Aaron Kotler and members of his family are nearby, as are Reb Moshe Feinstein, the Belzer Rebbe, and the

Mattersdorfer Rebbe.

May their souls be bound up in the bond of everlasting life

Love, Papa and Mama

P.S. Aunt Chaye Dube is holding up well under the circumstances, but her grief is profound, and her life has undergone a drastic change. She had a very loving relationship with Uncle Nochum Dovid and they were always together in heart and mind. Of course, her very devoted children Reb Shmuel Yitzchok and Chaya Pearl, Reb Mordechai and Goldie (Elefant), and several grandchildren are all by her side. Papa and I and our entire family are very close to her, as she has always been a sister to us. May Hashem comfort her and give her the strength to continue in her many charitable activities.

✍ ✍

The rainy season was over. The warm, spring day with fleecy clouds sailing briskly through the blue sky was the perfect day to dry the clothes that had just come out of my washing machine.

I went out on my balcony to hang up the freshly laundered linens, and looked down at the brown earth. Lo and behold! The bushes that had been bare just a few weeks ago, were filled with blooming roses in shades of baby pink and scarlet red. As I watched the budding flowers swaying gently in the breeze, a comforting thought came to my mind.

If blooming roses can come forth from bare branches, a body buried beneath the earth does not mean eternal death. The soul lives on in a better world, and one day, our beloved departed will return to us in the full glory of their physical resurrection.

My beloved brother, Reb Nochum Dovid left a rich heritage of good deeds that he planted in his garden of life. May these continue to grow and bring forth beautiful fruits.

Taking Everything "in Stride"

IT SEEMS THAT I WAS destined to learn the art of walking several times in my life. As a one-year old, I took my first, faltering steps. After the birth of my son, Yisroel Meyer, in Mir, Poland, I became paralyzed and had to learn slowly and arduously how to walk again. Many years later, while living in Yerushalayim, I fractured my right femur and required a new round of lessons in walking. When I repeated that "feat" by fracturing my left femur, I again had to be taught how to use my legs. By now I am a pro, and hope and pray that I shall not need any more lessons.

I was relieved to learn that there had been much medical progress since my first orthopedic surgery in Yerushalayim. At that time, a Smith-Peterson plate was screwed into my thigh to keep the bones together until they healed, and I was not allowed to stand on that leg for over two months. This time, I had "sliding nails" inserted, which, according to the nurse who witnessed the surgery, was a real plumbing job.

Whatever it was — plumbing or carpentry — I was able to stand on that leg just two days after surgery, with the help of the physiotherapist and a walker.

Dearest Children,

I'v done it again! This time I fractured my left femur, so now it matches my right femur, which, you will recall, I broke seven years ago.

This is how it happened: Papa and I were sitting and waiting for the bus on our way home from a visit to his neurologist for Papa's regular three-month checkup. The doctor had just given us a very positive report — the medication was controlling the Parkinson's Disease very well — and we were both in a good mood.

I had just finished telling Papa that since Chanukah was only a few days away, he should get his appetite ready for the latkes I would be making for him. The bus pulled up, and as Papa stood up he tripped lightly but caught himself. However, since I was holding his hand when he tripped, I lost my balance and fell to the pavement with a heavy thud. I realized immediately from the intense pain that engulfed me and blacked me out for a moment, that I had broken a bone.

Two kind passersby came to our rescue. While one stayed with us, the other telephoned for an ambulance to take me to the emergency room of Shaarei Zedek hospital. Papa was understandably very upset and wanted to come along with me, but I felt it would be too much of a strain for him. I asked our kind helpers to please take Papa to Aunt Bessie's, and tell her about my accident and where I had been taken.

Lying in the ambulance, my main thought was, "Well, there go Papa's Chanukah latkes." About an hour after I got to the emergency room, Aunt Bessie and Reb Simcha hurried in, very upset and concerned about me. First, they assured me that Papa was being well taken care of, and I should not worry. Then, they wanted to see if I was being well taken care of, and *Baruch Hashem* I was.

By that time, the X-rays had shown what I had already known, that I had fractured my femur, and I'd need surgery. A very capable orthopedic surgeon who was on duty would be able to operate later in the day.

In the meantime, Aunt Bessie called the Levitts, and Hemla and Chana arrived a short while later, visibly worried about me. Aunt Bessie and Reb Simcha were able to leave, as Hemla stayed until after the surgery, and Chana remained by my side the entire night.

So you should be assured, children, that our relatives and friends have rallied to my side, and I am thankful for their physical and moral support, especially the care they are giving Papa. Don't worry — everything is under control.

Love, Papa and Mama

P. S. Chana gave me a wonderful surprise and remained with me over Shabbos in the hospital. She has a friend who is a nursing student, so she was able to share her room, in the dormitories, close to the hospital. She certainly made Shabbos as restful and enjoyable as it could be.

✍ ✍

Dearest Children,

I understand you are receiving reports about my progress, which is good, Thank Hashem. I have a session with the physiotherapist every morning, and I am happy to report that I can already walk the length of my room with my walker — no small feat for a person of my age. In fact, the physiotherapist marveled at my determination. In her experience with elderly patients, she usually has to use all kinds of psychological approaches to get them to cooperate, "but in your case," she told me, "I have to hold you back, because you want to do too much too soon."

Of course she was not aware that my emotional impetus is knowing how much Papa needs me. The first time Papa visited me in the hospital, he broke down and cried. Naturally

I cried too, and the other three patients in the room promptly joined us.

Love, Papa and Mama

Dearest Children,

There is a Yiddish expression that asserts: "One mother can take care of ten children, but ten children cannot take care of one mother." This is certainly not the case in our situation! Be assured that Papa is being cared for lovingly and capably by many "children." Let me share the details with you. Avrohom Yitzchok comes from the Yeshivah every night. He helps Papa get to bed, and spends the night in our house. He takes care of Papa's needs in the morning and returns to the Yeshivah after breakfast. Thank Hashem, that we have a grandson here.

Mindy Altusky, Frume's daughter-in-law, has practically moved into our house with her new infant. She is in charge of seeing that Papa receives all his medication throughout the day, and serves Papa and Avrohom Yitzchok breakfast.

Polly Altusky, another of Frume's daughters-in-law, prepares and serves Papa lunch, and relieves Mindy for a few hours.

Papa eats his main evening meal by Aunt Bessie, and is there for the entire Shabbos.

A woman was hired to do the housecleaning, and another takes care of washing Papa's clothes. I am not sure who does the shopping, but most probably it is my next-door neighbor.

When I see how the work has been divided up, it is difficult to believe that until now I have taken care of all of it, and everything else that makes a house run smoothly. I also kept up with the correspondence, and went to a *shiur* from time to time; we had an active social life, relatives and friends visited us, and we visited them.

I am not trying to prove my prowess. I only hope that Hashem will help me once again to be able to take care of

Papa, and do everything else I was doing, so that I can give our devoted relatives and friends a reprieve.

Love, Papa and Mama

I certainly did not look forward to my stay in the hospital during Chanukah, as this Festival has always been a very joyous time for Reb Moshe and me. To my pleasant surprise, however, I found it to be much better than I had anticipated. Every night, a volunteer visitor came to light Chanukah candles in the rooms. There was a cheerful atmosphere throughout the ward, with the staff and volunteers trying their best to lift the patients' spirits. Many visitors came, bringing Chanukah gifts and spending time with the patients.

Just as the spirit of Chanukah prevailed in the hospital, so did the spirit of Shabbos enter every week, with Sabbath observance evident even in the smallest details. A non-Jew accompanied the doctors and nurses on their rounds and wrote the pertinent information on the patient's chart. Even the signal that summoned the nurse was a special one designed to be halachically permissible for use on Shabbos. On *erev Shabbos,* girl volunteers distributed candles to light. A rabbi recited the *Kiddush* both Friday night and Shabbos morning, and made *Havdalah* on Saturday night.

Though my accident and subsequent surgery were an ordeal, it was surely a *zechus* to be in Shaarei Zedek hospital. By the way, my surgeon, like so many of the doctors here, was a religious Jew.

Dearest Children,

I am having an ongoing argument with the head nurse and the social worker. My therapist recommended that I enter a rehabilitation facility for an additional two weeks after leaving the hospital. She feels I definitely need more physiotherapy before I can go home.

I explained to them that Papa has been awaiting my return impatiently, and that I want to be with him, which would be my best therapy. I can also have a physiotherapist come to our house. I think I am succeeding in convincing them that I am ready to go home.

I will try to get help with the housework, and I hope I will recover quickly and be able to take over before long.

Love, Papa and Mama

✍ ✍

I had an interesting experience while still in the hospital. The head doctor of the geriatric department visited me and asked if I would consent to be interviewed by him at a symposium of doctors, nurses, and therapists who dealt with elderly patients. My surgeon had recommended me because of my age, and the excellent progress I was making.

I accepted, as I was delighted to be wheeled out of my room for an outing. Had I been given advance notice, I would have worn my wig and dressed up for the occasion, but I guess the way I looked, in bathrobe and kerchief, emphasized the fact that I indeed fitted into the "elderly patient" category.

The topic of the symposium was the motivation of the elderly to recuperate after orthopedic surgery. I was considered a model patient and rated a high mark from all who attended. I am convinced that one cannot separate the emotional from the physical in any aspect of our lives.

✍ ✍

Dearest Children,

Despite the fact that reading Hebrew has been a part of my life since early childhood, and that I have been living in Yerushalayim for more than eighteen years, I still have not mastered the art of speaking Hebrew fluently. Since Kiryat Mattersdorf has so many English-speaking families, I do not have the opportunity or need to converse in Hebrew. I find that when I do speak Hebrew, many times I think in English and translate the English word into Hebrew, which certainly can get me into "hot water," both figuratively and literally, as you will see.

As you know, I'm still in the hospital, and last night, at about 2:00 A.M., I needed the bathroom facilities. I rang my bell and after several minutes the night nurse appeared. She must have been a new one, as I did not recognize her. Since I did not want to awaken the other patients in my room, I whispered in Hebrew, "*Ambatyah,*" the word which I thought meant "bathroom." The nurse looked at me condescendingly and answered in Hebrew, "No, no, not now — in the morning," patted me, and off she went.

I was astonished at her attitude. I waited for fifteen minute and rang my bell again. This time it took her quite a while to put in an appearance. I repeated my request in Hebrew, this time in an emphatic tone: "I need the *ambatyah.*" She was very annoyed, and answered sharply, "I told you that you will have to wait until the morning." But before she could escape, I sputtered in English, "I absolutely cannot wait until the morning for the bathroom, and I need help immediately." For a moment she looked at me quizzically and then asked, "Oh! You mean *sherutim*?" I nodded my head emphatically.

As she helped me down from my bed and got me a walker, she gave me a lecture on the importance of using proper Hebrew. I realized that I had used the Hebrew word for "bathtub," which can also mean "bathroom" — but in Israeli apartments there are usually two "bathrooms": one for the toilet, and one for the bath or shower. The bathroom with the toilet is never called the "bathroom" in Hebrew! She must have thought I was an old, cranky American who wanted a bath at two o'clock in the morning, so I can understand her reaction.

I am grateful for my sense of humor, and I gave everyone a

laugh this morning when I recounted my nocturnal experience. I remember, when I taught vocabulary to my high-school students, that I always impressed upon them the importance of using the exact word to express their thoughts.

Well, I certainly needed that lesson myself.

Love, Papa and Mama

✍ ✍

I was quite surprised to learn that my son, Raphael Yitzchok, would be arriving in Yerushalayim the day after I was to return home from the hospital. I had thought all along that I was acting my role of courageous-mother-coping-well to perfection. Now I realized that I had not fooled my children when I had sent word that none of them needed to come.

Most probably, my well-meaning relatives had tattled on me and let our child know that I was not quite ready to dance a jig yet. I realized what a sacrifice it was for Raphael Yitzchok to leave his wife Yehudis, the children, and his teaching position on such short notice. I knew it would not be easy for Yehudis either, but it certainly would be a boon for Reb Moshe and me.

I left the hospital despite the recommendations of the therapist, nurse, and social worker that I go to a rehabilitation facility for additional therapy. Nonetheless, they were all very gracious in wishing me well.

Dearest Children,

Papa and I were delighted to welcome Raphael Yitzchok. One of his first actions was to print a sign and place it on our front door: "Please do not disturb between the hours of 1:00 P.M. and 4:00 P.M." It was certainly a wise move, as there was a steady stream of visitors and well-wishers at all hours of the day, and it was taking its toll. At least now, we had our regular afternoon rest period to ourselves.

Raphael Yitzchok has taken over all of Papa's care, and waits on me hand and "foot," not to mention all his help in other things. When he was serving us breakfast this morning, I mentioned to him the experience I had when I was last in the States and staying with Yisroel Meyer and Chaya.

I had been about to take a cup of tea, when Yisroel Meyer walked in from his Yeshivah. Before he even took off his coat, he said, "Please, Mama, let me serve you."

"Yisroel Meyer," I answered, "I am perfectly capable of taking a cup of tea by myself. Take off your coat and relax."

"Mama, one of the main mitzvos of *kibbud av v'em* is to serve food to parents. Do you want to deprive me of a mitzvah that I cannot buy for any amount of money?"

Of course, I handed him the cup and he served me the tea. He then gave me a smile of appreciation and said, "Now, I feel like a millionaire."

Raphael Yitzchok is certainly becoming a multi-millionaire with all his *kibbud av v'em.*

We have hired a fine girl to help with the household chores every morning. She will come in time to prepare breakfast and leave after making lunch. Our main meal is being delivered through a special *chesed* organization which caters to women after childbirth or surgery. I pay for the food, but the preparation is done by volunteers, who do it with graciousness. They even prepare a special, salt-free meal for Papa. There are many organizations to help needy people, and now that I have become the recipient of their kindness, I realize once more how blessed we are to be living in Yerushalayim.

Love, Papa and Mama

P.S. Thank you for your loving phone calls. It was good to talk to all of you. I hope that by the time Raphael Yitzchok leaves I will be much improved, as he is doing his utmost to, quite literally, get me back on my feet.

✍ ✍

Dearest Children,

By now Raphael Yitzchok is safely home with Yehudis and the children. I'm sure they missed him very much. After he left, we heard that there was a raging snowstorm in New York, and Papa and I were very anxious about his returning in time for Shabbos. We were very relieved when we heard that he had made it.

I am sure that by now he has given you a detailed account of his ten days here. His visit did wonders for Papa and me. Both his positive attitude and the physical help were the best therapy we could have had. Though we miss him, we are happy that he is home with his loved ones.

Now *Papa* hovers over *me*, instead of vice-versa, but I hope very soon to reverse roles. I am managing very well, with the help of the housekeeper in the mornings and our relatives and friends in the afternoons. The physiotherapist, who comes three times a week, said that I am doing so well that I will be graduating from the walker to two canes very soon, and hopefully will be able to walk on my own in the near future.

This experience has once again reminded me how much most of us take our daily activities for granted. Walking is simple for people who have healthy legs — most people — and they probably don't give a thought to the effort one must expend for every step. To me each step forward, in every sense, is an accomplishment.

May Hashem guide me and give me the stamina to continue to "make strides" in every path of my life.

Love, Papa and Mama

Dearest Children,

I forgot to mention all along that when I fell, I also cracked several ribs. The surgeon said that nothing could be done except to tape them up, and in time they would heal.

I find that even breathing deeply brings a twinge of pain, and I try to minimize any sudden movements. The other day I felt a sneeze coming on, and called out to Papa, "Moshe, I have to sneeze! Do something quickly to stop it." Papa hurried over, but by then I had lost control, and the sneeze erupted into a loud "*whoooop.*" Papa looked on so helplessly as I grimaced with pain, that I burst into laughter, which only added to my misery. I ended up laughing and crying together.

Until now, I had always been a great believer in laughter being the best medicine. I have had to reconsider.

Love, Papa and Mama

✍ ✍

Dearest Children,

Spring is in the air, and today Papa and I sat on our balcony basking in the sun. We watched the children playing in the schoolyard across the street, and for a moment I had a desire to be a child once again — running, skipping and jumping.

Well, I am not doing any of those things but I am thankful to Hashem for the many blessings He has given me. I am already using canes, and each day brings progress. It is very rewarding to be able to do little things for Papa and for myself. In fact, for last Shabbos, I prepared a special sweet kugel that Papa likes. It gave me a great sense of accomplishment.

Love, Papa and Mama

Love from Our Children

IT WAS ALWAYS a great joy when our children came to visit us in Yerushalayim, especially when they came to celebrate a *simchah.* In between times we shared *simchas* by mail and, sometimes, by telephone.

Dearest Children,

MAZAL TOV! MAZAL TOV!

Mashi, your early morning call, bringing us the wonderful news that you gave birth to a daughter, delighted Papa and me. We knew how very much you wanted a girl, especially after three boys. I remember that even as a little girl, you always wanted a sister, but had to be satisfied with your two brothers. Papa said that I sounded like a broken record on the phone, repeating over and over again, "How wonderful — it's really a girl — how wonderful — it's really a girl..." I ran to tell Aunt Esther, Uncle Chaim and Aunt Bessie, and the Altuskys the good news. There was a lot of hugging and kissing, and they all send their heartiest mazal tov. The rest of the neighbors heard the excitement, and they, too, join in sending good wishes.

We shall be anxiously waiting to hear more details, and the name you chose for your daughter. May she grow happily and healthily. Elimelech, how are you managing with the boys? What is their reaction to their new little sister?

Love, Papa and Mama

I left early for work that morning, hoping the office staff would be there, so I could share with them the good news about Mashi's new daughter. However, much to my disappointment, no one had arrived yet. A pile of letters to donors needed to be typed and sent, so I picked up the first one and began. But instead of typing the usual thank-you letter, I wrote the following:

Dear Mr. and Mrs. Y.,

I am very excited, as I received a call early this morning from my daughter in the States telling me that she gave birth to a daughter, after three sons. The other secretaries have not arrived as yet, and I feel the need to share the good news with someone, so I am taking the liberty of sharing it with you. Thank you.

I signed my full name instead of the usual initials that I placed at the bottom of the letter. Then, of course, I went on to write an appropriate letter thanking them for their generous donation. I did hope they wouldn't think I was a scatter-brained grandmother.

The rest of the staff arrived, and the girls in the office shared my excitement. One of the secretaries ran out and bought chocolate cake and other goodies, and they made a party during our coffee break to celebrate the event. It was rewarding to have such a close relationship. We shared many of our "ups and downs" with each other.

✍ ✍

To Elimelech and Mashi,

MAZAL TOV!

Your daughter was born on the twenty-eighth — *kaf ches* — of Cheshvan. She should have *kaf ches,* which spells *ko'ach* (strength), and you should have *ko'ach* to bring her up with *yiddishe nachas.* She is *bas Mashi* — *bas mem* — and if you add the letters *kaf ches* to *bas mem,* you get *bas chacham* — the daughter of a wise and learned man. *Berachah, hatzlachah,* and *kol tuv* to both of you and to your three little "musketeers."

Keep well, Papa

Several weeks after I had written to Mr. and Mrs. Y. about the birth of my granddaughter, I received an elaborate grandmother's card with good wishes from them. Since then a personal relationship has been established in our correspondence. I had always wondered if the donors ever bothered to read the thank-you letters from our Orphan Home, and this proved that some really did.

✍ ✍

Dearest Elimelech and Mashi,

Your call announcing that you are making plans to visit us this summer was electrifying news. It has been almost six years since we settled in Yerushalayim, and we have missed you very much. You know how much Papa and I have longed to have some of our children visit us and actually see us in our Yerushalayim surroundings.

We think it is an excellent idea to send the three boys to camp and bring the baby with you. I am sure the boys will love it in camp, even though they have never been separated from you. And especially since Yisroel Meyer will be the

Learning Director and Chaya, the camp mother, you will not have anything to worry about.

I have already started to get our extra room ready for you. There is a comfortable hi-riser that opens up to two beds. I am emptying several drawers in my chest, and also making closet space for your belongings. A neighbor offered to lend us a crib and a highchair for Esther Gitel.

Papa and I are awaiting you impatiently. May we meet with happy hearts in Yerushalayim.

Love, Papa and Mama

During Elimelech's and Mashi's visit to us, I wrote letters to the other children to keep them posted.

Dearest Children,

I was at the airport to greet Elimelech, Mashi and Esther Gitel when they arrived. Papa was waiting for us in front of our house when the *sherut* pulled up, and we had a loving, emotional reunion.

Having the children here with us is very exciting. Elimelech and Mashi are delighted to be with us, and, of course, being in Yerushalayim is a special added dividend. Esther Gitel is warming up to us. She certainly is a very sweet *maideleh.* Our relatives and friends have all been coming to welcome them, so we are kept joyously busy.

I have made plans for them to tour the country as soon as they rest up a bit from their trip. Of course, Papa and I will baby-sit. We are waiting to hear the news from the boys in camp. Mashi gave each one a dozen addressed air-mail letters, so it will be easy for them to write to their parents in Yerushalayim.

Love, Papa and Mama

The first two weeks of the visit were very rewarding ones for all of us. Elimelech and Mashi went up north to the Galil for a two-day trip with my nephew, Gershon Kaufman, a wonderful tour guide, and returned very enthusiastic. They also toured all of Yerushalayim. Most of the time, Reb Moshe and I managed with Esther Gitel, but once or twice when I became desperate, a relative came by to relieve me. I'm afraid it had been many years since I had to look after an 18-month-old baby.

Chazal say that Torah, *olam ha-ba,* and Eretz Yisrael are acquired through suffering. I don't know if visiting Eretz Yisrael falls into that category, but the first letters from the boys in camp certainly provided it.

Though I had been sure that the boys would love it, I guess I was overly optimistic. First of all ages seven, eight and nine are very young for going away from home for an extended period. Secondly, the knowledge that their Tatty and Mommy were so very far away from them added to their lonesomeness.

Their first letters give a good idea of the effect they had on all of us, especially on Mashi and Elimelech:

> *Dear Tatty, Mommy, Zaidie and Bubbie.*
>
> I am homesick. Please write more often. Aunt Chaya took care of me as I had a stomack viruss, and she gave me medicine. I want to come home as soon as you come back even though camp will not be over because I am homesick. Sorry to upset you. Please write more often, around every two days or even more. I just got another letter from you. Uncle Yisroel Meyer is trying to do something about my homesickness.

The second letter really got us down:

> I hate camp very much. That if you were here you woud want your mother to, who is buby.

For a seven-year old, he expressed himself quite clearly — to our dismay! We fervently hoped that the next batch of letters would be less depressing.

Dearest Children,

Last week, I was almost afraid to open our mailbox, which was stuffed to the brim with air-mail letters from camp. We opened them with trepidation, and found that although they were still quite gloomy, there was a slight improvement in the tone. And in this week's letters the word "homesick" has hardly been mentioned.

There was an up-beat sentence in one of the letters, which comforted us quite a bit: "I do not like it in camp. I really hate it, but swiming I like it." The letters also contain lists of the presents they want their parents to bring back for them from Israel. Elimelech and Mashi feel guilty about sending the boys to camp.

Love, Papa and Mama

Dearest Yisroel Meyer and Chaya,

We just received your letter, Chaya, which shows you handled each of the boys like a child psychologist would. Yisroel Meyer, we see from your few lines that you've been censoring the boys' letters! Still, it was good to read your comforting words: "It's not as bad as it sounds, and they were only a little homesick. Don't worry. Everything is under control." From afar, you know, the problem is magnified. I can well imagine that both of you had your hands full, though, especially at the beginning, and we are all very thankful that you are there to ease the situation.

I wrote a separate letter to Raphael Yitzchok and Yehudis thanking them for making a special trip up to camp to spend time with the boys on visitors' day. All the boys wrote positive letters about the visit and all the treats they brought them. It made Elimelech and Mashi feel better.

Love, Papa and Mama

The days flew by, and before we knew it, Elimelech, Mashi, and Esther Gitel were about to leave. They spent their last week shopping for gifts for the boys, which they hoped would appease them and make them forget their homesickness.

Of course, we would miss them terribly, but Reb Moshe and I have always adopted a positive attitude in life. Instead of bemoaning our lonesomeness, we are thankful to Hashem for the time our children spent with us, and the loving memories they would leave us with.

Dearest Elimelech and Mashi,

Papa and I were anxiously awaiting your call, when it came early this morning. It certainly cheered us both up to know the boys looked healthy, and the camp experience did not leave everlasting traumas! Your description of the welcome you received from them was very humorous, with their "take it or leave it" attitude. We were so sure that they would not want to remain one minute longer in camp after you returned, and now you say, surprisingly, that they all want to stick it out. Who can understand little boys? But all's well that ends well!

I am sure you will tell the other children all about our life in Yerushalayim, and about Eretz Yisrael in general. It might whet their appetites for a visit to us in the near future.

Love, Papa and Mama

✍ ✍

Dearest Children,

Sukkos is *zeman simchasenu,* and this year it was especially a time of rejoicing. Having Raphael Yitzchok, Yehudis, little Aidel and Yocheved with us during *Yom Tov* enhanced our *simchah* by far. Though their visit was relatively short, from before Yom Kippur until after Sukkos, each minute was filled with joy.

Papa and Raphael Yitzchok spent many uplifting hours together learning in our sukkah, while Yehudis and I went out with the children. Time and physical separation have not diminished Yehudis's and my close and loving relationship. We are truly blessed that the children who married into our family are as much our children as those born to us.

The little ones livened things up for us during their stay, and the generation gap was quite obvious. Raphael Yitzchok and Yehudis were not alarmed at all when fifteen-month-old Yocheved suddenly stood up in her highchair and tried to climb out alone or when she stood swaying back and forth on one of our dining room chairs, whereas Papa and I covered our eyes so as not to witness the inevitable. Of course, nothing happened, but it always seemed as if it were about to...

We see Hashem's guiding Hand in giving babies to young people, and not to old ones like us! Now that they have gone, we miss them very much — highchair and all.

Love, Papa and Mama

✍ ✍

Reb Moshe and I had a very special treat with Yisroel Meyer's and Chaya's first visit to us. It was very exciting for all of us to be together again after many years of separation. For Chaya, who was born in Yerushalayim, it brought back nostalgic memories of her childhood.

Chaya's father, Rabbi Moshe Berman, came here as a young boy. His parents, who lived in Boston, wanted him to receive a true Torah education, so they sent him to an uncle in Yerushalayim, a great *talmid chacham*, who was childless. The uncle brought him up as his own son. Rabbi Berman subsequently married Peshe, who came from a well-known Yerushalmi family, and Chaya and her younger siblings were born in Yerushalayim.

Back in Yerushalayim after so many years, Chaya was very

excited.When she was unpacking her suitcases after their arrival, I noticed she had taken along a box of matzah. I looked at her questioningly, and she smiled, "You know, Mama, before we left the States, I saw this box of matzah in my food cupboard and I stuck it in. I guess subconsciously I must have been afraid of going hungry again in Yerushalayim, as strange as that sounds today!"

Chaya had been a young child when the War of Independence broke out. Yerushalayim was under siege for some time, and she and her family had lived mostly in a shelter. Chaya, who was the oldest of her family, knew what it meant to be very hungry. In fact, one of her first visits on this trip was to a Mr. Friedman, a close friend of her father's, who used to save a slice of fresh bread for her daily, during the siege of Yerushalayim. Chaya never forgot this special gift from Mr. Friedman, and remained everlastingly grateful to him.

When Chaya was ten years old, her father, an American citizen, managed to get Chaya and her younger brother and sister to the States. She became the little mother, with the responsibility of their care. In time, Rabbi Berman was able to send for his wife, Peshe, and the rest of the family.

Chaya had many relatives living here, whom she had not seen since she was a little girl. She was constantly on call, and there were many happy greetings. She walked again through the streets of Meah Shearim to the house where she had lived. The old Shaarei Zedek Hospital stood as a reminder of those days. She had in fact been born there.

The first time we went to the *Kosel* brought tears to Chaya's eyes, for she remembered visits to the *Kosel* from way back in her early childhood, before the War of Independence, when there was access to it under the British mandate.

Her visit brought back memories of sadness, of the hunger and suffering she and her family had experienced during the war, but it also brought many hours of joy to be back in

Eretz Yisrael.

After they left, I said to Reb Moshe, "Life certainly does have its unexpected twists and turns. Here we are, American-born, and living in Yerushalayim, and Chaya, who was born here, is living in the States."

May we all be reunited one day in Yerushalayim.

✍ ✍

When Elimelech and Mashi wrote that they were considering coming to Israel with their children to celebrate their son Shimon's bar mitzvah in Yerushalayim, Reb Moshe and I were delighted. We had already missed several grandsons' bar mitzvahs since the cardiologist had advised him not to travel to the States because it would be too much of a strain on his heart. This, their second visit, would be a special event for us, and we encouraged them to start making preparations.

Of course, I got busy also, looking for a furnished apartment to rent for them and their five children. I searched high and low for weeks, looking for one close to our house, that had all the facilities they would need for a comfortable ten-week stay. The summer rental prices were very high. Many of the families in Kiryat Mattersdorf earned much-needed funds by renting their apartments out and moving in with relatives for July and August. I finally rented a suitable place from a family I knew. They charged a fair price, and were happy to use the rental money toward their expenses for a trip to the States to visit with relatives.

Before our children were due to arrive, Reb Moshe set down some basic rules. "Kiryat Mattersdorf is almost a town in itself now, with heavy traffic — buses, cars and bicycles. We must be sure to watch the children carefully, especially the boys, when they cross the street. And we will have to be very careful that they don't lose their way when they go into town or on little trips."

I had a few do's and don't's of my own to add: All drinking water must be boiled — no drinking water from the tap. They must be sure to drink enough, as Yerushalayim has a very dry climate; we would have to be especially careful about their drinking during *chamsin* days at the end of the summer. I bought *meimiyot* — water canteens — with shoulder straps for each of the grandchildren, so they could wear them wherever they went. All fruits and vegetables would have to be scrubbed with a solution of soapy water. I would also have to make sure that they protected themselves from the strong Middle Eastern sun between the hours of 10:00 A.M. and 4:00 P.M.

We were ready and set for our most welcome guests.

Dearest Children,

You can well imagine how excited we were as we looked forward with great anticipation to the moment of Elimelech's, Mashi's, and the children's arrival. As you know, we had not seen the boys since they were very small, Esther Gitel since she was an infant, and we had never seen baby Aidel.

We decided that Papa would await them in their apartment, and I would go to the airport in the large van I had hired. I knew they would have loads of luggage, especially since I had been sending them lists and lists of what to bring to make their stay easier: paper dishes, paper towels, wax paper, toilet paper, aluminum foil (yes, still!), instant cereals, baby food, cans of salmon, and, of course, clothes and linens.

The plane arrived later than scheduled. I tried to catch a glimpse of them in the crowd, but I could not get very close, for there were crowds of people pushing and shoving. After what seemed hours, they finally appeared, tired and a little dazed. Mashi was wheeling little Aidel in the stroller, and holding Esther Gitel's hand. Elimelech and his sons were each wheeling a cart piled high with suitcases. The three boys had grown so tall I hardly recognized them.

There were excited greetings and *Shalom aleichems*, and I hugged Mashi and the girls. The boys kept at arms' length, too "grown up" to be kissed or hugged. Though the driver of the van did his utmost trying to fit all of us plus the luggage into the one van, it was impossible. I hired a taxi for the rest of the luggage, and Elimelech and Avrohom Yitzchok shared it with other passengers who were going to Yerushalayim.

It was much past midnight when we finally arrived at the apartment. I could see Papa standing on the balcony watching for us, anxiously, because of the long delay.

Elimelech and the boys lugged up the twelve heavy suitcases and the hand luggage. When Aaron Dovid walked into the house and put two of the suitcases down, Papa shook his hand and said warmly, "You are doing a great *chesed* helping my children with their luggage." Papa soon discovered, to his shock and amazement, that the tall, lanky, helpful "stranger" who towered over him was none other than his own "little" grandson!

When they were finally ready for bed, Papa and I left, telling them we would be there in the morning to help them get settled. As we walked to our house, Papa looked at me and said sheepishly, "Well, Ruchoma, I don't think we will have to hold their hands when they cross the street; perhaps it will be the other way around." I grasped Papa's hand as we crossed the street together.

Love, Papa and Mama

✍ ✍

It took a few days until the children were settled and got their bearings. There was a shopping center conveniently located across from their apartment, so Elimelech and the boys would pick up the groceries and fruits and vegetables on their way home from shul. Reb Moshe began studying regularly with the boys for two hours every morning, and he also started reviewing the *Haftarah* that Shimon would read on his bar mitzvah.

In the afternoons, the boys went here and there on the bus, and got acquainted with the different parts of Yerushalayim, which they began to know better than we did. They were already planning organized tours of the country for after Tisha B'Av. Esther Gitel was kept busy a good part of the day, playing with her cousins of the same age, and she was also a help keeping little Aidel busy, giving her mother a respite.

Mashi began learning how to be a good Israeli housewife and was following some of the rules I had laid down. She boiled all the water and scrubbed the fruits and vegetables dutifully, but when the children ran into the house, they made straight for the tap, and so the carefully boiled water remained in its jars. The children began to look like sabras in no time, with their tanned and freckled faces.

Dearest Children,

Elimelech, Mashi, and the children are all enjoying the experience of living in Yerushalayim and being near us. The grandchildren run in and out of our house several times a day. They're always asking me to tell them stories about Zaidie Herman and about our lives in Mir. They need the attention of a Zaidie and Bubbie, and, as you know, we are the only ones they have, since Elimelech was orphaned when he was a child. We decided that each of the grandchildren would have a turn eating *seudah shelishis* alone with us. In this way, we can give them individual loving care and attention — food for the soul as well as food for the body.

Shimon will be called up at the Isbee minyan for his bar mitzvah, and we'll have a Kiddush afterwards. We are postponing the *seudah* until right after Tisha B'Av.

Papa stops into their apartment every day on his way home from the Yeshivah, and I meet him there. Mashi caters to him, and prepares all the food she knows he likes. It is a special treat for all of us to have this time together.

I am sure you are looking forward to their return, and to hearing first-hand the many incidents they have to tell you about, which I have not included in my letters.

Love, Papa and Mama

Though the sun was still strong and bright in the deep blue sky, the heat of the summer day continued unabated, and the streets were full of children playing, nevertheless there was a tangible feeling that summer was waning. Elul would soon be here, and our children would be leaving.

Their visit had been exhilarating for all of us. The boys made strides in their learning with their grandfather, and gained much just by spending time with him every day. Shimon's bar mitzvah gave us all *nachas,* and made us very proud of him. It was a *simchah* Reb Moshe and I will always remember.

After ten weeks, the children and grandchildren had become so much a part of life in Yerushalayim, that it was hard to think that they could not settle here, at least not at this time. We continue to pray for the *geulah shelemah,* when all of our loved ones will be together with us.

✍ ✍

The visits of our children and grandchildren over the years gave Reb Moshe and me not only the opportunity to get to know all of our grandchildren, but also to become ever closer with our loving children.

Our oldest son, Yisroel Meyer, wrote the following heart-warming poem during his second visit to us. This time he came with our granddaughter, Gneshe, whom we had not seen since she was a very young child.

One morning, I noticed him busily writing. When he

finished, he said to Reb Moshe and me, "I have a present for you." It was the 12th of Elul, our wedding anniversary.

> To Papa and Mama on your 48th wedding anniversary. May you have many more healthy, happy ones. The poem consists of 48 lines:

When I thought of the idea, I was overwhelmed,
The task seemed much too great.
It certainly required a prolific writer,
A poet who is top rate.
The problem was not the lack of material,
There was no difficulty on how to start.
The task was putting feelings into words,
Which are deeply rooted in my heart.
Even of the most mediocre parents,
Children would have many pages to write,
To express their appreciation and gratitude
For their toil and many a sleepless night.
How much more difficult then is it for me,
With parents comparable to none other,
In fact, we must search the entire globe,
To find such a special father and mother.
Parents with such devotion one to the other,
Is really a rarity nowadays.
This *chinuch* without words made a deep impression,
And taught — how our children we should raise.
Our *chinuch* was always in this unusual manner,
Not by demanding or scolding did we learn.
Just by living at home and observing your actions,
Right from wrong we were able to discern.
The atmosphere you created in our home,
Was one of warmth and deep concern.
For all our needs, we were convinced,
That to you we could always turn.
Our meals were always a source of joy,
When we sat at the table all together.
We would discuss things of great importance,

And also trivial such as the weather.
The talks we had at these times and others,
Gave us great *chizzuk* and inspiration.
You showed us the beauty of the Torah life you lead,
The emptiness without it needed no explanation.
Your going to Mir was genuine *mesiras nefesh* for Torah,
Not the cliche so often used these days.
Each year you spent there was another seed planted,
For your family tree to grow and continue in your ways.
Any *middos tovos* which we may have attained,
To your credit are certainly due.
As everyone can testify that your *bein adam l'chavero,*
Has been achieved by so very few.
Let me just say, Papa and Mama,
Thank you for all you have done.
It certainly was my greatest mazal,
That to you I was born a SON!

Yisroel Meyer

From the Depths of Their Heart

WHILE LOOKING THROUGH some of my important papers, I found the letters that Yisroel Meyer and Chaya had written to us after the tragic loss of their oldest son, Lezer Yitzchok. It brought back a flood of memories of those sorrowful days, when Lezer Yitzchok suddenly became critically ill and passed away ten days later.

For us, it was a twofold suffering. Not only did we mourn the loss of our first grandson, but we also suffered for our children, Yisroel Meyer and Chaya, grieving for their oldest son.

Rabbi Maurice Lamm, in his book *The Jewish Way in Death and Mourning,* describes death in the following manner: "Death is a night that lies between two days — the day of life on earth and the day of eternal life in the world to come." He goes on to say that the night of death is an interlude, with the darkness inevitably proceeding to dawn. The deceased is going from a world of darkness into eternal light.

But what about the living who remain with conflicting emotions, as Rabbi Lamm states: "Bewilderment, agony, numbness, fear, and pain." How does one cope when tragedy strikes? Thank Hashem, through the entire ordeal our children proved what it meant to live a life of Torah. Yisroel Meyer and Chaya grew spiritually closer to Hashem. In one of Yisroel Meyer's letters, soon after Lezer Yitzchok's passing, he wrote how thankful he was to Hashem that they were given a reprieve of ten days to do *teshuvah, tefillah* and *tzedakah* before He took Lezer Yitzchok's *neshamah* to *Gan Eden.* Chaya wrote the following heartfelt tribute to her son and asked me to distribute it among our friends and relatives:

AN INVITATION TO A MITZVAH

During the coming month of Kislev, our son, Eliezer Yitzchok Isaac, *zt"l,* was destined to be led to his *chuppah* with great rejoicing, to greet his *kallah.* Yes, twenty-three years had passed since the joyous day of his birth, and, at last, the dream of parents to walk their child down the aisle to his *chuppah* was about to become a reality.

A person plans, but Hashem had other plans for our son, Eliezer Yitzchok Isaac, *zt"l.* Instead of walking him to his *chuppah,* we walked him to his *kevurah.* We made a covering for his body, but Hashem made a *chuppah* for his *neshamah.* His *chuppah* was in Heaven, and the good angels created by his good deeds and his Torah learning accompanied him. Hashem sanctified his *neshamah,* and our son sanctified his *kallah*: the Torah he had learned on earth.

His loved ones here can participate in sending him presents all the way to Heaven by:

Saying Amen with *kavanah.*
Reciting *Tehillim* in memory of his soul.
Learning extra Torah for his sake.
Giving *tzedakah* for his sake.
Avoiding falsehoods, as he was careful to do.
Not talking during prayers, especially during *chazaras ha-shatz.*

Not speaking *lashon ha-ra.*

If all the above are done with the thought of increasing our son's merit in Heaven, they would be very precious wedding gifts indeed. Lezer Yitzchok's "Thank you" would be in the form of his being an intermediary on your behalf.

I wrote the following to Yisroel Meyer and Chaya:

A tribute to my dear grandson,
Eliezer Yitzchok Isaac Shain, *zt"l*
niftar on the 28th day of Tishrei, 5741

A child was born in holiness,
Fragrant and pure.
The Earth sang songs of gladness,
And the trees stretched their leafy arms to Heaven
With thankfulness for this magnificent gift.
He grew from child, to youth, to man,
Strong in body and soul.
He wore the crown of Torah proudly,
And walked in the ways of his great fathers.
Suddenly, he was struck down.
For ten days the earth prayed, the trees pleaded,
We need him here.
Heaven issued her decree.
He is wanted up Above.
He was yours for twenty-three years.
His holy soul was welcomed by the angels,
Fragrant and pure.
Heaven sings hymns of gladness,
And the skies shine down on earth,
With thankfulness for this magnificent gift.

✍ ✍

Dearest Children,

After going through some of the letters that Yisroel

and Chaya wrote after Lezer Yitzchok passed away, I had a great desire to visit his *kever* on Har Hazeisim. [Our grandson was brought here for burial, where he is buried near a relative after whom he was named.] However, since it was difficult to get transportation, and I had no one to go with, I had to postpone it. The next morning I received a call from the family of a close friend who had recently passed away. They would be going to Har Hazeisim for her *sheloshim*, they explained, and if I wanted to come along they had room for me.

While approaching Har Hazeisim, I hoped that my friend's grave would be someplace in the vicinity of Lezer Yitzchok's, so I could visit him, also. However, I did not really hold out too much hope, as the cemetery is spread over a vast mountainside. As we drew closer, though, the minibus seemed to be driving in the direction of his grave, and I was astonished when we finally reached the top of the mountain and made our way to my friend's grave, to find that it was just two graves away from Lezer Yitzchok's. After the prayers, I asked the people to come over to my grandson's grave to say prayers as well, and my heartfelt ones mingled with theirs.

We cannot underestimate the continued closeness we have with our loved ones "Upstairs." Papa said, "The *tzaddikim* are fully alive only in the other world." And I feel that Lezer Yitzchok, from the other world, read my thoughts and knew how much I wanted to visit his *kever*.

I don't think I ever wrote this to you, but a few days after the funeral, Papa told me the following: "When Lezer Yitzchok's coffin was brought to Yerushalayim, I went over to him and asked him, among other things, to be a *melitz yosher* for a *refuah shelemah* for me, because of the great pain I was having in my leg. Since then there has been tremendous improvement."

Though Lezer Yitzchok was so young, only twenty-three when he passed away, he accomplished much in his lifetime. You may know that after his death, Yisroel Meyer found among his possessions a lot of his writings on Torah.

May we live to see the *geulah shelemah* and *techiyas ha-meisim*, when our loved ones will return to us.

Love, Papa and Mama

Dearest Papa and Mama,

I want to share with you a very unusual incident.

Several months ago, Raphael Yitzchok dreamt that he was the *ba'al koreh* in the Yeshivah and was reading *parashas Chukas* from the Torah. He read the word *zos* and when he looked for the following word, *chukas*, it was missing. So another *sefer Torah* was taken out, and this time it was opened to another reading, *parashas Ki Sisa*. When he awoke, Raphael Yitzchok tried to interpret the dream, but none of his interpretations seemed to fit.

As I said, he dreamt this several months ago. Last Friday, Rabbi Trenk asked Raphael Yitzchok if he would read from the Torah on Shabbos, not only the weekly *parashah*, but also *parashas Parah*, for the *ba'al koreh* would be away. All of a sudden it dawned on Raphael Yitzchok that this might fit into his dream, for this Shabbos the reading was *Ki Sisa*, and the reading of *parashas Parah* is from *parashas Chukas*. The connection to his dream seemed obvious, so he decided to check the *sefer Torah* from which he would be reading.

Lo and behold! He found a word in *parashas Chukas* that had a faulty *mem* — with part of the letter missing. He then checked a second *sefer Torah*, and again in *parashas Chukas* he found that the letter *yud* was faulty. He then checked the *sefer Torah* from which he would be reading the *parashah, Ki Sisa*, but found that to be kosher.

It was a great *zechus* for Raphael Yitzchok that through his dream, the reading of *parashas Parah*, which is a Torah commandment, was done from a kosher *sefer Torah*. What do you think of that?

All my love, Yehudis

Dearest Raphael Yitzchok and Yehudis,

Your dream, Raphael Yitzchok, reminded me of something my father asked me on one of my visits to Yerushalayim, when he was living here: "Ruchoma, do you realize that a *sefer Torah* is alive?"

Then he went on to tell me that one Wednesday night he could not fall asleep, so he decided to review the weekly Torah reading in his *sefer Torah.* Doing so, he noticed that one of the letters was faulty. Had this been discovered on Shabbos, he would not have been able to complete the reading. Of course, he immediately brought it to his *sofer* and asked him to repair it in time for Shabbos, as this was the *sefer Torah* that he had always read from since he was a young man. We can see from what Zaidie told me, and from your dream, that Torah is indeed *Toras chaim* — a living Torah.

Don't forget that we have always been "dreamers," and have certainly had some very remarkable dreams with special messages. You know that my mother's dream, which my father interpreted, saved my brother, Nochum Dovid, from the Hebron massacre, when he was studying in the Hebron Yeshivah as a young man.

Love, Papa and Mama

[Author's note: In my book *"All for the Boss"*, I wrote about my mother's dream on p. 101, and my father's dream on p. 390.]

✍ ✍

Our granddaughter Gneshe Basheva was born prematurely at the end of the sixth month, and weighed 400 grams (less than a pound). She was given but a few minutes to live but, as Raphael Yitzchok wrote, she fought a valiant battle and lived for almost twenty-eight days, much to the astonishment of the doctors and nurses who attended her.

Raphael Yitzchok wrote the following letter to us shortly after she passed away. His words gave us the *chizzuk* we needed.

Dearest Papa and Mama,

Hashem has given and Hashem has taken away; blessed be the Name of Hashem" [*Iyov* 1:21].

We knew all along that the baby's chances for survival were slim, yet, as the days passed and she fought so gallantly and with such fierce determination, we began to hope against hope that somehow she would pull through.

We visited her in the hospital many times, and each time we saw different expressions on her tiny, sculptured face: anger, hurt, determination, and towards the end, a sort of detachment and peace.

There is a terrible ache in our hearts, for over the last twenty-seven days we became very attached to her, and she crept deeply into our hearts. But we know that her holy *neshamah* will find its rest in a special place in *Gan Eden.*

In Koheles 7:2, it says: "Engrave it into your heart."

We must not allow this experience to be forgotten, but we must learn the true meaning of caring and loving others. We must fill our hearts with the significance of life. We must replace the void in our lives with more *avodas Hashem* and more *yiras chet.*

Our Torah learning must reach new heights, and thereby, as we are told in *Yeshayahu* 25:8, Hashem will wipe our tears away.

She passed away on Friday night at 10:00 P.M., just a few hours after the yahrtzeit of her great-grandmother Gneshe, after whom she was named. May her *neshamah* merit to be in the same exalted place as Bubbie Gneshe's.

Gneshe Basheva Shain, our beloved daughter — "*Tzeischem b'shalom.*"

Raphael Yitzchok

"Fringe" Benefits

WHEN I LEARNED the wonderful news that my granddaughter Aidel, Yisroel Meyer and Chaya's daughter, was engaged, I realized that for this *simchah* I would have to travel back to the States. Reb Moshe was not allowed to travel because of his heart condition, but he and our children insisted that I go. "We're certain that all the relatives will take good care of Papa," the children reassured me. And Reb Moshe was adamant too: "Just because *I* can't go, that's no reason for *you* to disappoint Aidel and our children."

And so I went, and shared the great joy and excitement of being at my granddaughter's wedding. It was a wonderful experience and a great privilege, but it was good to come home to Reb Moshe and Yerushalayim.

Dearest Children,

Thank Hashem, I arrived home safely. I am very tired, but

happy to be back with Papa in Yerushalayim. He was outside in the street waiting for me when the taxi pulled up in front of our building. We did not need words to express our lonesomeness for each other. Though Papa was wined and dined by our relatives while I was away, he was very relieved to have me home with him again.

Although we are grateful for all *simchahs*, may Hashem provide us with the *simchahs* of our children and grandchildren in Yerushalayim, so that both Papa and I can attend them together.

In all my excitement over coming for Aidel's wedding, I forgot to tell you about the experience I had as I was *leaving* Yerushalayim. I had ordered a taxi to the airport for 4:00 A.M., and I was concerned about how to get my luggage down to the street at that hour. Of course I did not want Papa to strain himself because of his heart condition, but I knew I couldn't lug the suitcases down easily by myself.

The night before I left, I said goodbye to Uncle Chaim and Aunt Bessie, and mentioned what time I would be leaving the house. I did not get too much sleep that night, as you can imagine, and at 3:45 A.M., I said to Papa, "We'll take one valise at a time, slowly, and slide it down the stairs to the elevator. We'll manage somehow."

The predawn quiet was all-encompassing. "I hope we don't wake any of the neighbors," I said, lowering my voice to a whisper as I went to unlock the front door. I opened the door, gasped, and jumped back in fright.

There in the darkness, standing quietly outside our door was — Uncle Chaim! "Reb Chaim," I cried, "what are you doing here so early?"

"Sh-h-h, the neighbors are sleeping," he replied. "Ruchoma, I came to take your suitcases down to the street, because I did not want Reb Moshe to strain himself," he added matter-of-factly.

He then took one suitcase down and came up for the other, and in no time we were waiting for the taxi. I was the last one to be picked up, as there were already six passengers sitting in the taxi. The driver jumped out to load my luggage, and suddenly froze as he caught sight of Uncle Chaim, with his *tefillin* on his head, his several layers of *taleisim* and his many pairs of *tzitzis,* all the fringes swaying in the morning breeze.*

Without uttering a word, the driver quickly grabbed my suitcases and strapped them to the luggage rack on the roof of the taxi. In the meantime, the passengers stared with a mixture of wonder and reverence at the awesome figure of Uncle Chaim in the early dawn. I climbed into the taxi and with Papa's and Uncle Chaim's blessings of "*Tzeischem l'shalom*" ringing in my ears, the taxi sped off.

The passengers sat as if thunderstruck, and there was complete, able-to-hear-a-pin-drop silence during the entire ride to the airport, which the driver made in record time. Surprisingly, no one questioned me at all. Perhaps they thought that I, too, had come from another planet.

We can learn from Uncle Chaim how *chesed* should be done.

Love, Papa and Mama

✍ ✍

About a year after my visit to the States, we received yet another "fringe benefit."

Dearest Children,

The wonderful news that Papa and I have become GREAT

*For reasons known only to himself, my brother-in-law Rabbi Scheinberg has for years followed an unusual custom: He wears many pairs of *tzitzis* and *taleisim,* and he also wears his *tefillin* all day. We, and all who know him, have grown so accustomed to seeing him dressed in this manner, that we cannot imagine the impact his startling appearance makes on those who see him for the first time.

GRANDPARENTS certainly thrilled us. Thank Hashem, this is our fourth generation. I have heard that those who are blessed to live to see a fifth generation are assured of a place in *olam ha-ba.* But I imagine that they have to have some good deeds to their credit also, to get up there.

Papa and I will have to wait about twenty years or so for Dovid and Aidel's son to get married and, G-d willing, have a baby. By that time, we will be very old. May Hashem give us long and healthy years to live to that day.

It is hard to believe that Yisroel Meyer and Chaya are grandparents, and that Aidel is a mother — I recall so vividly the day that she was born. Chaya had gone into labor on December 31, the last day of the secular year. Since they lived quite a distance from the hospital, they came to stay with us to make sure they would get there on time. When we arrived at the hospital, the doctor and nurses greeted Chaya with the exciting news that her baby might be the "lucky"one to be the first baby born in the new year! Of course, the newspapers would be alerted and they would send reporters to take photos and write up the story. Knowing how Chaya shies away from attention, she went into a panic and prayed that she should not be subjected to all the hullabaloo. Hashem answered her prayers, and another woman gave birth just after midnight, a few minutes before Chaya did.

Our heartfelt mazal tov to the Zaidie and Bubbie, to the Tatty and Mommy, and to the uncles and aunts. May our great-grandson follow in the footsteps of his great-great grandparents and bring pride to our family and to *klal Yisrael.*

Love,
"Elter Zaidie and Elter Bubbie"

Heartfelt Days

WHEN REB MOSHE and I left for the little hotel where we had been spending Pesach the past few years, we had no premonition that our lives were about to undergo yet another metamorphosis.

The letters that I wrote to our children tell it all: the pain and heartache we faced, the strength and stamina we found to cope with them, the care and devotion of our relatives and friends, and above all, the insight that Hashem in His Infinite Mercy was guiding us through this difficult period in our lives.

Dearest Children,

My telephone call told you only a little about what occurred, but in this letter I shall try to give you the details as they happened.

The Seder was spiritually uplifting, and Papa's active

participation gave much pleasure to the other guests at our table. The food was plentiful and delicious. On the first day of *Chol Ha-Mo'ed,* Papa and I were basking in the sun on the porch adjoining our room, which had a breathtaking panoramic view of Yerushalayim. I felt a deep sense of contentment. The *erev Pesach* rush was over, and now it felt like a holiday. Papa felt well, and we were enjoying the excellent service and company.

When Papa slipped and fell, on the second morning of *Chol Ha-Mo'ed,* I had no inkling that it was anything more than a slight bruise, as he was able to walk afterwards without too much pain. It was only later that night, when he suddenly found he could not stand or walk, that I summoned a doctor, who sent us to Hadassah Hospital's emergency room.

After what seemed endless hours of waiting our turn, Papa was finally examined and it was discovered that he had a fracture of the neck of the femur (the upper thigh bone). The orthopedic surgeon advised immediate surgery; however, because of Papa's rare heart condition, I suggested that first, a cardiologist should examine him and give us his opinion about the surgery. But by the time the cardiologist reached Papa, he had developed pneumonia, and the surgery had to be postponed.

I will keep you informed, and just keep up your prayers for Papa's *refuah shelemah.*

Love, Papa and Mama

Yisroel Meyer and Raphael Yitzchok flew in at a moment's notice when Reb Moshe's condition became critical, and their visit was like an emotional vitamin injection for me, giving me renewed vigor and strength throughout the difficult ordeal. Then Mashi came two weeks later, and her presence with Reb Moshe and at my side gave me the added physical stamina I needed to keep going. Before she left, she organized a twenty-four-hour shift among our relatives and friends, so that someone would be near Reb Moshe all the time, and I would be able to get some rest. I had been spending many hours in the hospital, as I did not want him to be left alone. It was indeed a great strain on me. With Mashi's arrangement, I still spent a lot of time with him, but I got the chance to go home to rest up and recoup my energy.

I have no doubt that his partial recovery was due to having our loving children near him. All of them, wives and husbands, wanted to be here with us; but we felt the presence of those who could not be here, and could hear their heartfelt prayers from afar.

Thank Hashem, Reb Moshe's condition improved after surgery, and we prayed that his health would continue to improve.

✍ ✍

Dearest Children,

The doctors in Hadassah have been discussing with me the idea of transferring Papa to a geriatric convalescent hospital, where he would receive physiotherapy and all the special care he needs to get him back on his feet. I think it is a good idea, for I don't see that anything more can be done for him at Hadassah after these eight weeks.

I had a humorous experience when I entered Papa's room a little before seven this morning. Last night, none of the "regulars" was available for the midnight to 7:00 A.M. shift, so I hired a young man from a *bikkur cholim* organization. The young man greeted me this morning quite perplexed. He explained that whenever Papa awoke during the night, he kept asking him for something, but he could not understand what it was that Papa wanted. He had questioned him with great patience over and over again, in both Hebrew and Yiddish, trying to understand what he meant, but the young man could not grasp what Papa wanted. Since he does not speak English, he had called some of the night nurses who understood English, to see if they could discern what it was that Papa was saying, but they too were mystified and said that they had never heard the word before.

"What word was it?" I asked curiously.

"Well, it sounded something like 'Rokoma'," the bewildered young man told me. At that moment Papa opened his eyes and saw me. "Racoma," he said, "I've been waiting for you."

The young man burst out laughing. The mystery was solved. I explained that "Racoma," my English name, comes from the Hebrew "Ruchoma."

Papa feels a little better, *baruch Hashem.* Keep up your prayers.

Love, Papa and Mama

✍ ✍

Dearest Children,

I am writing to you from the geriatric hospital, where Papa was transferred yesterday. I am hoping that it will only be a temporary stay, and that he'll be home very soon. I can hardly wait. My thoughts are constantly with him, even when I am home.

Although Papa will be getting intensive physiotherapy, his condition is complicated because of the Parkinson's Disease, which makes his muscles stiff. I am waiting for the moment he is out of the wheelchair and able to walk with a walker.

May Hashem answer our prayers.

Love, Papa and Mama

Dearest Children,

Papa awaits my arrival every morning. When I rush into his room, I am greeted by his welcoming smile, which is ample reward for my hurried morning preparations. The weather is lovely, so I usually wheel Papa out to the patio, where I read your letters to him, show him photos of our grandchildren, keep him updated on tidbits of life in our Kiryah, and tell him generally about what is going on in the world.

The doctors and nurses are very supportive and have all grown very fond of Papa. And no wonder! One of the nurses said to me, "There are two kinds of problematic patients: one is the patient who never stops complaining and drives us all crazy; and the other is like Rabbi Shain, who hardly ever complains, so that we never know if anything is bothering him." However, since I spend so much time with Papa, I am aware if there is any change in his condition, and they depend upon me to alert them.

The physiotherapist has not had too much success with getting Papa to stand up, but I still have high hopes that he will eventually get back on his feet, literally and figuratively, and be home soon.

Love, Papa and Mama

✍ ✍

As the days went by, I began to feel that I was part of the staff in the geriatric ward. I tried to be of help to the other patients, especially those in Reb Moshe's room who had grown to depend upon me. There were four other beds in his room; one patient was long-term, and the remaining three beds were occupied on and off. I also formed close friendships with the families of the other patients, as we faced many similar problems.

One day, an elderly man was wheeled into Reb Moshe's room with a case of pneumonia. His daughter, who accompanied him, whispered to me that her father was 102 years old! After a short while, I readily understood the secret of his longevity. With his indomitable spirit, he kept things very lively, refusing to be strapped into the wheelchair, and thumbing his nose at the food if it did not appeal to him. The nurses sighed in relief when he was discharged, but I missed him, as I had admired the remarkable character of this man so advanced in age.

I had a rewarding experience with one of the woman patients on the ward. She had suffered a major stroke several weeks before, and ever since had been oblivious to her surroundings. Every day when I passed her sitting in the wheelchair, I greeted her with a bright and cheery "Good morning," and patted her gently. She did not respond or show any indication that she heard me, but just stared blankly into space.

Then one day when I passed and gave her my usual greeting, she suddenly gave me a lop-sided smile of recognition. There was a gasp of astonishment from all those who were nearby.

This brought into sharp focus another experience I had many years before when Reb Moshe and I first came to Yerushalayim. A friend of ours had given us a plant which I became very attached to. I gave it special care, and it grew until its green leaves covered half of our window.

One day when I had been out of the house for many hours, I returned to find that the leaves of the plant had fallen off and were strewn on the floor. I looked with dismay at the bare stalks of what had been my beautiful plant. Reb Moshe found me in tears, and shared my consternation, knowing what the plant had meant to me.

Just then a neighbor walked in, and I pointed at the plant and said, "Look what happened to my beautiful plant — I just haven't the heart to throw it out." "Don't!" she exclaimed. "I've known plants that have become rejuvenated. Just keep watering it, touch it, and talk to it." I did not hold out any hope of it coming back to life, but, as I said to Reb Moshe, "What do I have to lose?"

Of course, I made sure that I was alone when I fussed over the dried-out plant, as people might have thought I wasn't normal! For weeks and weeks, the plant remained bare, as I spoke to it and patted its spindly stalks, and I became disheartened, but something inside urged me to keep on. One day in early spring, what did I discover but a single, tiny leaf sprouting from the dry stalk, and then another emerged, and another, until the plant once again covered half of our window with its flourishing green leaves.

This taught me a valuable lesson which I did not forget. If a withered plant could return to full bloom by means of loving care and patient attention, why not a human being?

Dearest Children,

Although our lives have undergone a drastic change in the four months since Papa had his accident, my life has not lacked moving and interesting moments. Today, for instance, after helping Papa with his dinner, I went over to a patient who was struggling with her meal. I finally spoon-fed her, and wiped her clean. Then another patient beckoned to me to wheel her into her room for a nap. When I returned to the dining room, a woman who had been visiting a newly-arrived patient remarked, "You certainly deserve credit as a volunteer, for the devoted care you give these elderly patients. And that rabbi over there "— her voice rose to a higher pitch, as she pointed to Papa — "certainly gets a giant share of your attention." She was quite surprised when I informed her that "that rabbi" was my beloved husband!

You know, children, now I understand for the first time the significance of the phrase "second childhood." Some of the patients whom I have been helping become very annoyed if I am not always at their beck and call. But who can blame them? They are in an infantile situation, dependent and helpless, and revert to infantile patterns of behavior. The nurses do try to give each patient attention, but they are understaffed and harried, so they appreciate any assistance I can give them.

Papa's condition remains stable, Thank Hashem, but I am praying for the miracle of his walking again. Time passes, and the physiotherapist has not given me much encouragement, but I have not given up hope.

Love, Papa and Mama

In my book *Reaching the Stars*, I included a poem, "What Do You See, Nurse?" (pp. 208-209) from a patient in an old-age home, in which she expresses her feelings about the seemingly callous attitude of the nurses. Afterwards I received a letter from a reader with the following poem, in which a nurse answers the patient. I think it is very appropriate to add it here.

Nurses' Answers to Old Patients

What do we see, you ask, what do we see?
Yes, what are we thinking when looking at thee?
We may seem to be hard, when we hurry and fuss,
But there are many of you, and too few of us.
We would like more time to sit by you and talk,
To bathe you and feed you and help you to walk;
To hear of your lives, and the things you have done,
Your childhood, your husband, your daughter, your son.
But time is against us, there's too much to do,
Patients too many — nurses too few.
We grieve when we see you, so sad and alone,
With nobody near you, no friends of your own.
We feel all your pain, and know of your fear,
That nobody cares, now your end is so near.
But nurses are people with feelings as well,
And when we're together, you'll often hear tell
Of the dearest old gran in the very end bed,
And the lovely old dad, and the things that he said.
We speak with compassion and love, and feel sad,
When we think of your lives, and the joys that you've had.
When the time has arrived for you to depart,
You leave us behind with an ache in our heart.
When you sleep the long sleep, no more worry or care,
There are other old people, and we must be there.

So please understand, if we hurry and fuss,
There are many of you, and so few of us.

✍ ✍

Dearest Children,

Despite the fact that Papa has been receiving excellent medical care, he developed an infection and was given strong doses of antibiotics intravenously. I refused to leave him at the beginning and remained at his bedside for eighteen hours straight. As I was saying *Tehillim* in the middle of the night, in walked one of the doctors to examine him. I asked the doctor if there was any improvement in Papa's condition, and he answered gently, "Keep up your prayers — they surely help."

It is truly a doctor of caliber who not only prescribes medication, but also understands the emotional and spiritual needs of his patients and the family. Papa began showing marked improvement, *baruch Hashem,* and no longer needs the IV.

I have begun to accept the fact that for the foreseeable future Papa cannot return home. He needs constant convalescent care which he could not possibly receive at home. I know that Papa accepts the situation too, although we have never discussed it outright.

I live one day at a time, spending much of the day with Papa, keeping his spirits up and mine also. I know Hashem watches over us and will give me the strength to continue to help Papa.

Love, Papa and Mama

✍ ✍

Ten weeks had passed since Reb Moshe was admitted to the convalescent home — ten weeks, and for me a lifetime. Every day when I left the hospital and took the bus home, it seemed I was stepping into another world, a world where birds still chirped, teenagers strolled, people laughed, and talked, and shopped, where little children played and shouted, and where there was the sound of music.

But I didn't feel part of this bright and busy, noisy world. My world had become centered among the elderly patients: those who sat in their wheelchairs with blank faces, devoid of expression; those whose eyes were filled with despair, hopelessness, lost dreams, and lives waning; those who drooled, overturned their cups, and were forever groping for something they could not reach; and those whose heads were bent over, who were too tired and discouraged to keep them up. I had also touched death several times. When I walked into the ward in the early morning and found a bed bare, stripped of linens, I knew that death had visited that night.

This had become my world, and in it — my beloved Reb Moshe, whose hand I clasped, who always gave me a smile to show that he knew I was near, and who lived every day with dignity.

✍ ✍

Dearest Children,

Papa has developed pneumonia once again, as he has very little resistance to infection. Though the doctor is concerned, he comforted me, saying, "Rabbi Shain has pulled through several infections, and I hope he will make it once more."

Chana is remaining with Papa for Shabbos, to give me a chance to regain my strength. I hope to return right after *Havdalah.*

Papa's seventy-ninth birthday will be this coming Monday. May Hashem continue to answer our prayers for his *refuah shelemah,* and may he have many more HEALTHY years.

Love, Papa and Mama

P.S. Chana copied this poem from a book that she was

reading. She certainly understood that it was just what I needed at this time.

I know not by what methods rare,
But this I know — God answers prayer.
I know not when He sends the word,
That tells us fervent prayer is heard.
I know it cometh — soon or late;
Therefore, we need to pray and wait.
I know not if the blessing sought,
Will come in just the way I thought.
I leave my prayers with Him alone,
Whose Will is wiser than my own.

Anonymous

Farewell

Dearest Children,

Today was the last day of the *shivah* period for Papa, and as is the custom in Yerushalayim, I went with a large minyan of relatives and friends to his *kever* on Har Hazeisim.

As the cars wended their way through the narrow, winding streets of the Old City, I had to tell myself over and over again that Papa had passed away. The day was very warm, the sky an azure blue, with an occasional stray cloud floating above. Papa is up there, looking down, I thought, and my heart cried within me.

As we lifted our voices in prayer for Papa's *neshamah,* a single tree very close to his grave bent her leafy boughs and shielded us from the blazing sun. The little tin marker with Papa's name on it was dug into the fresh brown earth. It stared at me forlornly, as if sharing my sorrow. The *matzevah* will be ready in time for the *sheloshim.*

As I stood looking out at the Temple Mount in the distance, I recalled the day Aunt Bessie and I bought the plots, about fifteen years ago. I had come home elated with the exciting news. "Moshe," I said, "we have prime plots on Har Hazeisim, right near Mama and Zaidie and Bubbie Andron. They are very special and face the *Makom Ha-Mikdash.*" Papa did not fully share my enthusiasm, as he always shied away from any talk of death. "Moshe," I consoled him, noting the expression on his face, "when the *geulah* comes, we can pitch a tent on our plots, and we'll be in the front row, watching all the action that will be going on in the *Beis Ha-Mikdash.*" This had brought a bright smile from Papa.

Now I thought sadly: We won't be pitching that tent together.

Children, although we have been in close touch by telephone, and I've told you a lot about the past days, there are other experiences that I want to share with you in writing.

I was with Papa late Saturday night, and since his condition was stable, both the doctor and the nurse urged me to go home and get some rest. I left Ephraim Shraga to spend the night with Papa, telling him, "Be sure to sit right near Zaidie. I'll come first thing in the morning, so you won't miss the davening or the morning session in yeshivah."

Once I got home, I was very uneasy somehow and could not fall asleep, so when Hemla and Chana knocked at my door at 3:30 A.M. (after the hospital had phoned them), I jumped out of bed and, with shaking hands, unlocked the door. One look at their faces told me the news. Though I knew Papa had been very ill, I had not allowed thoughts of death to penetrate. Now I was faced with it. My first reaction was: I accept. "*Baruch Dayan Ha-Emes.*"

How fortunate we are that even in our most difficult times, we feel the closeness of Hashem and can accept His decree. The taxi sped through the dark, quiet streets on the way to the hospital, and we were all silent. My mind was in turmoil, almost afraid to face reality. Ephraim Shraga, still in shock, awaited me, and the nurses burst into tears when they saw me.

Ephraim Shraga told me that he had been sitting right next

to the bed, when suddenly Papa's usual labored breathing became softer, as if in a deep sleep, and his holy *neshamah* left him.

Chana had spent the last Shabbos with Papa, and told me about Simcha Kaufman's visit that day. As you know, Simcha visited Papa every Shabbos, since he lived within walking distance of the geriatric hospital. On that Shabbos, a number of hours before Papa passed away, Simcha came and greeted him with his usual "*Gut Shabbos.*" Papa had spoken very little in the past few days, and did not respond to Simcha's greeting. But Simcha persisted, repeating over and over again, "*Gut Shabbos.*" Then, as if awakening from a deep slumber, Papa had opened his eyes and said clearly, "*Gut Shabbos.*" There was finality in his words, which were his last. It comforted me to know that Papa's life ended on a note of *menuchah.*

After Papa's death, Simcha told me that a month before, when he was visiting on a Shabbos afternoon, a strange thing happened. Papa had suddenly said in Yiddish (as Simcha does not understand English), "Simcha, *men hot mir ongezogt, az ich darf zich peklen* — I was told that I have to start packing." Simcha did not tell me about it at the time, realizing how I would have felt. It seems Papa had some forewarning that his life was drawing to a close.

I also had a strange experience a few weeks before Papa passed away. I used to help him put on his *tefillin* every morning, as it was difficult for him to manage them alone. One morning, as I was about to help him, he whispered, "Not now, Racoma, the *Shechinah* is here." I waited, trembling, not knowing what to do. A little while later, he said to me, "I'm ready now." I recalled reading that the Divine Presence visits a sick person, as we learn from *Bereshis,* when Avraham *Avinu* was visited by the *Shechinah* after he was circumcised, and that pacified me.

Now I want to fill you in on the details of the funeral: A car with a loudspeaker drove through many sections of Yerushalayim announcing the time and place of the funeral, which set out from Yeshivah Torah Ore, where Papa spent many years learning Torah. Also, large placards with information about the funeral and the *shivah* were posted in different areas throughout the city.

The funeral was a very large one, with standing-room-only in the Yeshivah, and many people waiting outside. Uncle Chaim made a moving *hesped,* as did Reb Moshe Aaron. I sat through the eulogies, telling myself, "It's Papa's funeral," but not really absorbing it.

It was only after I returned home and sat down to *shivah,* that the full realization of Papa's death struck me. A well of tears flooded me and a great loneliness enveloped me, and I prayed to Hashem to give me the strength to endure.

I know how much you wanted to be with me during the funeral and *shivah,* and it would have been consoling to all of us, but you know that I felt your nearness throughout the ordeal.

I'm very tired now, so I'll continue in my next letter.

Love, *Mama*

P.S. I was so used to signing "Papa and Mama" that I almost did it now, and then I caught myself.

✍ ✍

Hundreds of people came to pay condolence visits, and each one spoke about Reb Moshe's outstanding *middos,* as well as his greatness in Torah. Among those who came was the head of the geriatric hospital. "Mrs. Shain," he told me, "one never knows. Here you were always worried about Rabbi Shain's heart condition, and ultimately he passed away from pneumonia."

Reb Moshe had a heart condition that had never been properly diagnosed in the United States. We were under the impression that his condition probably stemmed from the rheumatic fever he had as a child, which had left him with a heart murmur. It was only after we had been in Yerushalayim for two years, and his heart acted up, that it was discovered that he had a congenital heart condition that is usually fatal in infancy or early childhood. In fact, an article on the subject was published in an international medical journal in March 1984, which stated that Reb Moshe was the only known person surviving his heart condition at the age of seventy-three.

This got me thinking: What *zechus* did he and I have, that we merited fifty-six rewarding years together, and he lived until the age of seventy-nine?

My thoughts went back to the days when I was a young teenager, and Reb Boruch Ber Leibowitz, the *Rosh Yeshivah* of Kaminetz, was staying with us, one of the honored guests in our house. One rainy day, when he had to go out, his galoshes were nowhere to be found. Finally, after much searching high and low, I crept under a deep cupboard and fished them out. Reb Boruch Ber, very pleased, exclaimed, "May you get your true *zivug* (marital match)."

At a later time, when he was leaving the United States to return to Kaminetz, hundreds of people came to our home to receive his blessing. My father pushed me through the throngs, into the back room where Reb Boruch Ber was seated, so I could get one too. Again Reb Boruch Ber gave me the identical blessing: "May you get your true *zivug.*" At that time, young as I was, his blessing did not make a deep impression upon me.

Now, looking back, I realize that when a *gadol,* a great man such as Reb Boruch Ber, gives such a blessing, it meant that Reb Moshe, my true *zivug,* and I would be married for many years. I think that this goes all the way back to what my father told my sister Esther when she was a little girl: "We've 'cornered the market' of the great mitzvah of *hachnasas orchim,* and all the dividends that we shall earn from this hospitality will remain with our family for ever and ever."

Reb Boruch Ber was our *ore'ach*, one of our many guests, and his blessing was one of the dividends...

Dearest Children,

Selichos prayers have begun, and since the Isbee minyan is just a half-floor down from me, I attend each morning at 6:00 A.M. It is very moving to see how many young school children come also, even though the services start at such an early hour.

These last days of the month of Elul remind me that soon after we were married, Papa said to me, "Elul is a special month for me. First of all, of course, it is the prelude to Rosh Hashanah, when we all prepare ourselves for the Day of Judgment, a time of spiritual growth. But for me, it holds an added reward because I was born on the sixteenth of Elul, and we were married on the twelfth — two very important landmarks." It gives me consolation to think that Papa's death on the fifteenth of Elul, one day before his birthday and three days after our anniversary, all in a period of five days, was another landmark for him, as he passed into his special place in Heaven. May his holy soul rest in eternal peace!

Every morning in my prayers, I recite *pesukei d'zimra,* but it was only yesterday that the following words took on a very special meaning: "Hashem watches over strangers, and causes the orphan and widow to endure."

Let me tell you how He is watching over this widow. I had to take care of some technicalities regarding my changed status, and I was advised to go to a certain office on the second floor of the National Insurance Institute between the hours of 8:00 A.M. and 12:00 noon. It was a blazing *chamsin* morning when I boarded the bus to my destination. I arrived a little before 10:00, and since the elevators were not working properly, I trudged up the two steep flights of stairs. The waiting room was crowded with people, and I hoped that my turn would come before noon, when the doors would close, and those remaining were usually told, "Come back tomorrow."

I found a seat, took out my *Tehillim,* and became engrossed in saying the Psalms for the day. When I looked up a while later, I noticed that quite a few more people had entered the waiting room, and each one was holding a little green slip. "What is that slip?" I asked the woman who had walked in last. "That's my number. Haven't you got one?" she asked me. "No," I answered. "I didn't realize that I needed a number." "Well, you'd better go down to the information desk and get one — otherwise you won't be called in," she advised. "And what is your number?" I asked, my heart sinking at this new problem. She looked at her slip and said, "Number 68."

I rushed down the two flights of stairs, hurried to the information desk, and quickly said, "Please give me a number," explaining to the clerk which office I needed it for. She handed me a green slip with the number 69. As I walked away from her booth, I noticed a woman dash over, throw her little crumpled green slip on the desk, and say something very excitedly. I could not grasp exactly what she said, but I assumed that she had become exasperated at having to wait so long for her turn, and had decided to go home.

The clerk called out to me, "*Geveret, Geveret,* come over here." I returned to her desk, and she said, "Give me back the ticket I gave you, and take this one." I unfolded the creased little ticket, and saw that the number was 49. I hurried up the stairs once again, and the woman whom I had questioned before asked me what number I got. When I showed her my number, she looked at me in surprise and asked, "How did you get this number?" "The clerk gave it to me," I said simply. She shook her heard in wonder. I had just sat down, when the secretary came out of her office and called out, "Number 49."

Not only did I attend to my needs in that office, but I had to get another document in the same building and was able to make it before noon. As I walked to my bus, I thanked

> Hashem for the special attention He gives widows.
>
> Children, I am comforted that you and the grandchildren have undertaken extra hours of learning Torah and are performing additional good deeds for Papa's *neshamah.* It will surely be spiritually uplifting for him.
>
> May the New Year bring with it peace to our Jewish Nation and the *geulah shelemah* which we all await.
>
> *Love, Mama*

✍ ✍

I received many letters of condolence from relatives and friends, and although Reb Moshe was a great *ben Torah,* most stressed his exceptional personality.

Dora Leiser, whose friendship with Papa and me goes back many years, wrote the following:

> It has taken me a few days to realize that Rabbi Shain is no longer with us physically, but his spirit will be forever with all of you, and with all those who came in contact with him.
>
> The picture I have of Rabbi Shain is one of a smiling, kind, and soft-spoken man. He was a devoted husband and father, an excellent teacher to his many students, and a good friend to all! His gentle manner and intelligent advice made everyone feel comfortable.

My niece, Mindy Stern, also mentioned, among his other attributes, the following:

> Everyone recalls Uncle Moshe with a smile — his gentle nature remains vivid in our memories. You may not remember this, but twenty-five years ago I became engaged, and my *chasan* needed to learn the *dinim* of marriage. Since his father was not living then, it was to Uncle Moshe that he turned for instruction.

Yes, Reb Moshe was gentle and soft-spoken, yet firm in Torah principles. He gave us the impetus to follow his direction.

Bracha Kosoff, a good friend of mine, was very devoted to him. Every week she spent several hours visiting him in the geriatric hospital. She sent me a clipping from the *Jewish Press*, that she felt would give me comfort:

> In this moment when death has triumphed, when your heart is heavy, when your spirit reels in sheer bewilderment, what should you say? What do you say and do now when the book of life has closed on your loved one? You must continue to live, to think and to do. He was his own profile in courage. You must carry on. He left a shining example of the meaning of life. Keep this spirit alive by living the kind of life you know he wants you to live. You cannot argue with God's decision to take him to Himself. Your duty is to keep on living.

This clipping certainly depicted Reb Moshe, and I knew he wanted me not only to keep on living, but also to give our children and grandchildren *chizzuk* and continue to accomplish things in the years that Hashem blesses me with.

My Life with Papa: A Chronicle

IN TIMES OF TRAGEDY, everyone finds his own way to assuage his suffering and grief. I have found that expressing my innermost thoughts through writing has been the catharsis that eases my emotional pain and distress.

Writing letters to my loving children, reliving many incidents of my life with my dear Reb Moshe, gave me inner peace and the strength to carry on through the sorrowful days after his passing.

Dearest Children,

I used to read a poem about time to my high-school students, and one of the lines comes back to me now: "Time is too long for those who grieve."

The last weeks have stretched interminably for me. It is difficult to believe that it is only thirty days since Papa has passed away. Hashem, in His infinite mercy, guides us in mourning every step of the way. During the first three days of *shivah,* I gave full vent to my emotions. For the rest of the *shivah* period I was comforted by the many relatives and friends who came to console me, and the three weeks between the end of *shivah* and the end of *sheloshim* was a time for grief and even for a kind of guilt. I felt the agonizing pain of deep loneliness, coupled with the nagging question, Why was I not with Papa when he passed away? Would it have been easier for him if I had been there to hold his hand?

Today, at the *sheloshim,* there was a large gathering at Papa's grave. As I stood there, I felt his nearness, as if death had not separated us at all. Somehow, I could hear Papa's loving voice comforting me, and for the first time since his passing, I felt a sense of inner peace.

I recall something that your cousin Shmuel Yitzchok said at Uncle Nochum Dovid's *sheloshim,* which he addressed to his mother, Aunt Chaye Dube. "Mama, for you it is the end of the period of *avelus.* Hashem understands exactly how much each one should grieve, and, surely, we do not have to be more merciful than Hashem. Now you have to continue with your life once again."

I know that Papa would want me to continue with my writing and other activities, and be a strong mother and grandmother to our children and grandchildren.

As much as you knew Papa, as the kind, understanding father, and the epitome of the true *ben Torah* — truthful, modest and soft-spoken — I nevertheless feel the need to talk to you, children, about our life together.

How wise my father was in choosing Papa and encouraging me to marry him! I was a naive seventeen-year-old when we married, and until then had lived a sheltered life in my parents' home. I looked up to your Papa as all-wise, because he was five years older than me, was an ordained rabbi, and had a B.A. degree from the university.

Three months after our wedding, we sailed for Mir, Poland. It was a period of great adjustment for me, because not only did I have to adjust to a primitive style of living, but I also had to learn to become a housekeeper, learn to speak Yiddish, and make new friends. Papa smoothed the way, making allowances when the dinner was either half-raw or scorched. We ate lots of eggs, which were cheap and easy to prepare on the kerosene stove. Fortunately, at that time, I had never heard of cholesterol!

Papa understood me, and instead of relegating me to wifely duties only, he helped me grow spiritually. When he returned from yeshivah, he would discuss the *musar* talks he heard from the *Mashgi'ach,* Reb Yerucham Levovitz, and later from Reb Chatzkel Levenstein. Of course, we were not angels, and we had our share of normal disagreements, but they always resulted in bringing us closer together.

As you know, I gave birth to Yisroel Meyer in Mir, in the midst of a howling snowstorm, with a midwife in attendance. Our happiness was marred by my very serious illness, blood poisoning, which resulted in paralysis in both my legs. The local doctor despaired of my life, and suggested, "Maybe prayers can help." The Yeshivah and the townspeople all prayed for me, and Hashem answered their prayers. Your Papa devoted days and nights to me, and though there were times when I was almost unconscious, I knew he was there.

When I recuperated enough to be moved, we sought the advice of an orthopedic doctor in Vilna, who sent us traveling to a certain spa near the Polish-German border, where I could benefit from all kinds of mineral and mud baths; however, he really did not hold out too much hope of my walking again. Through many trying months, Papa stood by, giving me the courage to keep going. Again prayers helped, and about a year after Yisroel Meyer's birth, he and I each took our first steps.

On the eve of the Second World War, when we had been living in Mir for almost six years, Zaidie Herman wrote that we should make preparations to return home. It was not easy leaving Mir, after being part of yeshivah life and becoming close to the townspeople.

As the clouds of war gathered over Europe, our farewells

were made with conflicting emotions. We were reluctant to leave, and yet we looked forward to being home again with our loved ones. Our homecoming was marred by the news of your Aunt Frieda's death several months before. It had been kept a secret from us, knowing how very attached I was to my beloved sister.

When we arrived in July 1938, the Depression was in full swing. We moved in with my parents, but slept in a bedroom at the neighbor's, one floor down. My father was struggling to keep his *hachnasas orchim* going by selling *chalav Yisrael* during the year, and matzos, as well as prunes and spices, for Pesach. Miraculously, my mother always had more than enough food for every Shabbos guest, so much that we ate the leftovers all week long.

We sent Yisroel Meyer to nursery school, where he received a nourishing lunch every day and learned to speak English. Papa tried his best to get a position as a Rebbe in a yeshivah, but none was available. So he joined a *kollel* and received a stipend of ten dollars a week; half of it went to Zaidie, toward our upkeep.

In September of that year, Papa finally found employment at the Rabbi Jacob Joseph Yeshivah as a first-grade Rebbe. With his salary of twenty-five dollars a week, we were able to move out of my parents' home, into a tiny apartment of our own nearby.

It was in an old tenement house that had been renovated. The landlord had recently installed "indoor" bathrooms, in a closet-like room adjoining the kitchens. Until then, they had been "outdoors," in the hallway. For Papa and me, our little closet toilet seemed a real luxury since we had spent our six years in Mir with an outhouse that really was outdoors.

Our kitchen had an interesting feature; a bathtub, as the little toilet closet was too small for one. It was covered with a white enamel top, and it doubled as a utility table. Every time one of us wanted to take a bath, I had to clear the dishes, pots and pans off the top. We had a small icebox with a pan beneath it for the water that accumulated from the melting ice. The pan had to be emptied two or three times a day, so it kept me from leaving the house for more than a few hours at a time.

From an auction house, we bought second-hand furniture, and from a stall in the marketplace, factory-damaged pots and pans. Bubbie Herman and Bubbie Shain contributed plates, tin forks, spoons and knives. Early every morning, I would frequent Orchard Street, where the pushcarts were, seeking bargains in fruits and vegetables. We ate an abundance of overripe bananas, mushy tomatoes, limp cucumbers and carrots, and potatoes which had seen better days. I passed up the luscious-looking cherries, peaches and plums, as we could not afford them. Uncle Noach, who was working as a *shochet* in a slaughterhouse, would bring us the cheeks of the cow, which was the cheapest cut of meat — at ten cents a pound! I cooked them for hours and hours, but they remained rubbery. I finally got a meat grinder, and we had a daily meal of meatballs with cooked vegetables.

Despite the poverty and deprivation of material possessions, we all thrived. Our little home was our private palace. Papa was my king and I his queen, and Yisroel Meyer was our little prince.

Only two things were lacking to make our lives complete. A year after we returned to the States, your Zaidie and Bubbie Herman decided to leave for Eretz Yisrael. It was a great blow to all their children, but especially to us, as we had grown very close to them, living with them and then spending all our *Shabbosim* and *Yamim Tovim* with them after we moved out. Papa and I also realized that Yisroel Meyer, who was such a little boy, would miss being part of their lives and their greatness. Of course, we had the loving devotion of Zaidie and Bubbie Shain, but they lived in Brooklyn, and we did not get to see them that often.

We also longed to have more children, not only for our own sake, but also for Yisroel Meyer, who needed a sister or brother. I finally had a series of medical tests when he was five years old, and I received the depressing results on *Chol*

Ha-Mo'ed Pesach. "Mrs. Shain," the gynecologist told me, "I'm sorry, but according to all the test results, you cannot bear any more children."

I cried all the way home. Papa tried to comfort me, saying, "Racoma, *Chol Ha-Mo'ed* is not a time for tears. Hashem has performed great miracles for us: You are alive, you are walking, and we have Yisroel Meyer. We should be very thankful for His blessings." How noble Papa was! Although he, too, was greatly disappointed at the news, he sought to comfort me with his soothing manner and wise words.

Papa made it easier for me to accept Hashem's decree that we would have only one child. However, Hashem, the Doctor of all doctors, had other plans for us. When Yisroel Meyer was eight years old, we were blessed with our daughter, Mashi. Papa and I were elated, and our joy knew no bounds at this special unexpected gift from Heaven. And then thirteen months later, Hashem blessed us once again with a son, Raphael Yitzchok.

Now we were a "real" family, baruch Hashem, with two sons and a daughter, and not the object of pity anymore from our relatives and friends. Our lives were full, and our tiny apartment bursting. We moved into a larger one, though it, too, was by no means roomy: four small rooms in a "railroad flat," so called because the rooms were arranged in a line, like the cars in a train. But it had two great luxuries: a refrigerator and a real bathroom with a tub.

The first night in our new apartment, I was so excited I could not sleep. I kept running into the kitchen and putting my hand into the refrigerator to make sure it was keeping the food cold. No more ice to buy, no pans of water to empty. And a real bathroom! I felt rich beyond description.

I bought flowery plastic drapes for ninety-nine cents apiece, and Papa hung them up in our small dining room. How proud we were of our new home! As soon as we had settled in, I invited some friends of ours to visit. We spent an enjoyable evening together, and when they were leaving, I escorted them to the hall. Not realizing that I was still within earshot, one said to another, "How poor the Shains are living." I ran into our apartment and burst out, "Moshe, our friends think we are poor!" Papa looked at me lovingly and said, "Racoma, we are very rich, but most people don't really understand what the word means."

These were busy years for Papa and me. You were growing up, and each stage of your lives was a new challenge for us. Each of you had his own distinct personality, and place in the family. Yisroel Meyer was the big brother, with the younger children looking up to him. He also became our built-in babysitter. Mashi, even as a two-year-old, had a mind of her own, and insisted on choosing by herself the clothes she would wear every day to nursery school. There was much lively sibling rivalry between Mashi and Raphael Yitzchok, and he also had a mind of his own.

We had quite a time with Raphael Yitzchok when he was little. He was a lively youngster, who tried to defy the laws of gravity, climbing on everything, including Papa's bookcase, and dangling from the top ledge. It usually took a lot of coaxing to get him down. One morning, I took Mashi and Raphael Yitzchok to the park, and before I had the chance to grab Raphael Yitzchok, he had climbed to the top of the monkey bars and was swinging back and forth. Since he was barely two years old, I watched him with trepidation, praying to Hashem to get him down safely.

Two women who were sitting on a nearby bench pointed to him swinging away, and I heard one say to the other, "That child's mother should be arrested for allowing him to be in such a dangerous position." I grabbed Mashi and started to wheel the stroller out of the park, motioning frantically to Raphael Yitzchok to climb down. But he thought I was giving him a friendly wave, so he waved back hanging on by one hand! I closed my eyes and waited for disaster. Suddenly, there he was next to me, innocently looking up and tugging at my skirt. I wanted to smack him and kiss him at the same time, but I did neither, only dragged him home. When I told Papa of his escapade, he said to me, "Raphael Yitzchok is a bundle of energy. May he use that energy to become a great *ben Torah.*" Papa always knew how to say the right words at the right time.

When I discussed Raphael Yitzchok's energetic activities with our pediatrician, he said, "Your son simply needs lots of space, and you keep him cooped up in a tiny apartment. What do you expect?"

Summer was approaching, and we started looking for a suitable place in the mountains to spend the summer months. Hashem blessed us, and we found the Leiser bungalows, a *shomer Shabbos* colony — a rarity in those days. We spent ten enjoyable summers there while you were growing up. It was the ideal place for us, and we made lasting friendships.

As you surely remember, Papa would gather all the boys for a Torah study session every morning, much to the gratification of all the parents. In the afternoons, when I had finished my housework, and you were all busy with your various activities, it was time for Papa's and my daily walk. We would walk down a country road, lined with green, leafy trees, blackberry bushes laden with fruit, birds singing everywhere, and surrounded by the peace and beauty of the countryside.

Although we had a loving marriage already, those walks enhanced it. We could discuss our innermost thoughts, knowing we understood each other. Sometimes we would walk silently, when words seemed superfluous. About a mile down the road, there was a farm where we stopped to buy fresh, sweet corn. We would return from our walks refreshed, our arms filled with corn and our hearts filled with peace.

I'm sure you recall the time when a group of the younger boys went out to the field behind the bungalows to try out the "art of smoking." One of them accidentally dropped a lighted cigarette onto the dry grass, which shot up in flames. Papa and I suddenly heard someone shouting, "Fire, fire!" Unruffled, Papa filled a cup of water and went to extinguish the blaze, only to discover that it was out of control, and the fire department had to be called. But to this day, people remember the picture of Papa calmly walking toward the blazing fire with only a cup of water in his hand! Yes, children, Papa always had a way of bringing calm to every situation.

The summer after Yisroel Meyer graduated from high school, we were up at the bungalow colony as usual. Since Yisroel Meyer was an honor student, the principal at the English department had asked Papa which college he would be going to in the Fall. He was astounded when Papa told him that he was not going to college at all, but to the Mir Yeshivah.

One sweltering, blistering day in late August, Yisroel Meyer came over to me and said, "Mama, Thursday is *Rosh Chodesh Elul,* the opening day at Yeshivah. I'd like to leave on Wednesday afternoon. Could you get my clothes ready?"

"Have you discussed this with Papa?" I asked.

"I just did," Yisroel Meyer replied, "and he thinks it's all right." I dashed out of the bungalow, and found Papa studying Gemara.

"Moshe," I blurted out, "I'm sure no one will be in the Yeshivah on Thursday, especially with this heat wave. If he leaves on Wednesday, he'll have to take the bus, but on Sunday he can get a ride straight to the city with one of our neighbors. You can learn with Yisroel Meyer the entire Shabbos, so he won't miss any learning."

Papa waited for a minute until I calmed down, and then answered, "Yisroel Meyer is on the right *derech.* The only way to grow to be a true *ben Torah* is not to look for the easy way out." I realized that I had been rationalizing, and that Papa and Yisroel Meyer were both on the right track.

On Wednesday afternoon, lugging his suitcase full of clean clothes and the batch of cookies I had baked, off he went into the scorching heat. Papa and I walked him down the road, and as he turned the bend, he waved to us, and we waved back in salute.

That night I could not sleep from the heat, and I imagined how Yisroel Meyer must be sweating in the boiling city. I decided to write and let him know how proud we were of him. The poem seemed to write itself.

The Yeshivah Boy

I walk over to the window,
And see a young boy sitting there;
I know he is learning the Torah,
For each word is a spoken prayer.

His life is one of holiness,
With understanding that brings him joy;
His life is clear like a bubbling brook,
This young but wise Yeshivah Boy.

Suddenly, I am thrust aside,
As strange eyes gaze and look;
They peer through the window, and they ask,
"What is he doing with that book?"

"Why does he sit and waste his time?
What can he hope to attain?
Why does he not seek to learn a trade?
Then, perhaps, something he will gain."

"What have you attained, you foolish eyes,
With your seeking fame and wealth?
At the end of the road, you have but naught,
You've lost even your bit of health."

"It is Torah and Torah only,
That sustains this whole wide world;
For us it is our guide in life,
Like a banner we keep it unfurled."

I gaze again through the window,
And send thanks to the One Above;
That the Yeshivah Boy who is learning,
Is my son, whom the Lord does love.

I know our Father in Heaven,
Will guard him like a budding flower;
My heart is peaceful within me,
Each moment of every hour.

So, mothers of all Jewish children,
For a Torah life do pray,
And teach them, your little ones,
What is truly the only way

That will give them lasting happiness,
Contentment and Heavenly joy;
To sit and learn the Torah,
And just be YESHIVAH BOYS!

Yisroel Meyer's answer arrived a few days later:

Dear Mama,

It was worth the effort to be in the Yeshivah on *Rosh Chodesh Elul* just for your poem. I am blessed that Papa and you always taught and encouraged me to be a Yeshivah Boy.

Thank you for everything,
Yisroel Meyer

Love, Mama

✍ ✍

Dearest Children,

I am sure you remember the excitement when we moved to our apartment on the East River Drive. Our dream had finally come true, and we had a roomy home. It seemed unbelievable at first with the large picture window in the living room, the terrace, and two walk-in closets that were almost as large as the tiny rooms in our previous apartment.

I wrote to my father in Yerushalayim, telling him the glad tidings. His answer came promptly: "Before you consider buying any new furniture, you should first purchase a *sefer Torah* for your new home." Papa and I discussed it, and wrote to Zaidie asking him to send us a *sefer Torah* from Eretz Yisrael as soon as possible.

Shortly afterwards we ordered bookcases built according to our specifications. Papa made a sketch of one that had three sections, with bookshelves on either end, and a built-in *aron* for our *sefer Torah* in the middle section.

It was an uplifting day for all of us when our *sefer Torah* arrived and Papa placed it carefully in the *aron.* Having our *sefer Torah* brought holiness into our lives in general, and also played a vital role when there was stormy and inclement weather and we couldn't get to shul for *Shacharis*: we simply had a minyan in our house. It also solved discipline problems with the children. Whenever you got into squabbles in the "Torah room," Papa would say, "Children, you must show respect for the Torah. You cannot fight in this room." By the time you cleared out of the room, most of your arguments had petered out. When Papa returned from the Yeshivah or Bais Yaakov, he usually made straight for his armchair in the "Torah room," where peace and quiet reigned.

The next few years were fulfilling ones for both of us. Papa was teaching ninth grade in the Yeshivah, and doubling as principal and teacher in the Bais Yaakov evening seminary. With his encouragement, I jumped into teaching and found it challenging and exhilarating. You were all growing up with the normal ups and downs of each phase of growth. Papa and I "weathered" the sunny and stormy periods together, always loving you and proud of your accomplishments.

An incident when Raphael Yitzchok was about twelve years old left a lasting impression on us. He had been saving his allowance for months, and finally had about half the amount needed to buy the bicycle he so wanted. Papa and I felt he deserved one, so off we went to the store to purchase it. He chose a beautiful red bicycle with shiny handlebars and chrome fenders. We also bought a heavy lock and chain to keep it safely stored in the special carriage room in the basement of our building. He rode it home proudly, with Papa and me following him and enjoying it vicariously.

A few days later, Raphael Yitzchok was scheduled to go to camp. Though it was difficult for him to part with his new bicycle, he locked it securely in the carriage room, and sort of patted it lovingly, as we walked out of the room. In each postcard, he mentioned his bicycle and how he was looking forward to riding it again.

The day before his return from camp, I went down to the carriage room to dust his bicycle and ready it for him. Much to my dismay, all that was there was part of a chain — and no bicycle. The chain had been cut, and the bicycle stolen. Papa found me very upset when he returned from Yeshivah. "Moshe," I asked tearfully, "What are we going to do? Raphael Yitzchok will be heartbroken, and I cannot bear the thought of greeting him with the news that his precious bicycle was stolen. Perhaps we should buy him another one and not even tell him anything." Papa and I sat for hours discussing how to handle this potentially traumatic situation.

We had heard that there were hooligans terrorizing the Jewish boys on the East River Drive by grabbing their bikes forcefully, and riding off with them. This helped Papa and me to decide how to cope with this overwhelming problem.

With a quaking heart, I went to meet Raphael Yitzchok's bus the next afternoon. Suntanned and skinny, carrying his canvas bag over his shoulders, he gave me a bear hug, and looked at me expectantly. I knew what was coming.

"How's my bike?" he asked.

"Raphael Yitzchok," I began, my voice shaky, "as you know, Papa and I have always looked for *hashgachah pratis* in every happening in our lives, and Hashem always watches over us. For the last few weeks, rough gangs in the neighborhood have been pushing Jewish boys off their bikes and stealing them. In fact, one of the boys was hurt pretty badly, because he would not give up his bike.

"Knowing you, Papa and I are sure that if this ever happened to you, you would never give up your bike without a good fight, and who knows how seriously injured, God forbid..."

Raphael Yitzchok did not give me the chance to finish my sentence. "Mom, what happened to my bike?"

I poured out the terrible words in one breath: "It was stolen from the carriage room. Yesterday I found the chain cut and the bike gone."

Tears welled up in his eyes and in mine, too. We walked together, not saying a word. When we neared the house, he said, "Well, that's the end of my bike, right, Mom?"

"Raphael Yitzchok, Papa and I faced a very difficult decision when I found your bike stolen. The easy way out would have been to buy you another bike without ever letting you know, but we did not feel it was the right way for us to act in this instance. Money was not a consideration at all. As I told you, we looked to *hashgachah* for direction. Papa and I understand that this is very bitter pill for you to swallow, but we must be thankful to Hashem that he saved you from what might have been serious harm."

Papa was waiting for us when we returned home. He saw our tear-stained faces, and tears filled his eyes also. Raphael Yitzchok never mentioned the bike again.

This incident brings to mind another that also involved Raphael Yitzchok and some bullies. After we moved to the East River Drive, he would go to the Yeshivah on Thursday nights for the weekly late night session. One night, as he was on his way home alone, very late, a group of tough boys surrounded him, and one of them asked in a threatening voice, "What school do you go to?" Raphael Yitzchok was very frightened and blurted out, "Rabbenu Yaakov Yosef." The boy then answered, "You're lucky — if you went to R.J.J., we'd beat you up."

It seemed that some non-Jewish boys were making trouble for the young yeshivah students. In our home, we always called the Yeshivah by the name that Zaidie Andron had given when he founded it: "Rabbenu Yaakov Yosef," after the Chief Rabbi of New York. However, most everyone else shortened it and called it simply R.J.J. (Rabbi Jacob Joseph). Raphael Yitzchok was saved from a beating!

Then there was the summer that Mashi went to Camp Bnos as a junior counselor, and Raphael Yitzchok went to Camp Yeshivah as a waiter. The *zeman* had not yet ended in the Mir Yeshivah where Yisroel Meyer was studying. Not wanting to spend the weekend without any of you, Papa and I decided to spend it in the mountains, so we could visit Mashi and Raphael Yitzchok at camp. We made reservations in a hotel where Uncle Ralphie and Aunt Clara were vacationing.

As soon as we arrived, we asked Uncle Ralphie, who had a car, to drive us to the camps. As we were riding along, Aunt Clara said matter-of-factly, "I think you should know that Mashi hurt her leg, but it's really nothing serious."

Mashi greeted us wearing a cast from her toes until above her knee! Aunt Clara's interpretation had certainly been an optimistic one, but she had not wanted to shock us. Mashi had fractured her ankle while skating with the campers, but realizing how concerned we would be, she had decided not to let us know. When I suggested we take her home, she refused, saying, "I'm having a great time now that the doctor fitted a heel on the cast, so I can hobble around and even go on trips with my group." We left Mashi, with her decorated cast signed by many of the girls in the camp, and headed for Raphael Yitzchok's camp.

As we rode along discussing Mashi's accident, Aunt Clara cleared her throat and said hesitantly, "By the way, Raphael Yitzchok banged his hand, but really it was a very minor injury." Papa and I gasped. "What happened to his hand?" I asked excitedly. "Tell me — tell me!" But before she had time to explain, we had arrived at the camp, jumped out of the car, and rushed to Raphael Yitzchok's bunk, not knowing what to expect.

He came toward us waving his hand, which was bandaged up in a splint. "Hi! It's nothing to worry about! I just fractured some fingers playing ball, but it's nothing to worry about. I can even keep on doing my job as a waiter," he assured us cheerfully. Of course, he would not think of leaving camp.

We learned that they both had their accidents the same day, and while Mashi was being treated by the doctor, lo and behold, in walked Raphael Yitzchok with his hand injury. There was astonishment all around, and the doctor exclaimed, "The Shains are breaking up the mountains!"

✍ ✍

Papa and I first realized that Yisroel Meyer was a mature young man and ready for marriage, when Aunt Esther called us about an excellent girl from a very special family, who would be just right for him. How right she was! Much to our joy, he became a *chasan* to Chaya, and she a daughter to us.

They were married on a very hot day in August, in a wedding hall which had no air conditioning, as you all surely remember, but Papa and I were too excited to notice the heat. Yisroel continued his studies in the Mir Yeshivah, while Chaya taught school. A year later, Papa and I were blessed with our first grandson, and our status changed to Zaidie and Bubbie — titles which we wore proudly.

Mashi graduated from the Bais Yaakov seminary, and got a position as a fifth-grade teacher in a Bais Yaakov school, and Raphael Yitzchok left New York and entered the Yeshivah of Philadelphia. The house seemed subdued, but Papa and I were kept busy with our many activities.

It was a great honor for us when the *Gaon*, Rabbi Aaron Kotler, suggested a match for Mashi: Elimelech, who had been studying in Lakewood Yeshivah for a number of years. Mashi and Elimelech were very suited to each other, and we welcomed him joyously into our family as an additional son.

It was a happy time for Papa and me, as we prepared for their wedding. I'll never forget when the four of us — Papa and I, Elimelech and Mashi — drove to the wedding hall to make arrangements with the owner, with whom I had made an appointment a few days earlier.

As we were ushered into his office, the owner, a middle-aged man, took one look at Mashi, and cried excitedly, "*Mein maideleh*!" She smiled, and said, "Good evening, Mr. B.," as Papa, Elimelech, and I looked on in astonishment.

We all sat down and proceeded to hear the story behind Mr. B.'s friendly greeting. When Mashi graduated from high school, she had worked as a secretary in Manhattan, and attended the Bais Yaakov seminary in the evenings. Since she could not get home in time to have dinner, I had suggested that she find a suitable restaurant near the seminary and eat her evening meal there. She took my advice, and whenever I questioned her about the meal at the restaurant, I was gratified to hear that she was eating nutritious meals at a low price.

Mr. B. then took up the story. "For years, I had a restaurant in Brooklyn, and many Bais Yaakov girls came to eat there. One evening about three years ago, a young girl came in and after greeting me, asked for the 'special.' There was a sign in my window: 'Special: Main dish, no trimmings, reduced price.'

"She began to come in regularly, and I noticed her exemplary behavior. Every evening she would go to wash her hands, make a *motzi,* start to eat, and become engrossed in her *sefarim.* After the meal, she would take out her *bentsher,* recite the grace after meals, pay me, thank me, and say politely, 'Good evening.'

"This went on for months, without any conversation other than her asking for the daily 'special,' and her greetings as she came and left my restaurant. I was very impressed with her courteous manner, her modesty, and her diligence, and without her noticing, I began to add 'extras' to her meal for the same price. Once when she didn't come to the restaurant for several days, I grew anxious. When she returned, I asked her why she had not come, and she told me that she had been ill with the flu.

"For about two years she came to my restaurant almost daily, and I felt as if she were part of my family. One evening, she mentioned that she was graduating from the seminary and thanked me for the service and very good meals I had served her. That was about a year ago." Then Mr. B. turned to Elimelech and said, "You are fortunate to have this *maideleh* as your bride."

We then made all the necessary arrangements for the wedding, and he quoted us a very fair price. When Mr. B.

asked us if we wanted to order a smorgasbord for the reception before the meal, we declined, as it would have been too expensive, and decided on drinks and cake instead. As we were leaving his office, he told us, "I will prepare the wedding as if it were for my own daughter."

When we left, Papa remarked, "Mashi, you were being watched by human eyes for almost two years without your even noticing it. Imagine how careful our actions should be, knowing that Hashem's eyes are on us every minute of the day." Papa's words left a great impression on all of us.

When we arrived at the hall on the wedding day, we were greeted by the most elaborate smorgasbord, including hot and cold dishes, with *two* waiters doing the serving! I said to Papa, "Moshe, Mr. B. must have misunderstood — we didn't order the smorgasbord. What should we do? How will we pay for it?" Just then, Mr. B. came out of his office with a hearty "Mazal tov" and asked us, "Well, how do you like the smorgasbord?"

"I think it is really very beautiful and luxurious," I answered, "but we didn't order one."

"I know you didn't order it," he smiled, "but I told you I would make a wedding as if the *kallah* were my own daughter, didn't I? Well, this is the smorgasbord I would have prepared for my daughter, and it is my present to the *kallah.*"

Their last *sheva berachos* was to be held in Lakewood, where they would be living. They loaded up their old car with all their wedding gifts and clothes, and set out early in order to be there by 2:00 P.M., when it was called for.

At about 3:00 P.M. I received a call from their friends in Lakewood, asking why they had not arrived yet. I was frantic, and didn't know what to do. A little while later the phone rang. "Ma? It's Mashi. Our car broke down in some hick town, and we were towed to a garage. I have no idea how long it will take to fix it, so please call Lakewood and tell our friends that we'll be late." Well, their last *sheva berochos* was celebrated in Lakewood without the *chasan* and *kallah,* for by the time they arrived it was late in the evening.

Papa and I decided, children, that before considering any *shidduchim* for you, we would consult Zaidie Herman, for we realized that he was blessed by Hashem with great insight. I discussed Yisroel Meyer's and Mashi's *shidduchim* with him, when I visited him in Yerushalayim.

When Raphael Yitzchok's turn came, Zaidie was quite old, and though his mind was clear, his memory was failing. Uncle Nochum Dovid, who was living in Yerushalayim, asked about several girls who had been suggested. Among the names was Yehudis Greenbaum.

Uncle Nochum Dovid wrote to us that when Zaidie heard Yehudis's name, he had asked, "Who is she?" Uncle Nochum Dovid had explained, "She is the granddaughter of Rabbi Shraga Feivel Mendelowitz." Zaidie had answered quickly, "It's a good *shidduch.*" Zaidie had known Rabbi Mendelowitz in the States, and was aware of his great dedication and self-sacrifice for Torah in America. Knowing that Zaidie's memory was weak, though, Uncle Nochum Dovid had questioned him about the girls at different times during the day, and each time, though Zaidie had already forgotten that he had been asked before, he gave the same reply.

It was only after Raphael Yitzchok and Yehudis had become *chasan* and *kallah* that we told them why we had advised him to meet her before any of the other girls. And so Yehudis became our youngest daughter, and now we had six children, *baruch Hashem.* As Yisroel Meyer says jokingly, "It's the only family where three brothers married three sisters."

When we returned from the wedding, the house greeted us silently. "I'm happy that all our children are married," I said to Papa, "but I have a great sense of loneliness."

Papa comforted me. "Racoma, it's a normal feeling, and I feel the same way, but it will soon pass." And pass it did, especially when all the children and grandchildren got together at our house on many happy occasions.

As our family grew, we welcomed each new grandchild with

excitement and affection. I recall when Papa and I were pacing the hospital corridor awaiting the birth of one of our grandchildren, a nurse passed by and said sympathetically, "I understand how nervous you must be, becoming grandparents for the first time." I guess because we seemed so tense, she took it for granted that we were awaiting our first grandchild. "Oh, we've already become grandparents a number of times," I replied, "but each additional grandchild is like a first to us."

Although you were all married with families of your own, our loving relationship with you continued, with frequent visits to your homes and you to ours. Papa and I thrived on being fought over — "Who gets Papa and Mama next?"

Then in the summer of 1967, Papa and I visited Zaidie Herman in Yerushalayim, two weeks before he passed away. It was then that we made the decision to settle in Yerushalayim by his first yahrtzeit.

Dear children, this letter has taken many hours to write, and I have shed many tears, as I relived part of my life with Papa and all of you. As much as I wrote about Papa, words are inadequate to describe who he was and what he meant to me. You are fortunate to have had him as a father, teacher, and role model of what a true *ben Torah* should be.

I am sure you are asking the question, "How can Mama live without Papa?" The answer is very simple: I am not living without Papa. Of course I miss his physical presence very much, but he still lives on with me emotionally and spiritually, and I am surrounded by the wealth of memories of our life together.

Children, I am comforted that you are close to each other, and that you are following in Papa's footsteps, living a life of Torah and guiding your children to continue on that path.

May we be reunited very soon in Yerushalayim, with the coming of *Mashiach*, the *geulah shelemah*, and *techias ha-meisim*, when Papa, *zt"l*, will return to us.

All my love, Mama

En"gulfed" in War

DAWN GENTLY PRODDED the sleeping sun. As she awoke, she stretched her rays through the dark, heavy clouds, peeked through and said cheerily, "Good morning." I did not answer her, as I could not share her good humor.

I faced a new day in a topsy-turvy world, physically exhausted and in an emotional turmoil. At 3:00 A.M. on that morning, my neighbor had hammered at my door. When I quickly leapt out of my bed and rushed to open the door, she shouted, "It's war! Get your gas mask ready." I hurried to the closet where I had stored the taped-up box which I, along with all the nation, had received from the Civil Defense authorities several weeks before. I tore it open and checked the items: gas mask, filter, cylindrical box of powder, atropine injection, and a few packets of gauze. Would I really have to use them? I asked myself, as I shuddered inwardly at the thought of chemical warfare.

I quickly turned on the radio, and it blared the news:

"War has erupted in the Gulf, and the Allied Forces are bombing military installations in Baghdad. Have your gas masks and kits near you, and be ready to enter your sealed rooms. We must be prepared for every eventuality." I twiddled the knobs of my radio from one station to the other, eager for every bit of news and commentary, as the hours of night slowly faded into dawn.

The last weeks, with the January 15th deadline getting nearer and nearer, were nerve-racking ones for all of us, as we awaited the unknown: Would there be war? I had prayed constantly that the Middle East in general, and Eretz Yisrael in particular, would be spared bloodshed. Now the war and its consequent threat to Israel was a reality, and I had to come to terms with how to cope with the emergency.

Surprisingly, I ate a hearty breakfast that Thursday morning, more from habit than from appetite. At mid-morning, I attended the bris of a great-nephew. The synagogue was packed to capacity, and when we came to the words *Ana Hashem hoshia na, ana Hashem hatzlichah na,* they were recited with a great, heartfelt cry from all of us, a cry that I hoped would reach the Heavens.

Of course the only topic of conversation was the Gulf Crisis and its ramifications for us. There was a sense of euphoria, with predictions coming fast that the Iraqi air force had already been wiped out, and the war would be over within a few days.

This elation was quicky dispelled when the dreaded wail of the air-raid siren sounded all over Israel at 2:00 A.M. on Friday morning, warning us of a missile attack. Since I was dozing lightly, I awoke immediately, grabbed my gas mask kit and hurried to my neighbor's house. I had prepared a sealed room like everyone else had, but I felt it would be wiser to be with friends in an emergency.

Asa and Hannah Wittow, with whom I have been neighbors and close friends since I settled in Yerushalayim, greeted me warmly and invited me into their sealed room. Their daughter, Batsheva, and Asa's elderly mother, visiting from Denver and caught up in the war, were also there. Our building resounded with loud voices, wailing babies, and banging on doors to awaken neighbors, some of whom, astonishingly, were sleeping through all the tumult and din.

Then began what soon came to be a regular ritual: putting on the gas mask, which I found extremely uncomfortable. My eyeglasses could not be worn under it, and they did not fit properly on top of it, so I peered through a fog. I sat and looked at my neighbors, who looked grotesque in their gas masks, as I did in mine. We all seemed to have landed from some distant planet. Our voices were muffled, but we were in no mood for talk anyway, so we kept the conversation to a minimum and sat glued to the radio.

Haga, the Civil Defense Authority, gave a few initial commands: "Enter your sealed rooms. Put on your gas masks, and stay tuned to the radio for further directions." Then the radio broadcast music. I enjoy music very much, and it usually has a very calming effect on me, but this time it was a source of frustration. Who needs music now? I said to myself. Stop it! Stop it! All we wanted to hear were exact details on what was happening. Where were the missiles falling? Did they have chemical warheads? Were there any casualties — any damage? But the radio ignored me and kept right on with the lively music. If I get the opportunity, I decided, I will tell them to choose more soothing music.

(But as the war progressed, and we sat night after night in the sealed room waiting for the missiles to land, and as I went about my household chores during the day, the wonderful broadcasting on Israel radio showed me what an amazing and united People we are. News bulletins, emergency instructions, and simple reassuring talk was provided in all the languages that our People, ingathered from the four corners of the earth, understand best: Hebrew, English,

Russian, Amharic, Yiddish, Ladino, Arabic, Spanish, French, and more.)

My neighbors and I sat quietly, tuned in to the radio and our own thoughts. Finally, the news came on: "Missiles have fallen somewhere in the center of the country. There have been slight casualties and damage. Remain in your sealed rooms with your gas masks on." I understood that there could be few details given, because security did not permit the exact site of the missile attack to be announced; however, the report left me with a sense of further frustration.

After what seemed like *forever,* the all-clear siren sounded, and we were given permission to remove our masks and leave the sealed room. With aching jaw, as the gas mask had pressed heavily against it, I bade my neighbors a "peaceful" night, and thanked them for their hospitality. I returned home, where I spent the few hours until daylight with a throbbing heachache, unable to sleep.

All day Friday I walked around in a daze. The two sleepless nights had left me bleary-eyed. What plagued me and most everyone else was the unanswered question, "Is this just a preview of what's to come?"

Again, the answer came quickly with three air-raid sirens coming in close succession. The first came on Friday night at about 9:00 P.M., after our Shabbos meal, fortunately. The second, sounded at about 5:00 A.M. Shabbos morning, was claimed, later, to have been a false alarm, but wreaked havoc with our nerves anyway. The third alarm went off at about 7:15 A.M., just when the Shabbos Isbee minyan was getting started for *Shacharis.* The men quickly cleared out, each one hurrying to his home. Once again, I hurried to my neighbor's sealed room.

The Rabbanim had advised that the radio be plugged in before Shabbos and kept on low volume, so that we would be able to receive emergency bulletins on Shabbos if necessary. Again we heard very few details, except that the missile attacks were indeed very real ones, coming from western Iraq, and falling somewhere in the center of Israel, which meant the Tel Aviv area.

Then, as during all the attacks that followed, in those tense minutes between the siren and the news broadcast of the results of the missile attack, we all prayed and recited *Tehillim.*

Thank Hashem, these first attacks appeared to have caused almost no injuries. However, they left no doubt in our minds that Saddam Hussein was doing his utmost to provoke us and get us involved in the Gulf War. Would his diabolical scheme work, and Israel retaliate? And then what?

After the all-clear siren sounded, we did get a minyan together, but the inner peace of Shabbos was sorely missing. Though I always remember that Hashem is the Master Planner, I am only human. And although I appeared calm outwardly, when I heard the sudden cessation of radio broadcasting and the frightening code words repeated, and the eerie wail of the air-raid siren, my heart pounded, my muscles felt all tied up in knots, and my stomach seemed to leap to my throat.

Dearest Children,

What a shame we didn't buy stock in the telephone company before the war! I heard that during an ordinary twenty-four-hour period, there are approximately 3,000 international calls from the United States to Israel. On the day following the first missile attacks on Israel, there were 750,000 calls, including yours.

I appreciate your phoning and can readily understand your concern for my welfare. However, I am blessed that I do not have the conflict many others are facing at this time: to stay or to leave. As I told you on the phone, this is my home, and it is here in Yerushalayim that I intend to remain, with Hashem's help.

I certainly can make allowances for the many Americans and other "foreigners" who left Israel before the January 15th deadline, and after the first missile attacks. The yeshivah and seminary students, who came for a limited time, were under extreme pressure from their parents and relatives overseas to leave immediately. This was magnified when the American consul advised their nationals to leave Israel on the Friday before the war started.

Uncle Chaim was actually besieged by hundreds of students, young couples, elderly people, and others seeking his wise counsel about whether to remain or to leave. In addition, his phone rang all hours of the day and night from panicky parents and relatives from all parts of the globe, asking him to use his influence to see that their loved ones leave as soon as possible.

Uncle Chaim advised many to remain, but there were situations where mothers with several young children felt they could not possibly cope under these circumstances. It caused marital disputes, where husbands studying in yeshivah refused to leave, and their wives would not go without them.

Trying to leave Israel at the last minute was hectic. Our neighbor Asa Wittow, who is a travel agent, had his hands full trying to get accommodations for all those who turned to him for tickets. However, he was mostly busy with cancellations, as time and time again many changed their minds and decided to stay. It is a very difficult time for everyone, but knowing Hashem watches over us and guides us gives me a sense of security.

I am very gratified that Raphael Yitzchok and Yehudis did not apply any pressure on [their daughter] Blume Rochel to leave seminary here, but allowed her to make her own decision. She discussed the pros and cons with me, and had no qualms about remaining here. As she said, "I looked forward for so long to this year in Israel, and the only reason I would consider leaving would be if my parents insisted." She is remaining, along with the 31 other girls who have also decided to stay on, out of the 96 students who arrived at the beginning of the school year.

The assistant principal is a very understanding woman and has moved into the seminary dormitory to be with the girls and give them motherly care. They are continuing their studies, but do have a curfew and are not allowed out of the dormitory after dark. In their spare time, they are helping needy families. I am sure this experience will add much to Blume Rochel's spiritual growth. I am in close touch with her, and she is a real trouper.

Love, Mama

Dearest Children,

Though the war has brought many disruptions into our lives, I have found positive aspects, also. For instance, I listen to the hourly news broadcasts in Hebrew, something I did not bother to do before the war. After all my years here, I am suddenly making great strides in speaking and understanding Hebrew, which gives me a sense of accomplishment.

In fact, I recently listened to an interesting Hebrew program on the radio in which a psychologist was interviewed about the effects of the war on the emotions. He cited both insomnia and loss of appetite as normal reactions. I was very relieved to know that I am so normal, as I have both symptoms!

I heard that there have also been marital problems caused by the war, but the following "problem" had a happy ending: A middle-aged couple who were not on the best of terms were forced to be together in their sealed room during the first missile attack. This proved disastrous, as they had their own personal war with each other to contend with at the same time. They sought advice and were told to prepare two separate sealed rooms, one for each of them.

After enduring several missile attacks alone in her sealed room, the wife could not take the isolation anymore. She finally summoned up the courage, knocked at the door of her husband's sealed room, and asked if she could share it with him. By that time, the husband had also mellowed considerably, and was relieved to have her company. The last I heard is that they have resolved some of their differences. I do hope they live happily ever after — when the war is over.

However, it seems that the war is far from over, as we are still being bombarded with missiles. We have also been bombarded with constant quotes from the Scriptures and other sources predicting the coming of the *Mashiach.* The *gedolim* advise us not to delve into these matters and, instead, to concentrate on Torah study, acts of kindness, and faith in Hashem. However, it is quite difficult to disregard these rumors, as many people derive *chizzuk* from the thought that at long last the Redemption is nearing.

I, too, have found a verse that seems relevant to our times. You know how much I like the book *The Midrash Says* by Rabbi Moshe Weissman, which gives the weekly Torah portions and *midrashim.* Where it speaks about the Song at the Red Sea, in *parashas Beshallach,* I read the following:

> In the future, Hashem will reinstate to their former positions all the kings and leaders who oppressed *bnei Yisrael* — Hadrian, Nevuchadnetzar, Sancheriv, and all the enemies of the Jewish people after them, and, subsequently, He will take revenge upon them in public.

I subsequently read an article in a current English magazine describing Saddam Hussein in the following manner: "If Saddam Hussein is a new Hitler in George Bush's eyes, and a reincarnation of the *Babylonian King Nevuchadneztar* in his own..."!

Love, Mama

✍ ✍

Dearest Yisroel Meyer,

A very happy birthday to you, and may we share many more joyous ones. This week is Tu B'Shevat, Rosh Hashanah of the trees, and as you and the trees celebrate a new year together, I have many thoughts to share with you.

Yisroel Meyer, you have grown through the years from a young sapling into a stately, handsome tree. The loving dew (*Tehillim* 110:3) of your wife, Chaya, has enhanced the garden of your lives.

Sunshine has shone through your leafy, green branches, and brightened our days. Yet, with your soft shade, you have spared us from the harmful effects of its rays.

Your branches have produced delicious, luscious fruits. May Hashem bless you and Chaya that your garden continue to flourish through every season of your lives.

It is also my wish on this Tu B'Shevat that Hashem look down from Heaven and judge all the trees favorably, so that they flourish and bring fullness to our land. We have had an extremely dry winter, with very little rain. By this time, when most of the rain should have fallen, there is great concern here, and even talk about importing water from abroad.

Hashem has sent us many messages these last months that signal us to become closer to Him and ask for His sustenance. Rain in Eretz Yisrael is given on our merit, we are told. May He answer our prayers and bless our trees.

I want to end my letter with some lines from the poem "Trees," by Joyce Kilner, that has always been one of my favorites.

> I think that I shall never see
> A poem lovely as a tree.
> A tree that looks at God all day,
> And lifts her leafy arms to pray.
> Poems are made by fools like me,
> But only God can make a tree.

Yisroel Meyer, your birthday has given me some respite from the continued tension of the Gulf War. For the first time since it started, I feel a deep sense of relaxation. Thank you!

Love, Mama

✍ ✍

Dearest Children,

What an upheaval there has been in our lives since the Gulf War started! Things we always took for granted have undergone radical change. For instance, all weddings, engagement parties, bar mitzvah celebrations, lectures, and other events scheduled for the evening hours have become afternoon affairs. Guests attend weddings in the middle of the day, all dressed up and carrying their gas mask kits with them, a reminder that war is still with us.

Yerushalayim has become a ghost town at night, with most people trying to get home before dark. Places of entertainment are mostly closed, and those which are kept open have very few customers. During the night hours, most of us are tuned in to the radio, listening for news and for the frightening signal: just before the siren goes off, the radio gives two code words — *nachash tzefa* ("viper"). Although I have heard it a number of times already, I still get a sinking feeling in the pit of my stomach when music is interrupted with those two dreaded words, followed by the siren. I guess one never gets used to the threat of danger.

Lately, when, at the rising wail of the siren, I make the dash into my neighbor's sealed room, although I take my gas mask along as usual, I have been lax in putting it on. The missiles so far have been "conventional" and have not carried chemical warheads, thank Hashem. I read an article describing the effects of chemical warfare, and it sounds like all the horrors that are prophesied in the war of Gog and Magog. May Hashem spare us from such catastrophe.

Love, Mama

Dearest Children,

Today, when I went out onto my balcony and gazed at the blue, cloudless sky, with the bright sun painting colored shadows here and there, I also saw what seemed like a mirage:

the schoolyard that faces us was filled with children running to and fro! The schools have just been reopened, and the children seemed like bright spirits freed from captivity. Of course, they have to keep their gas mask kits with them at all times, and there are lots of air-raid practice drills.

It is the middle of February, and the Gulf War is four weeks old. Can it be only four weeks? Time plays tricks on us — four weeks can seem like four days, and sometimes — like now — four weeks are a lifetime.

These last weeks have brought suffering and destruction, fear and anxiety. Yet, I have seen and heard how courage overcame calamity, prayers subdued panic, and faith battled despair.

We have witnessed many miracles through this difficult period. Although seven thousand five hundred homes have been damaged by the missiles, with six hundred of them completely demolished, miraculously there have been few casualties. Men, women, and children have walked out of their collapsed homes with hardly a scratch. Of course, losing one's life's possessions is a disaster, but gaining one's life is a special blessing from Hashem.

This past winter, as I mentioned in one of my other letters, Hashem has withheld rain from our land. Prayers were recited around the clock pleading not only for an end to the war, but also for much-needed rain. The warm, sunny days of December and most of January brought little satisfaction to us. The very few days of rain during that time were greeted with shouts of joy.

But with the fall of missiles on our land, Hashem sent us the blessing of rain. Many times He blew the winds to deflect the missiles to unpopulated areas, which caused no damage.

There have been many revealed miracles, and this has resulted in great awakening to seek Hashem, knowing it is only He who can bring peace and security to us. May He continue to hear our fervent prayers and answer them.

Love, Mama

Early Purim morning we heard the news that Hashem had performed miracles for us as he had for the Jews in the time of Queen Esther. I listened to President Bush's announcement at 4:00 A.M. Israel time that an unofficial cease-fire had gone into effect, and I felt a great sense of relief.

I thought of the miracles that had taken place during the entire war. A war was fought, and we were attacked with deadly missiles, but not one Israeli soldier was lost, and much bloodshed was spared. Many of the missiles failed to hit their targets. The Jewish Nation turned to Hashem and became stronger in faith.

We see that everything that happens has deep significance. The number 39, for example, holds a very important place in our tradition. There are 39 activities that are forbidden on Shabbos. There are 39 lashes that the *beis din* meted out as punishment for certain sins during the time of the *Beis Ha-Mikdash.* And someone recently pointed out to me that we had 18 missile attacks in which 39 missiles fell, and by multiplying 39 times 18, we come up with the total of 702, which is the *gematria* — the numerical value — of the word *Shabbos*!

It certainly gave me much food for thought.

Once again Purim had brought deliverance to the Jews. And the joy of Purim was great. The threat of missiles was lifted and, instead, the air was full of a crackling, tearing sound from all directions: hundreds of people *un*sealing their rooms! The garbage bins were overflowing with plastic and old tape!

Night and day blended together, as there was no fear to venture out after dark. We, in Yerushalayim, celebrated Shushan Purim on Friday, so we could not extend the celebration into the night because of the coming of Shabbos, but everyone made the most of it during the day.

The *mishlo'ach manos* had a share of *Saddam-tashen*, instead of *Hamantashen*, but they looked and tasted the same! I guess Haman and Saddam Hussein depict the same despotic tyranny.

The joy of Purim, however, was marred by a tragedy. Just when the war was over, and the *Intifada* seemed to be lessening, a yeshivah boy was stabbed to death in the Old City. We are still facing many enemies who seek our destruction.

✍ ✍

Dearest Children,

Several weeks have passed since the end of the war. A number of people have asked me, "What did you gain from the Gulf War?" They surely expected an entirely different answer from the one I gave them: "An alarm clock."

I did not think it was necessary to elaborate on the many miracles we witnessed. Everyone, except perhaps blind bats, saw clearly the great *chesed* Hashem did with us. Even many secular Israelis and newspaper reporters used the word "miracles" to describe the Gulf War. However, they omitted the most obvious fact: Hashem performed them all.

So where does my alarm clock come in? Ever since Papa passed away, and you decided that every week one of the couples would telephone me from the States, it has meant a lot to me. You understood how much it would help to overcome my extreme loneliness.

The time we decided would be best for the weekly call— Sunday morning at 6:00 A.M. Israel time — has become the highlight of my week, and I await each weekly call with great anticipation.

Normally, I go to sleep on Saturday night much past my usual bedtime, as I putter around slowly cleaning away the beloved signs of Shabbos, and bringing the weekday items back. Now, since I want to make sure to be up much before 6:00 A.M. on Sunday morning to recite the morning *berachos* before your call comes through, my Saturday night sleep is often very restless. Many times, I have awakened even before 5:00 A.M. and did not allow myself to fall asleep again for fear I might oversleep.

Of course, on Sunday mornings I am always on an emotional high after having spoken to you, but physically I walked around in a daze from lack of sleep. Somehow, it never occurred to me to buy an alarm clock.

Just before the Gulf War started, a young American couple with whom I had become very close called to tell me they were leaving for the States. They asked if I could use any of their possessions that they were not taking back with them. When I questioned them as to what they had, they mentioned, among other things, a radio-alarm clock. A sudden "ringing bell" flashed through my mind: an alarm clock — just what I needed! I jumped at the chance, and they gave it to me as a gift.

The alarm clock saved the day, children, or I should say my Saturday nights. I set it to go off twenty minutes before 6:00 A.M. With a soft, musical tinkle it awakens me in ample time to be ready for your loving calls. It also has a radio, and it was very convenient having one right near my bed during the Gulf War.

Children, I saw great *hashgachah pratis* in my receiving the alarm clock at the special time I needed it. Hashem knew that during the Gulf War I would need my sleep, because the screaming sirens disrupted my normal sleep pattern. He therefore made sure for me to have the alarm clock before the war started, so as not to lose additional sleep on Saturday nights.

This gave me a feeling of encouragement through the entire war. For if Hashem takes care of each one's individual needs, as small as they are, surely He will answer the prayers of *Klal Yisrael.* And He certainly does!

Thank Hashem for His precious gift — the radio-alarm clock — which keeps me "tuned" into Him.

Love, Mama

Afterword

Dearest Moshe,

It is a little over three years since you left me for your special place in Heaven. I have gone through periods of extreme loneliness since then, but I realized that I had to pick up the pieces of my life and try to put them into some semblance of order.

I felt that you would want me to continue my writing, because you had shared with me the "ups and ups" of writing *"All for the Boss"* and knew how rewarding writing was for me. I hoped in some small measure that it would fill the void you left and give meaning to my life.

As you know, I can only write about experiences that have touched my life deeply. I therefore decided that my second book would be about my teaching experiences. With your spirit ever near me giving me confidence, I wrote *Reaching the Stars.*

Baruch Hashem, I have just finished my third book, *Dearest Children.* The book contains the letters that I wrote to the children about our life in Yerushalayim, from the time we settled here in 1968 through 1988, when you passed away. Each letter was signed, "Love, Papa and Mama."

Yes, Moshe, I once again felt your loving presence hovering over me from the first letter through the last, which helped me throughout the writing of the book.

It is true that I shed many tears as I rewrote the letters, but they also brought back many loving and dear memories that warmed my heart.

I hope and pray that I will continue to "reach out" toward new horizons in my writing efforts.

I am sure you will always be near me, taking pride in my accomplishments, which you have always shared with me.

Though you are far away in a spriritual land,
I feel your presence nigh. I hold your hand.
How blessed I was to be your wife,
Your shining spirit still brightens my life.
I hear the angels with their voices raised,
Extol your virtues in song and praise.
Peace and joy fill my heart,
Which whispers to me, "We are never apart."

All my love,
Ruchoma

Glossary

The following glossary provides a partial explanation of some of the Hebrew, Yiddish and Aramaic words and phrases used in this book. The spellings and explanations reflect the way the specific word is being used herein. Often, there are alternate spellings and meanings for the words.

AL HA-NISSIM: lit., "for the miracles," a prayer which is a declaration of thanks for the miracles of Chanukah and Purim.

AM YISRAEL: the People of Israel.

ARON: a cupboard; a coffin.

AVODAS HASHEM: the worship of God.

BA'AL TESHUVAH: a penitent; a formerly non-observant Jew who returns to Torah observance.

BEDIKAS CHAMETZ: the search for leaven conducted on the night before Pesach.

BEIN HA-ZEMANIM: the semester break in a YESHIVAH.

BEIS HA-MIKDASH: the Holy Temple.

BERACHAH (-CHOS): blessing(s).

BIRKAS HA-CHAMAH: the blessing on the sun.

BIRKAS KOHANIM: the priestly blessing.

BITACHON: faith and trust in God.

BLECH: (Y.) a special Sabbath warming tray.

BNEI TORAH: learned, observant Jews.

BNEI YISRAEL: the children of Israel.

BUBBIE: (Y.) grandmother.

CHAG: a Festival.

CHAMSIN: a hot, dry wind from the desert.

CHAREDI: ultra-Orthodox.

CHASAN: a bridegroom.

CHAZAKAH: an established claim.

CHEDER: (Y.) a religious primary school for boys.

CHESED: lovingkindness.

CHEVRAH KADISHA: (A.) the burial society.

CHILLUL SHABBOS: the desecration of the Sabbath.

CHIZZUK: strengthening; encouragement.

CHOL HA-MO'ED: the intermediate days of the Festivals of Pesach and Sukkos.

CHOLENT: (Y.) a traditional, savory Sabbath stew which is kept hot overnight and served for lunch.

DAVEN: (Y.) pray.

ERETZ YISRAEL: the Land of Israel.

EREV: the eve of; the day preceding.

ESROG: a citron, one of the Four Species used on Sukkos.

FREILICH: (Y.) happy.

GADOL: a great Torah scholar.

GAN EDEN: the Garden of Eden.

GEMAR TOV: the traditional greeting between Rosh Hashanah and Yom Kippur, wishing one a good Divine judgment for the new year.

GEVERET: a respectful form of address to a woman.

GEULAH SHELEMAH: the Final Redemption.

GUT SHABBOS: (Y.) "Have a good Sabbath."

GUT VOCH: (Y.) "Have a good week."

HACHNASAS ORCHIM: hospitality.

HAKAFOS: lit., encircling; the seven circuits made in the synagogue, carrying Torah scrolls on Simchas Torah.

HAMANTASHEN: (Y.) triangular, jelly-filled cookies for Purim.

HASHGACHAH PRATIS: Divine Providence.

HAVDALAH: the blessings recited at the conclusion of Sabbaths and Festivals.

ISH EMES: lit., a man of truth; a righteous man.

KADDISH: a prayer recited for the soul of the deceased.

KALLAH: a bride.

KASHRUS: the Jewish dietary laws.

KEVER: a grave.

KIBBUD AV V'EM: honoring one's father and mother.

KIDDUSH: sanctification of the Sabbath and Festivals, usually recited over wine.

KINOS: lamentations.

KLAL YISRAEL: The Jewish People.

KOLLEL: an institute for advanced Torah learning for married men.

KUGEL: (Y.) a baked pudding, often of noodles or potatoes.

LACHMANIYAH (-YOT): roll(s) or bun(s).

LASHON HA-KODESH: the Holy Tongue (Hebrew).

LATKES: (Y.) pancakes; potato pancakes.

LECHEM MISHNEH: the two loaves of challah placed on the table on Sabbaths and Festivals.

MA'ARIV: the evening prayer service.

MACHZOR: the prayer book for Festivals.

MAIDELEH: (Y.) a young girl.

MAKOM HA-MIKDASH: the site of the Holy Temple.

MASHGIACH: the spiritual guide and counselor of a YESHIVAH.

MASHIACH: the Messiah.

MATANOS L'EVYONIM: gifts to the poor which are sent on Purim.

MATZAH (-ZOS): flat, unleavened bread eaten during Pesach.

MATZEVAH: a tombstone.

MAZAL TOV: "Congratulations!"

MESIRAS NEFESH: dedication; self-sacrifice.

MELITZ YOSHER: someone to pray and speak well for us in Heaven.

MELAVEH MALKAH: a celebration on Saturday night honoring the departing "Sabbath queen."

MIDDOS TOVOS: good attributes.

MIKVEH: a ritual bath.

MINYAN: a minimum of ten male Jews aged 13 and over, the quorum required for congregational prayer.

MI-SHEBERACH: a prayer for one called up to the Torah, for the benefit of the congregation or individual members, especially the sick.

MISHLO'ACH MANOS: gift packages of food traditionally sent on Purim.

MUSAF: the additional prayer service on Sabbaths and Festivals.

NACHAS: pleasure and satisfaction.

NASH: (Y.) snack.

NE'ILAH: the concluding prayer service on Yom Kippur.

NESHAMAH: the soul.

OLAM HA-BA: the World to Come.

OLAM HA-ZEH: this world.

ORE'ACH (ORCHIM): guest(s).

PARNASSAH: livelihood.

PETEK: a slip of paper.

PIKUACH NEFESH: saving an endangered life.

REFUAH SHELEMAH: "A speedy recovery!"

SANDEK: the man who has the honor of holding the baby on his lap at a bris.

SEDER: the Pesach night ceremony recalling the Exodus from Egypt, read from the Haggadah.

SEFER: a book; a holy book.

SEFER TORAH: a Torah scroll.

SEGULAH: a good omen.

SELICHOS: penitential prayers.

SEUDAH: a festive meal.

SEUDAH SHELISHIS: the third Sabbath meal.

SEUDAS HA-MAFSEKES: the meal eaten before a fast.

SHACHARIS: the morning prayer service.

SHALESHUDES: (Y., colloq.) SEUDAH SHELISHIS.

SHELOSHIM: lit., thirty; the thirty-day period of mourning.

SHEMITTAH: the Sabbatical year.

SHEVA BERACHOS: the seven blessings recited at a wedding; one of the festive meals held in honor of the bride and groom during the week following the wedding, at which the seven blessings are recited.

SHIUR: a Torah Lesson.

SHIVAH: lit., seven; the seven-day period of mourning.

SHMOOZE: (Y.) chat.

SHUK: the open-air market.

SHUL: (Y.) a synagogue.

SHTREIMEL: (Y.) a fur-trimmed hat worn by Chasidim.

SIMCHAH: joy; a joyous occasion.

SUKKAH: a temporary structure which Jews erect and live in during the Festival of Sukkos.

SUFGANIOT: jelly doughnuts, traditionally eaten on Chanukah.

TALMID: a student.

TATTY: (Y.) Daddy.

TASHLICH: the ceremony of symbolically casting away one's sins by tossing bread crumbs from one's pockets into a body of water on Rosh Hashanah, and reciting a special prayer.

TECHIAS HA-MEISIM: the resurrection of the dead.

TEFILLAH: prayer.

TEFILLAS HA-DERECH: the traveler's prayer.

TEFILLIN: phylacteries.

TESHUVAH: repentance.

TZADDIK: a righteous, pious man; a holy man.

TZEISCHEM L'SHALOM: "Go in peace."

YAHRTZEIT: (Y.) the anniversary of a death.

YOM TOV: a Festival.

ZAIDIE: (Y.) grandfather.

ZECHUS: privilege; merit.

ZEMAN: a semester, or school term, in a YESHIVAH.